Language
Exploration
& Awareness

A Resource Book
for Teachers

Larry Andrews

University of Nebraska—Lincoln

Longman
New York & London

Language Exploration and Awareness

Longman, 10 Bank Street, White Plains, N.Y. 10606

Associated companies:
Longman Group Ltd., London
Longman Cheshire Pty., Melbourne
Longman Paul Pty., Auckland
Copp Clark Pitman, Toronto

Senior acquisitions editor: Laura McKenna
Sponsoring editor: Naomi Silverman
Development editor: Susan Alkana
Production editor: Marcy Gray
Cover design: Anne M. Pompeo
Production supervisor: Anne Armeny

Library of Congress Cataloging-in-Publication Data

Andrews, Larry.
    Language exploration and awareness: a resource book for teachers
/ by Larry Andrews.
        p.   cm.
    Includes bibliographical references and index.
    ISBN 0-8013-0963-8
    1. Language arts.   2. Activity programs in education.
3. Teaching.   I. Title.
LB1576.A625   1993
428'.007—dc20   92-8256
                                                            CIP

1 2 3 4 5 6 7 8 9 10-MW-9695949392

For Kim

For her constancy, patience, questions, and support

Contents

Preface

What are some of the more vivid memories of your English language lessons in school? Grammar drills? Usage worksheets? Memorizing 25 spelling words for Friday's final test? Writing "S," "V," "IO" and "DO" above the subject, verb, indirect, and direct objects in sentences?

These activities represent what many students remember, with little affection for the memories. For them, these drills and worksheets asked them to analyze language aspects they thought were unnecessarily "picky," primarily because the activities are so far removed from their sense of the world around them or one they might face.

Ironically, these same students laugh uproariously at the language play in poems, novels, and comic strips, and in the jokes of television comedians. They are emotionally touched by song lyrics. They become angry when they or friends are the butt of name-calling, and are disillusioned when politicians, teachers, parents, or advertisements do not live up to their words. They knowingly smile at the seeming naiveté of the words to songs from previous generations, music they call "oldies." In each of these cases the students are making significant language observations.

I wrote this book in an attempt to broaden teachers' views of the English language arts curriculum, and thereby increase students' opportunities to examine a broader array of language elements (semantics, regional and social variations, discourse conventions, and the like). Language learning in schools ought to be more than recognizing aspects of correct syntax and good usage.

HOW THIS BOOK IS ORGANIZED

Section I, "Language Exploration and Awareness: The Rationale," describes what Language Exploration and Awareness (LEA) is and how LEA differs from the traditional approach to the study of language in schools. Section I discusses the weaknesses of the customary approach, and especially its emphasis on only one aspect of language: traditional grammar. Section I further describes the need for language to be viewed as a *social* activity, not a fixed code to be memorized for universal application; it advocates more learner engagement and more student talk in classrooms.

Section I provides the philosophical foundation for and the characteristics of an approach to language study—language exploration and awareness—that enables students to examine and explore numerous aspects of language in use. LEA is characterized by:

1. The study of genuine, authentic language rather than abstract and contrived textbook examples and models
2. An insistence on the premise that language-learning activities in schools be student-centered rather than teacher-centered
3. A requirement that students make observations of authentic language uses, then formulate generalizations based upon those observations
4. A recognition of the linguistic fact that "good English" is a rigorously enforced but floating social standard that is attained through varying uses of language, depending upon their diverse contexts of use. A social tax is assessed against those who violate the expectations and requirements for good English; these standards are embedded in every communication event.
5. Finally, LEA is based upon the proposition that as students' language continues to develop, this growth *in* language helps them grow *through* language.

Section II, "Language Exploration and Awareness: The Elements," is designed to serve two purposes. First, each chapter in the second section provides the classroom teacher with basic concepts, knowledge, and information about a number of important elements of language. I do not presume to say that each chapter is a complete or thorough examination of, say, the principles of how words are created and enter the language, the field of semantics, or regional and social dialects. Each chapter, however, is complete enough so that it provides either a review of basic linguistic topics and concepts for some teachers, or is a good introduction to aspects of language for those teachers who want or need the information.

FEATURES OF THIS BOOK

Student Explorations

Each chapter in the second part of this book concludes with a special section entitled Student Explorations. These explorations give illustrative activities the classroom teacher can use in a classroom to help adolescent and young adult students explore the aspects of language described in the previous chapter.

These illustrative explorations have a family resemblance. They satisfy a number of LEA criteria, which makes them significantly different from the typical seat-work lessons in traditional English language handbooks, workbooks, and other commercially packaged materials.

Ultimately, the best language explorations are those created by the students and the teacher and are the result of student-initiated observations and questions about language they observe on television, in newspapers, novels, school announcements, popular songs, conversations, sermons, menus, and highway billboards. The illustrative explorations at the end of these chapters serve as exemplars for other explorations that teachers and students may devise on their own.

For Your Inquiry and Practice

Throughout both Sections I and II of the text you will find additional sets of language explorations entitled For Your Inquiry and Practice. These are explorations pre- and in-service teachers should complete in order to enhance their own understanding and appreciation of various aspects and elements of language. Although the chapter-ending student explorations are suggested as exemplars for use in school classrooms, I also recommend that the teacher-readers complete some of them. The student explorations are not age-specific, and enable the reader to explore several aspects of language in greater depth.

Language explorations are not nomadic wanderings. To the contrary, as you examine the criteria for successful language explorations described in Chapter 1, you will observe a clear pedagogical method: The best way for people to learn about language is for them to observe language, ask questions about how and why language forms are used as they are in various contexts, make closer and more focused observations, and then form a tentative generalization.

This model was not arrived at by chance. It is the way you and I first acquired language. It is the way you and I continue to learn language.

Unlike many books about language and language study, this text has no glossary. You will find, instead, that when technical terms first appear they are presented in boldface print, and are defined in and through their context of use. This is the usual and normal way you and I encounter new language in real life.

References

Similarly, you will not find an additional list of recommended readings at the conclusion of each chapter. Instead, at each chapter's end is a list of titles referred to in that chapter. These are some of the most insightful language books available. Please accept my enthusiastic invitation to read some or all of them. They are my recommendations for further reading, enjoyment, and professional development.

WHO THIS BOOK IS FOR

This book is written for teachers of English and language arts. Most undergraduate methods courses are no longer built around a single, omnibus text, but use one or more texts for examining the pedagogies of teaching literature, writing, and language. *Language Exploration and Awareness* is the language teaching book.

Many universities offer special courses in teaching the English language and/or linguistics for upper-level undergraduate students and beginning-level graduate students. This text is designed for those courses. In some cases, it can be used in an Introduction to Language or an Introduction to Linguistics course, especially if that course emphasizes language study from a sociocultural perspective. This perspective will also make this textbook appealing to ESL teachers.

The subtitle of this book, "A Resource Book for Teachers," demonstrates that it is also written for current classroom teachers. I see it occupying a special place on the desk of every English language arts teacher in today's classrooms.

A desk or collegiate dictionary will be needed to accompany some of the learning activities in this book. Several editions are available at most bookstores. Unfortunately, the small, paperback dictionaries sold at supermarkets and discount stores omit word histories, variant spellings, alternate pronunciations, and too much other information to make them useful either to professional teachers or their students.

Finally, I hope that *Language Exploration and Awareness* will be as vital, enjoyable, and clarifying for readers as it has been for me, the writer. More importantly, I hope that student language learners will realize the same outcomes.

ACKNOWLEDGMENTS

Language Exploration and Awareness was conceived during the spring of 1990 while I was a visiting fellow at the University of London Institute of Education. Michael Stubbs, to whom I am indebted for many reasons, was instrumental in my receiving the appointment and in introducing me to the language exploration efforts under way in the United Kingdom. I want to thank Sir Peter Newsam and Denis Lawton, directors of the Institute, the faculty and staff at the Institute's Departments of English and Teaching English to Speakers of Other Languages, and the library. Everyone was graciously helpful. My stay in London and at the Institute was made possible by the support of several persons at the University of Nebraska—Lincoln: M.A. Massengale, John Yost, Jim O'Hanlon, Jim Walter, and Ronald W. Roskens.

Relatively little of the material in this book was previously published elsewhere, and I am grateful to the publishers for permission to include it here. The Chapter 3 section, "Language Learning Requires Practice," first appeared as Larry Andrews' "Putting More Talk in the Middle Level Language Arts," *American Secondary Education,* vol. 19, no. 1, 1990, pp. 9–12. Figure 6.2 in Chapter 6, "Dimensions of Language Variation," is from Michael Stubbs' *Educational Linguistics,* Oxford, Basil Blackwell, 1986, p. 21. The statement of language beliefs in Chapter 8 is an excerpt from Ann Ruggles Gere and Eugene Smith's *Attitudes, Language and Change,* Urbana, IL, National Council of Teachers of English, 1979, pp. 8–10. The classroom exploration in Chapter 8 entitled, ". . . them that speak leasing . . ." is from The Kerygma Program, *Shalom* Leader's Guide, Pittsburgh, PA, 1989, pp. 19–20. The appendix, "Non-White Minorities in English and Language Arts Materials," was prepared by the National Council of Teachers of English Task Force on Racism and Bias in the Teaching of English, 1978.

Several colleagues read part or all of the manuscript for *Language Exploration and Awareness.* While their comments made the book better, they should not be held responsible for its remaining faults: Mike Stubbs, Yasukata Yano, Peter Hasselriis, Dave Wilson, Karla Hawkins Wendelin, Sue Dauer, Roger Bruning, and Al Kilgore. Ken Hansen created the illustrations. Thanks to all of you.

A number of classroom teachers also contributed to this book, either by coaching my teaching and writing or by lending their classroom explorations. They are: Laurel Barrett, Jennifer Becker, Debra Bundy, Sonia Christiansen, Lynne Danielsen, Michele Diedrichsen, Joan Doyle, Linda Enck, Jim Fields, Amy Finlay, Pamela Gannon, Sheri Gross, Laurie Hokom, Joan Jorgensen, Jodi Knoll, Cindy Meyer, Jessica McAndrew, Paul Orvis, Bev Redwine, Lorilyn Rennings, Verla Ringenberg, Sheri Rogers, Dana Schaefer, Amy Steager, and Louis Whitmore. Leah Andrews, my niece, is not yet a classroom teacher but is a writer! She contributed several sentences you'll read in Chapter 1. Naomi Silverman, like an earlier Naomi, understood and had faith from the beginning. Her encouragement has been important to me. Sarah Crowley at Longman kept the manuscript and me on a timely and steady course with efficiency and good cheer.

I want to thank the reviewers of the manuscript: Miles Olson, University of Colorado at Boulder; Philip M. Anderson, Queens College of the City University of New York; Ruth K. J. Cline, University of Colorado at Boulder; Duane Roen, University of Arizona; and Allen Berger, Miami University. Their comments and suggestions were very beneficial.

For their continuing inspiration, I am grateful to my parents, to A. Sterl Artley, Ben and Betty Garrison (aka R and Martha), and to a special group of friends: LCGC.

Finally, my wife Kim and daughters Wyn and Sally, my severest but most loving critics, are my first-draft responders and reality-checkers in most things. They read initial drafts of this manuscript and endured the earlier mealtime conversations leading to it. Their comments are usually direct, sometimes not what I want to hear, but always helpful and what I need to hear.

Introduction

Language is the pliable adhesive that helps to form, identify and bind nations, communities, neighborhoods, groups, societies, and personal relationships. Language is also the means by which those groups give voice to their ideas, dreams, despairs, hopes, fears, memories of yesterday, and visions of tomorrow. Language can be used to disappoint or hurt; it can affirm or heal, as well. Language can be used to constrain or to liberate.

The English language is also a required subject studied in K–12 schools. This book is for those who learn and teach in those schools.

The study of the English language in most (thankfully, not all) schools in the United States has been and continues to be rudimentary forms of analyses of isolated sentences in which the students are to identify or duplicate correct examples of spelling, grammar, and syntax.

While studying syntactical and orthographic structures such as these may be a part of language study, ostensibly because it improves students' speaking and writing abilities, it should be only a *part*. For a number of lamentable reasons, however, the study of the syntactic structure of language has been the primary if not the only aspect of language study included in most school curricula in the United States for the past century. Consequently, many students leave our schools with severely truncated and erroneous notions about language, what it is, and how it is used.

To put it another way, imagine you are attending the first meeting of an Introduction to Computers class; the instructor greets you and the other aspiring computer users and asks all of you to open the computer owner's manual to the section explaining how the computer is physically assembled. Imagine further that the instructor devotes not only the initial session but the duration of the course to this section of the manual. Suppose even further that this course is required for four years and that assembling the computer and memorizing the names of its parts represent the major emphasis of the course. Wouldn't you wonder when the instructor would get around to helping you learn more about how you might actually use your computer for meaningful tasks? Assembling the computer is patently important, but your needs and interests go farther than that feature.

Going well beyond how the language is structurally assembled, LEA opens the door to a study of a variety of language topics. LEA invites classroom teachers, and their students in particular, to an alternate approach to the study of language, one that encourages students *to explore* many aspects of language, not just syntax. When students have the opportunity to observe and explore a larger linguistic universe, they become more proficient users of the vast diapason of aspects of language in its human contexts.

Many teachers express a desire to pursue such a program of language study with their students, but indicate that they know more about teaching literature or writing than language studies. This is not surprising. The English courses most school teachers complete throughout their teacher education or graduate programs are more likely to be literature courses. Few have taken more than one or two English language courses. *Language Exploration and Awareness* helps to fill that void.

Linguistics, the study of language(s), has undergone a number of significant changes in the past several years. Language is no longer viewed by professional language scholars as a depersonalized object to be examined and standardized, but as a complex and variable human activity to be observed and better understood.

School curricula can and should reflect these developments. A balanced language curriculum should give learners numerous opportunities to explore the many reasons they and others use language, where language comes from, and how it changes and varies according to who is using it, for what purposes, and in what settings. They should learn how to assess language effectiveness in these ever-changing contexts.

Among the many intended outcomes of this book, one is paramount: Children and young adults who have had the good fortune to explore many elements of language, in addition to the traditional single element of traditional grammar, will appreciate and understand that language use—especially that use of language frequently called "good English"—is an intensely and inherently social and human activity; it reflects an array of *choices* to be made, not unilateral *rules* to be obeyed.

Let's go exploring!

Language Exploration and Awareness: The Rationale

CHAPTER **1**

Language Exploration and Awareness: What It Is

The study of our language opens all kinds of doors.
—David Crystal, *Who Cares About English Usage?*

The English language has traditionally been studied in classrooms in the United States in order to help the students increase their language competence for higher achievement in a number of other areas: better speech, better writing, and better reading; to better prepare them for the next grade, for high school or college, and the work force.

With few exceptions, for a century the all-but-exclusive focus of language study has been on the *structure* of English—usually traditional grammar.

A considerable body of research, however, confirmed by the experiences, observations, and conclusions of thousands of classroom teachers and their students, makes it abundantly clear that the traditional approach to English language teaching and learning in classrooms, with its emphasis on traditional grammar, has been largely ineffective. This is especially apparent when one considers the amount of time and emphasis allocated to it.

Quite simply, as Hillocks shows, studying traditional grammar and parts of speech of the language—as they have been traditionally taught—has not made appreciable differences in students' reading, writing, or speaking performance.[1]

Ironically, no matter how convincing the evidence that seems to demonstrate that teaching traditional grammar and usage does not help writing or speaking, nothing seems to diminish the impulses and compulsions to con-

3

tinue to teach it in schools.[2] A number of possible reasons for this heritage are discussed in Chapter 3.

For the moment, however, let's consider one possible reason for the failure of traditional school language study to accomplish what its advocates say it either will or ought to. The reason is illustrated by the following (true) story.

A certified teacher hoping to gain a full-time position was serving as a substitute teacher in a large, metropolitan city in the Mid-west. She reported to temporary duty one morning in a seventh grade general music class. After the bell rang and the students were settled at their desks, she picked up the regular teacher's grade book and began to call the roll.

"Anderson?" (No answer.)

"Brown?" (Again, no answer.)

"Cunningham?" (Still, no answer!)

Being an experienced substitute, the teacher knew enough, she thought, to become wary of the students' collective refusal to reply. What's the next trick going to be, she wondered?

"All right, class, let's have some cooperation here," she directed.

"Davis?" (Still, and again, no reply.)

With this fourth unacknowledged name, the substitute teacher sat down, first glared at the class, then stared hopelessly at the grade book.

A youngster from the front row got up from his seat, approached the teacher's desk, and quietly said to her, "Lady, you're on the wrong page."

Like the substitute teacher, those of us who have labored to teach language by emphasizing traditional grammar and usage to the virtual exclusion of any other or all other features of language have been either on the wrong page, or on the *same* page for the wrong period of time. In addition to helping our students learn about the *structure* of language, we should have also been attending to some of the other "pages" of a larger and broader language curriculum; one which takes into account both a fuller picture of how and why language actually works in the real world, and a more accurate understanding of the learners, their interests, abilities, and stages of linguistic development.

If medical schools educated their students the way we traditionally teach the English language, the medical school curriculum would be limited to Anatomy I, Anatomy II, Anatomy III, and so on. Learning the anatomy of the human body is important, obviously, but it's not a complete curriculum for physicians. Similarly, learning the anatomy of language is important, but it's not a complete language curriculum.

METALINGUISTIC AWARENESS AND THE LANGUAGE ELEPHANT

Many of our students—those still in classrooms in the United States and those who have graduated—have followed what is described throughout this book as a "traditional curriculum" in English language study. As a result, they are, as Wilson describes them, like the blind men in the fable, each having "a limited personal experience of that elephant, language."[3]

The approach I am calling Language Exploration and Awareness (LEA) views the study of the English language from a larger perspective. A more comprehensive view will, as Wilson puts it, "help those of us blinded by our personal provincialities to see the [language] elephant whole."[4]

Before our students can gain significant insight into the way they and other speakers and writers unconsciously or deliberately manipulate language elements, patterns and structures, they should first become more aware of the *wholeness of language study*: regional and social variation (dialects), word formation processes, how dictionaries record the histories of words and their varied uses, social discourse conventions, and the like.

Another major purpose of the LEA approach is to provide learners with an opportunity to examine *language as language*. As you will observe elsewhere in this book (as well as from your own experiences), in the traditional curriculum the English language is usually studied primarily as a means to other student-outcomes. These outcomes are an important part of the English language arts curriculum, but it is also important to note that *language is seldom studied in its own right*.

In fact, Elbow points out that in the view of many people, English courses are "ancillary." English has tended to be, he says, "a handmaiden to the other disciplines in the humble sense of that metaphor: a 'service discipline.' "[5]

The view of English as a subject that enables students to write, speak, and think better in *other* school subjects and activities presents a number of

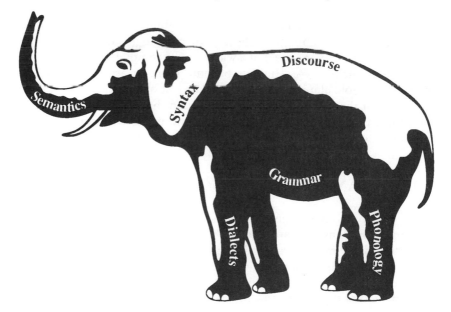

negative outcomes. "There is a depressing general ignorance of the nature of language and the complexity of linguistic issues in society," Milroy and Milroy observe.[6] Many of these language matters have widespread ramifications for our students beyond school, in areas like human relations and human rights, politics, and consumerism, just to cite a few.

LANGUAGE STUDY IN TODAY'S CURRICULUM

A recent analysis of 17 U.S. high schools with reputations for excellence in teaching English shows that both the teachers in these schools and their department heads estimate that they allocate approximately 50 percent of their time to the study of literature, 27 percent to writing, and about 10 percent to the study of language.[7] This analysis reveals an increase in the time devoted to writing since the Squire and Applebee analysis of high school English instruction, which was published some twenty-five years earlier.[8] "The increase in writing instruction came at the expense of language study, speech, and other activities."[9]

The traditional approach to studying language seems to assume that students are already aware of what constitutes, for example, either an act of communication, some of the ways of communicating other than through speech or writing, or how language use varies—normally and inevitably—both by *user* (dialect) and by *use* (diatype). All of these examples are relatively alien ideas in the traditionally homogenized, single-standard-of-correctness view of language structure and use found in the traditional English language curriculum.

One of the primary goals of an LEA program of language study is to enable students to develop their reflective or **metalinguistic** awareness (overt knowledge about language uses) of a wider, more complete range of language features and principles. As students become more aware of the totality of language (the whole elephant, that is, and not just one particular part like the skeleton, tail or the trunk) and its varying human characteristics and meaning-making uses, they will attain metalinguistic awareness, and consequently be more competent in using language confidently, deliberately, and intentionally.

GROWTH IN AND THROUGH LANGUAGE

There is widespread and general agreement, as Bolinger and Sears indicate, that thought and language are related.[10] The degree of this relationship has been discussed for many years and at great length by linguists, anthropologists, learning theorists and cognitive scientists.

For example, Vygotsky argued that the verbal behavior of a child precedes and *enables* cognitive growth.[11] Whorf[12] and Sapir[13] hypothesized that the vocabulary and structure of one's language *predetermine* how an individual will "name" and classify other persons, places, and concepts and, therefore, perceive the world. Piaget, on the other hand, suggested that the early cognitive concepts of children *establish a structure* for their subsequent understanding, learning, and using language.[14]

Like the age-old question of whether the chicken or the egg came first, there is no agreement on whether language creates thought, or thought creates language. Nevertheless, as the theories summarized above demonstrate, there is virtually no disagreement that language and thought are inextricably related and interdependent.

It is beyond the scope of this chapter to provide a more thorough discussion of these theories describing the relationship between language and thought. The relationship between thought and language is, as Aitchison describes it, "a vast and woolly subject."[15] Given this vastness and woolliness, you will come to see and appreciate, I hope, the fact that the LEA manner of language study is based not upon any *one* of these theories to the exclusion of others. The approach to language study advocated in this book recognizes the similarities among the several theories and that language development and cognitive development are separable but interdependent operations, usually growing in a mutually supportive fashion with each other.

Language has traditionally been viewed as a *vehicle of thought*, a means of shaping thoughts and ideas so that they may be made both clearer and more communicable.[16] Language is also sometimes thought of as the *content* as well as the vehicle of thought. Perhaps we can negotiate a compromise for the purposes of this book and agree that language is simultaneously *both* the medium and the message.

At the risk of oversimplifying, let it be said that as the school learner becomes more adept with language, and able to use language spontaneously and with increasing levels of elaboration and precision, thoughts and ideas— meanings—of a more complex nature can be formed, synthesized, evaluated, and articulated by the language user. Thus, as students grow *in* language they also grow *through* it.

ACQUIRING AND LEARNING LANGUAGE

You will encounter a similar interposition in this book with regard to how people acquire and learn language. As we will discuss in Chapter 2, language learning is a continuous process that certainly isn't completed by the age of five or six; the language of adolescents and young adults is still developing.

While some scholars adhere to psycholinguistic models of language learning, others believe that sociolinguistic paradigms are more accurate. I believe we must take *both* schools of thought into account as you and your students examine the personal and social uses of language.

Psycholinguistics is the study of language in relation to the mental processes used as people understand, acquire and produce it.[17] A psycholinguistic approach to language study examines what is happening *within* the individual—mentally, cognitively, psychologically—and usually does not consider the language learner's interactions with and among people.[18] Rather, the focus of psycholinguistics is more likely to be upon the roles of one's memory, perception, and concept development. The study of psycholinguistics has clarified what happens as a child acquires sound patterns (**phonology**), meaning patterns (**semantics**), and word and sentence structures (**syntax**), and has been the dominant school of linguistics in the United States for the past three decades.

Sociolinguistics, on the other hand, is the study of how language is used in relation to social factors such as social class, age, sex, ethnic origin, educational level, and type of education and geographic location.[19] Sociolinguists study, for example, how the social networks composed of family, friends, neighbors, and coworkers might shape a person's language choices. In summary, the study of how one's communicative competence is shaped through socialization processes is the domain of sociolinguistics.

Gee suggests that there are good reasons to claim that during the past several years the fields of psycholinguistics and sociolinguistics have been merging.[20] For example, Giles and Robinson[21] point out that although Noam Chomsky's *Syntactic Structures*[22] invigorated both linguistics and psychology, it quickly became apparent that there was more to acquiring language than Chomsky's psycholinguistic Language Acquisition Device (LAD). Language acquisition and learning also required a sociolinguistic Language Acquisition Support System (LASS).[23]

Chomsky's LAD helps to explain how the brain enables language learning. The LAD makes it possible for the language learner to perceive, understand, and ultimately reproduce the phonetic distinctions between /pin/ and /pit/ or /nip/ and /tip/ and to associate these oral or written terms with their respective referents. The LAD helps the language learner first to acquire, indirectly and incidentally without formal instruction, the rules underlying the morphology and syntax of one's language of nurture, and then to generate sentences that abide by these rules.

The LASS, on the other hand, recognizes that people do not acquire and learn language in isolation. As Wells observes, "Learning to talk is more than acquiring a set of linguistic resources; it is also discovering how to use them in conversation with a variety of people and for a variety of purposes."[24]

Examples of the LASS will be one's parent(s), older sibling(s), friends, and neighbors. The LASS both supports and shapes language as it establishes both specific and general norms and expectations. It informs the language learner, once again indirectly and incidentally, about the social rules governing language as it is used: when to say "Please" or "Thank you"; what to say in response to "Hello. How are you?" When "Once upon a time . . ." is more appropriate in some circumstances than is, "Hey, have you heard the one about . . . ?" (and vice versa). Or, how the term *neither* might be pronounced (NIGH-ther versus KNEE-ther).

The view presented in this book is a merged perspective. There are obvious psycholinguistic underpinnings that can help to account for the language that school learners have acquired. By the same token, as you will see in Chapters 2 and 3, this language is seldom isolated or decontextualized and is rarely used in a vacuum. Language and the social surroundings in which it is used are virtually inseparable. Anyone who has observed young adults for even a brief time will note that they have acquired the basic linguistic structures of language (psycholinguistics), but that regardless of their unique linguistic features, their language has many common elements (sociolinguistics). The same is true of bankers, teachers, preachers, and lawyers.

At the risk of either trivializing or proliferating language typology, I believe a combined socio/psycholinguistic approach is appropriate, both generally, and with particular regard to schools. Both LAD (psycholinguistic) and LASS (sociolinguistic) appear to be coworkers as we acquire and learn language.

FOR YOUR INQUIRY AND PRACTICE:

Leah wrote these sentences when she was five years old.

1. Mi dog went to another fens. she plad and had fun she stad overnit. mi dog ez nis. she ez prete i lik her.
2. Santa clos ez cmin 2 ton. he nos ef u r slepn he nos ef u r awak he nos ef u bn good r bad.
3. Santa clos bregs us toes. he es fat. 1 ov hes renders es namd rudof.
4. Valentnz ez soon. It will be on febuera 14. We will have a porte. we will hav koekes and candi. we wil hav fun.

What understandings about language has Leah acquired and learned at the age of five years?

LANGUAGE EXPLORATION AND AWARENESS: THE CRITERIA

LEA is an approach to the study of *several* aspects of English language—not just spelling, usage, and traditional grammar—which enhance students' sensitivity to and awareness of language as it is used in diverse contexts by real people for different purposes in real life.

LEA provides opportunities for students to learn about regional and social variations in pronunciations and word choices: how words come into and leave the language, and how dictionary publishers record these uses and changes; how sentences we exchange at church or synagogue, in grocery stores, at parties, in libraries, and hospital corridors follow predictable and rigorously enforced social discourse conventions; and how language can re-inforce stereotypes about men, women, and members of religious or racial groups different from our own.

The idea of "explorations" is not new to many educators. Many middle schools and high schools already have elective "exploratory" or "taster" courses in art, music, foreign language, the world of work and technology and the like, for an entire semester or for a shorter time. These exploratory periods give students opportunities to explore and investigate a field of study. Explorations in language not only provide this same introductory purpose, but also give students essential experiences with the larger domain of English language that are often omitted from more traditional school curriculums. Through these experiences, students become more aware of the complexity and diversity of language.

While elective exploratory courses are used in several schools today, the better language explorations are those that emerge and evolve naturally in the regular lessons and course of language study. In order to provide some guid-ance and coherence to student inquiry, the following criteria should be used. These criteria are the defining characteristics of language exploration and awareness as an approach to the study of language:

The Activities Emphasize Meaning

One of the most basic reasons human beings bother to communicate with each other is to impart some kind of meaning. To the extent that this is an accurate statement regarding the general public, it is all but axiomatic when we con-sider school-age learners! Consequently, the activities in the LEA approach will focus on the *meaning(s)* emerging from a language observation or event. While the structure of a discourse is obviously important, it should be dis-cussed only when a student question or comment about structure comes into the discussion, or when the learner's oral or written language is being dis-cussed with the teacher in an individual writing conference or small group discussion.

It is a questionable investment of time to assign to an entire class a work sheet asking the students to underline, circle, diagram, or identify in some other manner an isolated syntactical element. The time spent on activities like "Find the personal pronoun" will be much better spent if the students are engaged in a more productive language activity, such as browsing in the media center or classroom library, reading a book, writing in their personal or class journals, or talking with a friend about a good reading experience.

These alternatives produce useful aptitudes and attitudes because the students are engaged in meaning-generating work. Worksheets usually initiate a search for a "right answer" and do not stimulate much meaning-making.

LEA Activities Use Authentic Language Found in Genuine Social Circumstances

Real language frequently looks and sounds different from the textbook, other-world language often used to illustrate or describe language. Consequently, LEA stresses actual language as it is used by real people for real purposes. After all, this is the language people actually use in various social circumstances throughout their lives. Real people seldom write, for example, "practice" letters applying for a nonexistent job with a fictitious firm, an activity I observed recently in a classroom of 14-year-olds in which the focus was on "practical" English (whatever that term might mean).

The spurious activity built around the letter of application could have been replaced by a *real* letter to Reebok, L.A. Gear, Nike, or any other shoe manufacturer, written by a student who is angry about a pair of shoes that wore out too soon and are falling apart; or the student who disagrees with a local newspaper's or television station's movie reviewer might write a *real* letter taking exception with the reviewer's assessment of a current film.

The foregoing does not mean that the only legitimate form of writing real language is found in business letters. Students will also write **expressively**, creating free writes, poems, song lyrics, dialog and numerous other forms of written discourse. The distinction I'm trying to make is that their written uses of language should emerge from genuine contexts, not phony ones.

Alternatives such as these are much more real to the student. The letters represent a statement the students want to make, and they are more likely to "own" these letters than they will the mock-up. When students feel ownership in any activity, they are going to invest more care and attention to it; this much is common sense. It's also authentic.

The Activities Provide for a Developmental View

The activities should generally correspond with the level of language development attained by adolescents and must take into account the fact that young adults' language competence is still developing.

Classroom teachers who hold this view are patient. They see language development as a long-term process. They understand that the focus in their classrooms is on the students' continuing language development, not short-cuts to it or one-shot vaccinations which ostensibly provide for "correctness."

This view puts such notions as *standards*, *correctness*, *precision*, *accuracy*, and other judgmental criteria into a different perspective. Of course, these expectations are important! Adopting a developmental view, however, enables the teacher to respond to students with the knowledge and conviction that student language production will not duplicate or match adult competence, but will look and sound like language in the process of *becoming* more mature. While adult language may be incorporated in these activities, it will not be the centerpiece.

They Develop Awareness of Several Aspects of Language

Rather than stressing one feature of language (structure), the activities enable the students to examine a variety of elements and/or generalizations: signs, symbols, language change, regional and social variety, lexicography, semantics, morphology, spelling, and so on. While the ultimate goal of a K–12 language arts program is for the students to achieve control over language and be able to produce spontaneous, clear and elaborated oral and written utterances, LEA operates from the belief that reflective awareness is a prerequisite to control.

The Activities Are Student-centered and Inquiry-oriented

Lecturing adolescent students about anything, especially language matters, is risky business and ineffective teaching. Just try it and watch their eyes glaze over! Nevertheless, the best estimates of classroom talk indicate that the bulk of oral discourse in classrooms is carried on by the teacher, sending an implicit message that the most appropriate pupil response is passivity.[25]

An example of classroom discourse that promotes student passivity is the traditional lecture. Within the context of the lecture hall or classroom, everyone assumes it is the lecturer's job to talk and the students' responsibility to listen, and perhaps write notes on what they hear.

Another example of classroom discourse likely to induce student passivity is the following exchange:

(1) TEACHER: Who can tell me the capital of Texas?
(2) PUPIL 1: Austin?
(3) TEACHER: Right.
(4) TEACHER: What about Iowa?
(5) PUPIL 2: Des Moines?
(6) TEACHER: Good.

When students are lectured at for a substantial period of time during the school year, or for several years, or when they "participate" in a classroom discussion merely by supplying single-term responses, learner passivity should not be unexpected!

Normally people do not acquire language passively but through an active, rule-making, hypothesis-testing process. This notion is contrary to a popular language myth, which holds that there is a catalog or list of "approved" words, phrases, clauses, and sentences adult language users employ to symbolize ideas. The language learner is required to memorize the individual items in this catalog and the things they stand for. Harris calls this the "fixed code fallacy."[26] This view sees children as empty heads waiting to be filled with linguistic data in the form of words, names, and definitions that can be repeated.

A more accurate account of how language users learn language has children actively constructing possible ways of using language, based in part on what they have seen and heard and in part on the child's attempts to create language. For example, the child who observes that plurality typically is indicated through the -s marker will learn to use *cats*, *boys*, and *girls*, but will overgeneralize -s to form the plural *foots* and *mans*. In time, most students will learn the conventional uses of both the regular and the irregular plurals.

The point is that the children learn how to mark plurality by implicitly and indirectly observing and applying the results of their observations to their own language. Older students, adolescents, and adults follow similar patterns as they encounter new linguistic content, new language demands, and a widening circle of social contexts in which language is used.

Through similar applications, we arrive at a number of positive generalizations about how language works successfully; normal children grow up with the capacity to communicate with members of their language networks without (or despite) any direct teaching.

With some obvious modifications, activities in the LEA approach will follow the model of *active* language development as far as possible. It may sound simplistic to say it, but it's true: People who do not use a language do not learn it. Consequently, in order for LEA to work successfully, students must actively engage in the activities.

They Provide for Reflection

If learners are unaware of language options, they are not free to exercise linguistic choices and remain bound to and constrained by a smaller universe of competence, a realm Freire calls a *silent* culture, in which control of language is either withheld or wrested from the speaker.[27] Further, activities that do not cause the learner to reflect, but instead stress the recognition or recall of right answers are probably nothing more than disguised tests. If adolescent learners are to become reflective users of language and to develop metalinguistically (having overt knowledge about their own language), and be able to exercise a wider range of choice from a growing array of options, they must be reflective about language and its uses. This is a major cornerstone of the language exploration and awareness approach.

I ended a speech to an education honorary society several years ago by saying that there is nothing wrong in having nothing else to say, unless one goes ahead and says it! Even with this caution, there is one more thought I would like to share with you.

The LEA approach in this book is an alternative way for children and young adults to learn language. The traditional method of language teaching is used for contrast, since it remains today the more widespread method, despite its clear and long-lived record of demonstrated ineffectiveness in making appreciable changes in students' oral or written language proficiency.

Throughout this text I refer to the traditional method of language study, an approach to classroom language teaching (not necessarily language learning) that I believe is *prelinguistic*. It is not based on linguistic scholarship, but reflects a curious, if not gloomy, mixture of misinformation about people and language. Further, it often substitutes *statements* of preferred linguistic behavior for accurate *information* about language. The traditional method of language study stresses *externally* imposed rules of language, derived from *external* opinions of what satisfies a single criterion of correctness. Thus, this approach imposes upon students a voice other than their own.

Like most English teachers, I am frequently stopped in the corridor, on the street, at church, in the library and at the telephone by friends and colleagues with a question on what I consider a minor issue in word selection, punctuation conventions, and the like. The questions inevitably begin with either, "Is it alright if I . . . ?" or, "Is it permissible to . . . ?" These questions presuppose a catalog, code, or list of an approved way to talk and write.

My answers to their questions are always counter to this notion of a fixed code, so I typically respond by asking how they are using the language element, in what context, and for what purpose. My reply is intended to be true both to what I know of language use and the belief that language use is not a robotic but a human activity, driven by human needs, intentions, and choices.

Language exploration and awareness is consistent with my reply. Among the major aims of LEA is the enlargement of the language user's *internal*, or metalinguistic, awareness and control of language, which is derived from the individual's heightened sensitivity to multiple and varying requirements and criteria of effective language use. This means that students who successfully complete a language exploration and awareness course in language learning rely less on externally-imposed authority in language. Instead, they assume more personal responsibility and authority as they develop linguistic confidence, precision, and proficiency.

FOR YOUR INQUIRY AND PRACTICE:

Interview five or six persons from other career fields (no English language arts teachers), ask them about the forms and content of language study they remember from their school days. What was the emphasis or focus of study, as best they can remember? After you complete your interviews, review the notes you made. To what extent do your respondents' language studies agree or disagree with the six language exploration and awareness (LEA) criteria? Do you believe LEA represents an approach to the study of language that more teachers should use?

NOTES

1. George Hillocks, *Research on Written Composition* (Urbana, IL: National Council of Teachers of English, 1986), 227, 248.
2. Peter Elbow, *What is English?* (New York: The Modern Language Association and the National Council of Teachers of English, 1990), 15; and Patrick Hartwell, "Grammar, Grammars and the Teaching of Grammar," *College English* 47 (1985) : 105–127.
3. Kenneth G. Wilson, *Van Winkle's Return: Change in American English, 1966–1986* (Hanover, NH: University Press of New England, 1987), 37.
4. Ibid.
5. Elbow, *What is English?*, 112.
6. James Milroy and Lesley Milroy, *Authority in Language* (London: Routledge & Kegan Paul, 1985), 175.
7. Arthur N. Applebee, *The Teaching of Literature in Programs with Reputations for Excellence in English* (Albany: State University of New York, Albany Center for the Learning and Teaching of Literature, Report 1.1., 1989).
8. James R. Squire and Roger K. Applebee, *High School English Instruction Today* (New York: Appleton-Century-Crofts, 1968), 140.
9. Applebee, *Teaching of Literature*, 10.
10. Dwight Bolinger and Donald A. Sears, *Aspects of Language*, 3rd edition (New York: Harcourt Brace Jovanovich, 1981), 134.
11. Lev S. Vygotsky, *Thought and Language* (Cambridge: Massachusetts Institute of Technology Press, 1962).
12. Benjamin Whorf," A Linguistic Consideration of Thinking in Primitive Communities," in John Carroll (ed.), *Language, Thought and Reality* (Cambridge: Massachusetts Institute of Technology Press, 1956), 65–86.
13. David Mandelbaum (ed.), *The Selected Writings of Edward Sapir* (Berkeley: University of California Press, 1949).
14. Jean Piaget, *The Language and Thought of the Child* (London: Routledge & Kegan Paul, 1965).
15. Jean Aitchison, *The Articulate Mammal* (London: Unwin Hyman, 1989), 5.
16. Edward Finegan and Niko Besnier, *Language: Its Structure and Use* (New York: Harcourt Brace Jovanovich, 1989), 2.
17. Jack Richards, John Platt, and Heidi Weber, *Longman Dictionary of Applied Linguistics* (London: Longman Group, 1985), 234.
18. Aitchison, *The Articulate Mammal*, 1.
19. Richards, Platt and Weber, *Dictionary*, 262.
20. James Paul Gee, "Literacy, Discourse, and Linguistics: Introduction," *Boston University Journal of Education* 171 (1989): 5–25.

21. Howard Giles and W. Peter Robinson, *Handbook of Language and Social Psychology* (New York: Wiley, 1990), 2.

22. Noam Chomsky, *Syntactic Structures* (The Hague: Mouton, 1957).

23. Jerome S. Bruner, *Childs Talk* (New York: W.W. Norton, 1981).

24. Gordon Wells, *The Meaning Makers: Children Learning Language and Using Language to Learn* (London: Heinemann, 1986), 15.

25. Michael Stubbs, *Discourse Analysis* (Oxford: Basil Blackwell, 1983), 64.

26. Roy Harris, *The Language Myth* (London: Duckworth & Company Ltd, 1981), 10.

27. Paulo Freire, "The Adult Literacy Process as Cultural Action for Freedom," *Harvard Educational Review* 40 (1970), 205–221.

CHAPTER 2

Language Exploration and Awareness: Why It Is

They have been at a great feast of languages, and stolen the scraps.
—William Shakespeare, *Love's Labour's Lost*

THE FOCUS AND CONTEXTS OF LANGUAGE STUDY

In his history of English teaching in United States schools, Applebee records that the subject called *English* did not appear in school curricula until the end of the nineteenth century. Grammar was the first formal study of English to become widespread in schools.[1]

Not having an existing tradition of English instruction already in place to serve as a guide to how native language might be taught, the schools looked to other forms of formal language study—the teaching of the classical languages, Latin and Greek—for instructional methods and models.[2]

The emphasis in teaching the classical languages was grammar, and it emphasized two elements: learning the rules and learning their use. These two elements were learned through sentence parsing, analyses of sentences, diagramming, and the correction of usage errors. This approach to the study of Latin and Greek was generally adopted as the guide to the study of English. Consequently, what evolved in the study of the English language was a shift from a method of *teaching* a classical and foreign language to a method of *correcting* a native one.[3] Briefly and simply, this is how the prescriptive study of English grammar began.

In subsequent years educators suggested alternatives to this model of English language instruction. "The traditional rules of grammar, the efficacy

17

of parsing and diagramming, the clear alternatives between correct and incorrect usage were all boldly attacked and at least partially discredited."[4] Nevertheless, the prescriptive tradition and its associated attitudes toward language use remain healthy, despite recurring recommendations, suggestions, and pleas for other approaches.

There are a number of reasons for continuing the prescriptive approach to language. How English language study entered the curriculum is one contributing factor. Precedents exert strong influences, and the traditions they establish are difficult to alter.

Another reason, I believe, is that professional language scholars, linguists, have had less influence on the language portion of school curricula in the United States than their colleagues in the theories of literature or writing.

Some claim that linguists' ideas and writings are so arcane that they are difficult, if not impossible, to understand. Linguists are sometimes accused, in fact, of being too far removed from reality and too abstract. They float and dance in what one writer has called "celestial unintelligibility."[5]

Similarly, some educators talk about linguistics as if it were merely a newer kind of glorified method of analyzing sentences, which in my view is a gross oversimplification of its concerns.[6]

Moreover, and unfortunately, a number of potentially useful approaches to language study have failed to make a difference in K–12 classroom practices for a simpler reason. How some of these approaches might be translated into comprehensible, meaningful, and feasible classroom study in the schools either has not been attempted or has not been accomplished successfully. Consequently, many school curricula retain a traditional emphasis on one aspect of language rather than a wider array, more by default than by design.

Recent research suggests that most schools continue lessons that emphasize the structure of an isolated, decontextualized, and idealized English language, stressing parts of speech, sentence structure, word analysis, and the organization of paragraphs.[7] Unfortunately, these approaches are usually no more successful today than they were 25, 50, and 75 years ago. In fact, Hillocks' review of numerous research studies spanning several decades shows that this approach to classroom language learning is not only ineffective, but is a "gross disservice" that is actually detrimental to the students' ability to write.[8]

Nevertheless, the purpose of *Language Exploration and Awareness* is to **affirm** language study. The study of the English language is an important, if not the central, activity in any school. Language development is not completed by the first grade or by ages 11 or 16, and our students still have much to gain before they can be considered truly competent with language. Further, students who continue to grow in language are much more likely to achieve success in other school subjects, especially those that require reading and writing. Vygotsky suggests that conscious and deliberate mastery of language is one of the principal contributions of school.[9] It is not, therefore, the *study* of the English language in question here, but rather the general *method* or *approach* that needs to be altered.

Most students view the more traditional approaches to language study as far removed from their personal experiences with language and therefore *unconnected* from their want or need to use language differently from their current practices.[10] The traditional approach typically fails to present a more comprehensive view of language and language users, and has been ineffective for a variety of reasons which include, but are not limited to, the following.

WEAKNESSES OF THE TRADITIONAL APPROACH TO LANGUAGE STUDY

The traditional approach:

1. Has emphasized the structure of written language, rather than the meanings oral and written language help to create
2. Assumes a single standard of "correctness," and attempts to make language use uniform and standard, ignoring the obvious and inevitable features of language variation and change
3. Has used artificial, unnatural, and false language as an example of the type of language "good" writers and speakers ought to use, instead of authentic, natural, and true language as it actually is used by real people
4. Assumes a model of language attainment appropriate to adult mastery, instead of a developmental model considerate of young learners
5. Has emphasized control by the learner over isolated language elements before it helps the learner establish a level of awareness about the larger fullness of language

Emphasizes Structure Rather Than Meaning

In the traditional program, nine-, ten- or eleven-year-olds begin a six- to eight-year analysis of the traditional Latinate grammatical and syntactical structure of written language. In many cases it's a one-year program repeated six, seven, or eight times! Students memorize definitions of nouns, verbs, adverbs, and conjunctions, subjective and nominative cases, and the categories of phrases, clauses, and sentences. By labeling the parts of speech of the words in sentences, and through related analyses of individual sentences, the students are expected to be able, then, to create sentences that duplicate the adult models they have been studying.

In addition to confusing the distinctions between passive memorization and active learning, the focus of this type of language study is on the "pure meaning" of illustrative and "ideal" sentences that are supposed to represent adult language. The sentences are typically presented in list form and are examined independent of any real context of use.

For example, a recent English handbook gives a list of the following sentence pairs, each pair illustrating a type of sentence:

> A. A *declarative* sentence makes a statement.
>   1. Dexter grows broccoli in his garden.
>   2. Our boat has leaked since last fall.
> B. An *interrogative* sentence asks a question.
>   1. Wouldn't you like a pillow for your head?
>   2. What will an extra night in the hotel cost?
> C. An *imperative* sentence gives a command.
>   1. Wait for me, Mario.
>   2. Chauncey, stop that barking!
> D. An *exclamatory* sentence expresses strong emotion or surprise.
>   1. Willie's sister said her first word!
>   2. Oh, what a surprise I have for Lon![11]

I can make several comments about these categories and their illustrations. First, the categories are simplistic and are simply incorrect when we consider how people actually use language. For example, a structure seeming to be an *imperative sentence*, as in, "Give me your telephone number again," is really a *request* (asking) for information. Similarly, another structure which from a simplistic point of view might appear to be an *interrogative sentence*, as in, "Will you please close the door?" or "Can you pick up a loaf of bread on your way home?" is more likely a *command*. As we will see later, interrogative sentences are sometimes used to make *exclamatory statements*. The textbook categories are erroneous because they stress rudimentary and decontextualized structural features and not *meaning* as it emerges through authentic language use.

These incomplete textbook definitions of sentences have at least one other dubious feature: historical precedent. One of the examples cited earlier tells the reader, "An *imperative* sentence gives a command." This is very much like an older definition: "A sentence which gives an order is a command." The second definition comes from one of the texts in my personal collection of old books. This English language textbook was published in the United States over a century ago![12]

Can you imagine the public outcry if physics or geography teachers used facts, definitions, or concepts that denied the existence of twentieth-century knowledge? When English language curricula are based on outmoded notions, we are no better than the physics teacher who refuses to go beyond Newtonian physics or the geography teacher who continues to use maps with the warning, "Here there be beasties" emblazoned on the outer reaches of the oceans!

Other exceptions to the simplified categories can be found easily by randomly observing any fifteen minutes of authentic and normal conversations in school corridors, parking lots, or the aisles at church or the grocery store, or, in short, anywhere people congregate and use real language. These are the locations of authentic language; places where real people use language for sharing meanings.

You might take a few minutes at this point to examine the Student Explorations at the end of Section II. You'll notice that the language used for examination and analysis in these explorations comes from newspapers, magazines, road signs, picture books, novels, short stories, interviews, dictionaries, menus, conversations, and from students' naturally occurring oral and written language. These are examples of authentic language in which *meaning*, intentional and otherwise, is the major item of interest.

Secondly, the sentences used to illustrate the categories exist only because they demonstrate, at least in the judgment of the company producing the handbook, a particular grammatical feature. The sentences aren't real because they do not occur in a normal context of use. They're either wordroids or sentential robots. Further, sentence A-1 in the list is unrelated to A-2, sentence B-1 is unrelated either to the preceding sentences or to sentence B-2, and so on. The sentences pose as discourse, but their isolation reveals them as pseudodiscourse. The emphasis is on the syntactic purity of each isolated sentence. These are not real sentences because they do not represent real discourse; they are contrived illustrations. They are *like* discourse, but are *not* real discourse. These are clearly textbook sentences, with bona fide or genuine meaning serving only an indirect or secondary purpose.

While structure in language obviously is important, it is one of the last linguistic features the typical language learner attends to directly or intentionally; *meaning* is the first and, for most people, the most enduring interest and perceived need. From the onset of language acquisition until young adulthood and in many cases beyond, language users are most concerned with what they talk *about* rather than what they talk *with*.[13] The paramount and overriding linguistic interest of normal language users is meaning.

This does not mean that structure should never be included in the language arts curriculum. To omit structural studies completely would be as professionally irresponsible as teaching *only* structure, or syntax. I am suggesting, however, that the over-emphasis on syntactic structure is premature and entirely out of balance with most learners' needs and sense of what's really important.

In reality, people learn to use language because of what it can accomplish for them. As Thornton, Doughty, and Doughty observe, ". . . the important thing about a pupil's language is not what it sounds like; it is what [the pupil] can use it for."[14] The child learns to say "milk," for example, because saying the word *means something* and produces meaningful results.

Similarly, adolescents have learned—indirectly and incidentally—what language can accomplish. They know, for example, that adopting the code words of their respective social networks simultaneously establishes and symbolizes identity, group affiliation, and belonging. These are meaning-making speech choices of the most personal type, are virtually universal among all language learners, and are especially important to adolescents and young adults. Remember, the unstated but nevertheless nearly unanimous motto for most students in our schools is "death before uncool." The sense of the motto is relatively clear: Death is preferred to committing an act others might interpret as uncool or not hep! Of course the surest way to avoid being "uncool" is to gain the affirmation and identity that comes from group similitude.

School-age learners need language for several reasons. Among the important ones are: sharing ideas, dreams, secrets, and thoughts with their friends (or those with whom they want to be friends); negotiating and constructing questions, answers and interpretations of information in the world; and performing these communicative acts in a fashion their peers consider acceptable and "with it." Using language for all of these purposes is a tall order.

Further, it is a generally accepted sociolinguistic fact that people adopt the language of the group or network they either belong to or aspire to join; this is true for adults and adolescents alike. It is all but futile, therefore, for teachers to try to "take away" the adolescent's normal language and replace it with a another, even (or especially) when the replacement language is what adults prefer. The simple fact is, most adolescents do not want to be socially affiliated or identified with the adult society that teachers and textbooks represent. They have their own social groups and their membership in *these* groups—symbolized in large measure by discrete speech patterns and word choices—is what matters most.

You have no doubt observed that some adults, perhaps even some English teachers, identify themselves through their actions as language cops. These agents from the department of [language] corrections patrol classrooms and corridors, poised to pounce upon and apprehend miscreants who live outside the palazzo of paragraph purity.

One such teacher told me how he "handled" his students' use of the word *humongous* (huge): he told his students that they could use the word in his classroom, but since it is not in the dictionary, they *must not* use it anywhere else. (As a matter of lexicographical fact, *humongous* is in "the dictionary." It's included in two dictionaries in my collection.)

Sometimes attempts by language cops to command and control language use are downright funny. In a four-page text division headed "Frequently Misused Words and Phrases," for example, a language handbook cited earlier tells its adolescent audience, "Avoid using *amongst*, which is an outdated form."[15]

The most recently published dictionary on my desk, *Webster's College Dictionary*[16], does not use a *label of time*—a label used in dictionaries to show that a term is dated and is considered obsolete, archaic or older—for

"Yeah, I'm from the department of
corrections, and what you've been doing
with your passive sentences is known by us."

amongst. Why, one wonders, has this term been selected as one that is, presumably, "misused"? (No mention is made, by the way, of closely related terms like *whilst, amidst,* or *against.*)

The term *amongst* (like *whilst*) is routinely used by the Queen of England, the Archbishop of Canterbury, my friends Nan and Tony Tickner in Newcastle, and Graham and Kathleen Shaw in Barnes (a London suburb), as well as by millions of speakers and writers throughout the United Kingdom, Canada, Australia, and other countries where standard British English is used. Are these and and other language users—seen and heard frequently on news programs carried by ABC, NBC, CBS, NPR, CNN, and C-SPAN—guilty, as some language cop claims, of committing "outdated language"? Of course not.

It is true that *amongst* is used either more or less frequently, depending upon the habits and conventions of the language users we are considering. But this feature of usage is a characteristic of one's language family, and of regional and social dialects. *Why* different people use different forms of similar words in changing social contexts is a more productive and more honest question. (See Chapters 7 and 8.)

Since no amount of adult (teacher or parent) ridicule, discouragement, attempted control, or fun-making will cause Lisa or Brad to stop saying "humongous," or "like" as used in "Can we, like, go to 7-Eleven?" the teacher or parent who tries to control or eradicate a community or network usage such as "like" (or any other structural element) in the language of a school-age language user will encounter stony silence, cold, catatonic stares, or temporary compliance accompanied by resistant, under-the-breath mutterings.

When a communication is incomplete, language users of all ages seldom analyze the *structure* of the failed utterances; rather, they reflect upon the *meanings.* When communication fails, people are most likely to ask: "Why did she/he/I say *that*?"

Bolinger and Sears point out that the relationship between words and meanings is known to all speakers. When they struggle with an idea, they are not apt to ask themselves which structural element will help them say what they want to say; rather, they will say or think, "What's the right word?" (a clear indication that they are groping for clearer *meaning*).[17]

Assumes Language Homogeneity Instead of Language Diversity

Several years ago I asked my university to release me from my administrative appointment so that I could return to my first academic loves: teaching, reading, thinking, conducting research, and writing. Shortly after my decision became public knowledge, the dean of one of our colleges met me on the street. As our curbside conversation came to an end, the dean said: "By the way, do me a favor; make sure your students know *not* to begin sentences with 'Hopefully.' Teach them that adverbs don't begin sentences! That just drives me up the wall!"

People on my campus know this dean as a kind, intelligent, and tolerant person. He has worked to bring diversity to his faculty and student cohort. His comment demonstrates, nevertheless, just one of the many myths about the homogeneity of "proper" language.

"Hopefully" has for some reason been singled out as a major misuse of an adverb. Why "hopefully" in the sentence-initial position should create so much controversy remains a linguistic mystery.

Resistance to the use of *hopefully* has been voiced by several critics, Lipton among the more recent. He likens the relatively widespread use of *hopefully* to a relentless advance by a linguistic General Sherman as he observes that "*Hopefully* is marching roughshod through sentences, modifying every word on the Eleven O'Clock News but the right one."[18]

Few people given to criticizing the public's use of language vent their spleen in a similar fashion with other adverbs used at the beginning of sentences, like "Naturally, I think so, too.", "Surprisingly, we went first.", or "Fortunately, she was there." Amazingly, amid the fuss over "hopefully," other sentence-initial adverbs seem to be more acceptable.

Whether the issue is the proper placement of adverbs, the use of split infinitives ("To boldly go . . ."), the correct or preferred pronunciation of "mischievous," the dropping of either /r/ ("Pahk the cah heah.") or /ng/ ("Stop that runnin'!"), or a multitude of other possible examples, there is a persistent tendency among some language critics, classroom teachers, and textbook publishers to prescribe one use rather than another, and then to label the preferred use as correct and the other incorrect.

The traditional language program has followed the prescriptive approach to language study for a century in the United States, despite the indisputable evidence that language use *varies* in real time and *changes* over time.

For example, "butcher" once was limited to meaning "slayer of goats." "Silly" once meant "happy or prosperous." Similarly, my grandfather had no idea what "byte" might mean, but he was able to use "tug," "hayme" and "crupper" (pieces of harness used in farming) with precision. I don't recall hearing my grandfather speak the word "mischievous," but if and when he did, I suspect he made the word a four-syllable term with the second syllable the stressed one; that's how the other speakers in his language network pronounced it.

There are hundreds of similar examples of language diversity and change, but they are ignored in the traditional program that advocates a single standard of correct language use. This attitude is the result of several factors, no doubt. For example, James and Lesley Milroy suggest that written language has been studied, analyzed, and codified to a far greater extent than oral language and, consequently, teachers (and textbooks) impose the standards of written language on oral uses.[19]

While the Milroys' point is helpful, we must also remember that despite its codification and greater degree of standardization, written language varies, too. A letter applying for a job, a note to the mail carrier, a shopping list, a letter to a friend whose spouse has died recently, and a manuscript prepared for publication in a scholarly journal each will use a different style of written language. It is misleading to students to tell them, directly or indirectly, that the formal, written language in a scholarly manuscript or its equivalent is the *one and only* standard against which all other uses will be judged.

It is similarly misleading, if not downright dishonest, for students to hear one variety of language preferred when their choice is equally as appropriate and effective in a given context.

At the knowledge level, many prescriptive statements about language simply are wrong. Telling students that a double negative makes the sentence positive is a misapplication of a principle from mathematics. If a speaker says, "We don't have no money," only a knave or a fool would insist that the speaker has *some*.

At the human level, prescriptive statements are more horrific, especially when a student is made ashamed of the way she speaks. As Halliday, et al., observe:

> A speaker who is made ashamed of his own language habits suffers a basic injury as a human being: to make anyone, especially a child, feel so ashamed is as indefensible as to make him feel ashamed of the color of his skin.[20]

A modern English language arts curriculum ought to provide opportunities for students to observe which features of language are judged by a society or an audience as *acceptable* or *unacceptable* as the speakers, contexts, and communicative needs and intentions vary and change. The modern program should substitute information about language use and how it varies for unexamined assertions of personal preference, whether the preference is the teacher's or the textbook publisher's.

Emphasizes Artificial Instead of Authentic Language

The traditional program uses artificial language in a number of ways. First, it uses many contrived examples of "good English." As stated earlier in our discussion of structure versus meaning, many of the sentences in textbooks, guidebooks, and prepackaged workbooks were written by a professional illustrative sentence generator. The sentences are isolated and have no context of authentic use. Secondly, these sentences do not represent the ways real people use real language in real circumstances. They are, therefore, *misleading* inasmuch as they appear on a page out of nowhere, but nevertheless are held up to the students as good models.

For example, earlier in this chapter we examined the traditional classification of sentences, which tells us that there are declarative, exclamatory, interrogative, and imperative sentences. At the time, I suggested that the illustrative sentences exist only because they provide examples; they possess no "real" meaning because they are not naturally occurring statements arising from a true communication event among people.

If one accepts these sentences literally and out of any real context of use, then the definitions seem harmless enough. The fact is, however, *real sentences always appear in a context* and many sentences frequently mean "more" than their literal content. For example, "Are you kidding?" *may* be an interrogative sentence, using the traditional definition usually taught, but in real use this sentence will more likely serve an *exclamatory* function, especially when it is used in context in response to a question.

(1) MARY: Uncle Bill's coming to town Friday.
(2) GARY: Hey, great!
(3) MARY: He says he'll take us to dinner at La Cafe de Fama. Can you make it?
(4) GARY: Are you kidding?

Unless Mary overdosed on literal pills earlier in the day, she will take Gary's reply in statement (5) *not* as a question (interrogative), but as an exclamation actually meaning something like "Of course!" or "Certainly!" or "You bet!"

Only when sentences are placed in some real context can we accurately describe them and their uses. Few people use language in single, isolated, one-shot sentences. The traditional program tends to forget, nevertheless, that in real-time language use, people simply do not go around making unconnected, unprompted, and unsolicited statements or comments about the world.[21]

To the contrary, the language that people really use is more likely to be *exchanges* of interconnected discourse in which the speakers, their relationship, their intentions, and the setting affect the linguistic choices in one sentence, which affect the choices made in the next, and the next, and so on.

Observant adults will notice, for example, that in one circumstance the executive [E] will choose a more formal style of words and phrases when he is meeting with his staff [S] and a representative [R] from the national office to discuss the purchase of a new piece of software:

(1) E: It is certainly our pleasure to welcome Mr. Leeter who joins us today
(2)   bringing greetings from the national office.
(3) R: Thank you, Thomas. It has been several years since I've been here. The
(4)   reason I'm here today is to describe to you and to your staff the status of
(5)   the installation of the new spreadsheet. Yes, there's a question?
(6) S: With all due respect, Mr. Leeter, is this change necessary? The current
(7)   program has been very useful, I thought.
(8) R: For several years we've been examining the format of the quarterly
(9)   reports . . .
(10) S: [Interrupting] [We've heard that, Mr. Leeter, but my question . . .
(11) E: [Interrupting] [Mary, let's allow Mr. Leeter the opportunity to
(12)   explain. . . .

On the other hand, E will make a very different set of more informal language choices when coaching at a Little League baseball game later that day, discussing aspects of the game with his son and his son's teammates [T]:

(1) E: Guys, I'm here to tell ya. . . .
(2) T1: (Interrupting)   [Mr. Shaw?
(3) E: . . . Huh? Oh, ah, Tom?
(4) T1: Do we play next Thursday or Friday?
(5) E: I donno, Tom. If you'll . . if all . . when you guys . . .
(6) T2: [Interrupting]   [But, my mom
(7)   needs to know!

The traditional approach to language study, with its over-emphasis on explicit knowledge of prescriptive syntax through atomistic and analytic study of decontextualized, idealized sentences promotes a homogenized standard of English usage and seldom, if ever, recognizes the distinctions illustrated in these two passages.

The first example, for instance, is more formal; an employee, Thomas, is introducing Mr. Leeter, his superior and a district manager in the corporate structure. Thomas is more deliberate in his language choices. One does not climb the corporate ladder successfully by saying stupid things in front of superiors.

The second example, on the other hand, is very informal, and takes place in a casual context; Thomas's language choices are less deliberate and more spontaneous, but, as was the case with the first example, they are appropriate to the context.

The traditional language programs in schools seldom recognize distinctions such as those illustrated in these two examples. The result is a truncated and often erroneous view of both language and people, and how people actually use language.

Emphasizes Adult Instead of Developmental Models: Bronze Lullaby

In his autobiography, the British writer Laurie Lee recalls the anger and disillusionment he experienced his first day at the village school. After arriving at school, he was taken to a chair and told, "Well, you just sit there for the present." "I sat there all day," he writes, "but I never got it."[22]

Describing an older language user, Perera tells of the college student who wrote in a final exam paper about the "child development theories of P. R. J."[23] One of my colleagues tells a similar story about the piano student who was particularly fond of the music of the French composer, "W. C."

Despite the fact that the speakers in these examples come from greatly diverse age groups, one of the things they have in common is that when the participants were in relatively new territory their "model" of language and the predictions and understandings it created didn't work. The speakers imposed their own sense of reality on the language used by adults, a language reflecting a very different reality. Similar misunderstandings occur in English classes when the language model used is an adult model, whether the model is theoretical or practical.

The traditional approach to language study glosses over the fact that the language of adolescents is still developing. This is a serious error. The language of adolescents is neither fixed nor established. Young adults are still learning how to interpret the sociolinguistic features of speaker, intention, and situation or context in their daily conversations. Romaine found that the use of socially stigmatized forms (multiple negation, the use of *ain't*) is at its maximum in a speaker's adolescent years.[24]

Further, young adults are still developing their language fluency and will continue to use false starts, voiced hesitations and meaningless repetitions. Complex noun phrases, some modal auxiliaries (shall, may, ought to), relative clauses introduced by "whom" or "whose" and many other grammatical constructions are not that frequent in the language of some adolescent learners.[25]

These are just a few examples of normal language development among adolescent learners. These students are not substandard, stupid, or lazy. The examples illustrate simply that young adults are still learning the language; they are still serving their linguistic apprenticeships, largely unaware, rightfully and understandably so, that anyone might care about the use of adverbs in sentence-initial positions.

Despite what has been learned about continuing language development among learners in their early teens, English language handbooks and textbooks presuppose an "ideal speaker/hearer," equipped with an adult mastery of language. However, as most of their teachers know, many middle-school students do not possess this level of mastery.[26] Consequently, too many students experience needless frustration when they use these texts which are based upon inappropriate assumptions and models.

A more contemporary, linguistically-based approach is based on the recognition that language develops continually in gradations, not discrete steps, and that the concept of *continuum* of language development is a crucial underpinning to any curriculum of school language study.[27] More often than not, however, the traditional approach to language study assumes that the learners' language is already fully developed and that all that is needed are examples of how to use it correctly.

Emphasizes Control before Awareness

One of the greatest weaknesses of the traditional program of English language study is that it attempts to teach students how to control isolated features of language before many of the students are aware of their own language or the languages around them. Further, the traditional program too often emphasizes isolated features through negative examples, which is completely opposite from the normal way young people acquire and learn language.

Several years ago a group of us in our church assembled a coed softball team for one of the city leagues. Women my age came through the school system long before both Title IX or the newer physical education curricula. Consequently, for most of them, who had graduated from high school twelve to fifteen years earlier, the coed softball team was their first opportunity to play an organized team sport. At a team practice session one afternoon when I said, "Don't swing if the ball isn't in the strike zone!" the female batter turned to me and asked: "What's a strike zone?" I had been guilty of assuming the batter had control over something she wasn't even aware of.

The traditional English language arts curriculum makes a similarly false assumption, namely, that students can control individual facets of language before they are aware of the wholeness of language and its attendant complexity. This resource book is dedicated to the proposition that K–12 learners can indeed learn more about exercising control over language, but this aim will be realized only if they have opportunities to explore language, strip from it the mystification often imposed by traditional English language textbooks, and become aware of the complexity of language and how real people use real language for authentic and extremely varied purposes.

Moreover, language handbooks and textbooks frequently present examples of sentences which the students are to avoid because they are "confusing," "weak," or "unacceptable."[28] Including ungrammatical or negative examples under the heading of "Don't Say" seems to be counter to the ways language is acquired and learned. The traditional approach, therefore, stresses the wrong kind of control as well.

Pinker provides a thorough analysis of whether negative, ungrammatical evidence (models, prototypes, examples) is ever available to the language learner. "Obviously," Pinker states, "no one gives children ungrammatical sentences tagged with asterisks."[29] An asterisk conventionally is attached to ungrammatical and improbable sentences, as in *boy home the ran.

By the time most children begin formal schooling, at age six or seven, their language use demonstrates that they are capable of or are in the process of becoming more proficient in making a number of grammatical distinctions. For example, young language learners already employ constructions such as those in the left column, and implicitly understand that expressions such as those on the right are dysfunctional.[30]

Give me the car.	versus	*take me the car
Water the plant.	versus	*put the plant
Bill walked Mary home.	versus	*Bill went Mary home

Further, Macnamara illustrates the naming differentiations young children can make. For example, the child named Harry has learned the semantics that many namelike terms can be applied to *one* object or referent: *Harry* (the child himself), *you* (a pronoun), *boy* (specific), and *person* (generic).[31]

Exactly how children acquire and learn these and other complicated uses of words and language is not clearly known. Most linguists believe that language is acquired as children first observe how words are used in the contexts around them and then try them out in other contexts. Most of the feedback children receive from these efforts stresses the success of the functional, meaning-centered uses of their language in a home/social context and is not about grammaticality.[32] In whatever form the feedback might assume, then, grammaticality and negative evidence or examples are seldom used. Briefly, this is one reason why the negative examples in textbooks aren't likely to be useful to the learner's language growth. People do not appear to acquire language through negative examples.

A final point needs to be made about negative, ungrammatical examples. Simply put, what is ungrammatical to one generation or context may be or may become grammatical to another. Currently, we would identify the following sentences as either grammatical or ungrammatical:

1. He mailed me a letter.
2. She faxed me a letter.
3. *he satellited me a letter
4. *she televisioned me a letter

Can you imagine when sentences 1 or 2 would have been considered ungrammatical? Conversely, five, ten, fifteen, or twenty years from now will sentences 3 and 4 still be tagged with asterisks pointing out that they are ungrammatical? Your answers to these questions will be speculative, of course, but you get the idea. Several characteristics of traditional language curricula and textbooks are not in step with current linguistic thought. This chapter has described some of those characteristics in an attempt to provide a context for the approach I am calling Language Exploration and Awareness.

___

FOR YOUR INQUIRY AND PRACTICE:

Prepare a brief statement entitled, "My Language Story." How is your language different today from the oral and written language you used five years ago? Ten years ago? What and who have been the major influences on your evolving language?

___

NOTES

1. Arthur N. Applebee, *Tradition and Reform in the Teaching of English: A History* (Urbana, IL: National Council of Teachers of English, 1974), 5–8.
2. Ibid.
3. Ibid.
4. Commission on English, *Freedom and Discipline in English* (New York: College Entrance Examination Board, 1965), 20.
5. Cited in Jean Aitchison, *The Articulate Mammal* (London: Unwin Hyman, 1989), 164.
6. Peter Doughty, John Pearce, and Geoffrey Thornton, *Exploring Language* (London: Edward Arnold, 1972), 28.
7. See: Arthur N. Applebee, *Contexts for Learning to Write: Studies of Secondary School Instruction* (Norwood, NJ: Ablex Publishing Corporation, 1984); and John Goodlad, *A Place Called School* (New York: McGraw-Hill, 1984).
8. George Hillocks, *Research on Written Composition* (New York: National Conference on Research in English and Urbana, IL: ERIC Clearinghouse on Reading and Communication Skills, 1986), 248.

9. Cited in Margaret Donaldson, *Children's Minds* (London: Fontana Press, 1978), 99.
10. Doughty, Pearce, and Thornton, *Exploring Language,* 28.
11. Mary Ellen Snodgrass, *The Great American English Handbook* (Jacksonville, IL: Perma-bound, 1987), 27.
12. C.C. Long, *New Language Exercises for Primary Schools* (Cincinnati and New York: Van Antwerp, Bragg, and Company, 1889), 31.
13. Donaldson, *Children's Minds,* 87–88.
14. Geoffrey Thornton, Peter Doughty, and Anne Doughty, *Language Study: The School and the Community* (New York: Elsevier, 1974), 130.
15. Snodgrass, *English Handbook,* 36.
16. *Webster's College Dictionary* (New York: Random House, 1991).
17. Dwight Bolinger and Donald A. Sears, *Aspects of Language*, 3rd ed. (New York: Harcourt Brace Jovanovich, 1981), 52–53.
18. James Lipton, *An Exaltation of Larks* (New York: Viking Penguin, 1991), 13.
19. James Milroy and Lesley Milroy, *Authority in Language* (London: Routledge & Kegan Paul, 1985), 71–72.
20. M. A. K. Halliday, Agnes McIntosh, and Peter Strevens, *The Linguistic Sciences and Language Teaching* (Bloomington: Indiana University Press, 1964), 105.
21. For an excellent discussion of the study of genuine discourse see Michael Stubbs, *Discourse Analysis* (Oxford: Basil Blackwell, 1983), 150.
22. Laurie Lee, *The Edge of Day: A Boyhood in the West of England* (New York: Morrow, 1960), 45.
23. Katherine Perera, "The Language Demands of Schooling," in Ronald Carter (ed.), *Linguistics and the Teacher* (London: Routledge & Kegan Paul, 1982), 115.
24. Suzanne Romaine, *The Language of Children and Adolescents* (Oxford: Basil Blackwell, 1984), 108.
25. Katherine Perera, *Children's Writing and Reading: Analysing Classroom Language* (Oxford: Basil Blackwell, 1984), 121–124.
26. Perera, *Language Demands of Schooling,* 156.
27. Eric Hawkins, *Awareness of Language: An Introduction* (Cambridge: Cambridge University Press, 1987), 69.
28. These terms are used regularly in Snodgrass and in H. Ramsey Fowler, *The Little, Brown Handbook* (Boston: Little, Brown, 1980).
29. Steven Pinker, *Learnability and Cognition: The Acquisition of Argument Structure* (Cambridge: Massachusetts Institute of Technology Press, A Bradford Book, 1991), 6.
30. Ibid., 99.
31. John Macnamara, *Names for Things: a Study in Human Learning* (Cambridge: Massachusetts Institute of Technology Press, 1982), viii.
32. Pinker, *Learnability and Cognition,* 11.

CHAPTER 3

Language Exploration and Awareness: Three Prerequisites

> *Language is not an abstract construction of the learned, or of dictionary-makers, but is something arising out of the work, needs, ties, joys, affections, tastes, of long generations of humanity, and has its bases broad and low, close to the ground.*
> —Walt Whitman, from *Slang in America*

There are three prerequisites for the success of the language explorations approach to the study of language described in this book. Those prerequisites are the general topics of this chapter:

1. Language study should focus on realistic and genuine uses of language
2. Language success is assessed by the application of multiple criteria of effectiveness
3. There should be more opportunities in classrooms for student talk

To introduce and illustrate the first objective, here is an autobiographical vignette. The incident reflects what I call a monocular view of the world ("My way, or the wrong way!") which has a direct, if not an opposite, relationship to the expanded view of the English language curriculum described in this book.

---

* An earlier and shorter version of a portion of this chapter appeared as, "Putting More Talk in the Middle-Level Language Arts," *American Secondary Education*, Vol. 19, No. 1 (1990), pp. 9–13. Reprinted with permission.

The setting: We are sitting in a circle in the main lodge at summer camp, finishing our final day of counselor orientation. Most of the young campers who will join us tomorrow have some type of physical disability; many come from lower social classes. The staff session is planned to help us better understand, and therefore appropriately respond to the physical and other needs of each camper.

One of the directors at the session is finishing the description of how the family-style meal service will work, and concludes by reminding us: "Make sure the campers break their bread; they never do this and it looks just awful to see them chewing on a whole slice. Someday I'm going to have 'Break Your Bread' chiseled above the fireplace!" The counselors dutifully nod, implicitly agreeing to teach the campers the importance of breaking a slice of bread in half at mealtime.

USING REAL DISCOURSE AND MULTIPLE CRITERIA IN DETERMINING CORRECTNESS

This scene is worth sharing because it illustrates an unwavering insistence on only one way to define socially correct behavior. When applied to language behavior, it's an attitude that should have been eradicated decades ago, but, like teenage acne, it persists. This attitude toward language—as an abstract construction of the learned that is imposed upon people—remains widespread in American society and in many classrooms. However, the children and young adults in our classrooms know better. They have been observing real language at work for years, and have gained implicit understandings of how authentic language really works.

If you have overheard youngsters playing school, for example, you will recognize the following passage.

(1) MARY: Let's get quiet, boys and girls. . . .
(2) GARY: Teacher! Teacher!
(3) MARY: Gary, I'm not ready for your questions. You must pay . . .
(4) GARY: But, Teacher . . .
(5) MARK: Gary, siddown!
(6) MARY: Boys! Boys! [clapping hands] I'm
(7)   afraid I'm going to have to separate you if you can't behave!

In statement (1), Mary demonstrates her implicit knowledge of Teacher's routine way of talking to a class, directing its attention or activity, and redirecting focus when necessary. Mary learned her script and its rules through observation; she and other school-age children in the United States know how to play school in accordance with the rules without direct instruction.

The game would break down, on the other hand, if Mary began with, "Dearly beloved, we are gathered here . . . ," "Peace be with you brothers and sisters . . . ," or "Gentlemen, start your engines." While the "class" would recognize these sentences as grammatical, they would most likely also rule them invalid; this is not the way their classroom teachers typically talk.

Similarly, had Mary said in statement (7), "Ladies and gentlemen of the jury . . . ," Gary and Mark would most likely reject this alternative because it isn't right; it just doesn't fit the context. It doesn't follow the contextual or situational rules of classroom discourse.

In the several pretend or "playlike" games of young language learners, rule violators are dealt with. If one of the participants does not adhere to the rules of the game, that person suffers immediate consequences: He or she is reassigned to another role, ignored, or left out of the game altogether.

Adults treat rule violators similarly. How many times have you decided *not* to ask a colleague or an acquaintance a casual question for fear that you'd get a lecture instead of a simple answer?

GOOD ENGLISH IN CONTEXTS OF SOCIAL AVENUES

For a variety of reasons, these are important observations for teachers of English and the language arts. They remind us that kids learn easily and quickly how to shift their language to fit a particular circumstance; that "correct" language use is determined by its context; and as contexts change, so do the standards and criteria for judging correctness. They have learned that there is no *single* standard for what is considered "correct" in real-time language usage, but there are options within the sociolinguistic system. The correctness of the option selected is determined by the application of multiple criteria, or multiple "rules" if you prefer.

In short, young people implicitly understand that real language use is a context-determined and socially driven behavior.

Adolescent learners know, for example, what is "good English" when they speak with friends on the school bus. It is language that opts for nicknames, inside jokes, and a lot of *you know*'s, *like*'s, *sure*'s, *yeah*'s, *um*'s, and similar words that maintain bridges to social relationships. Similarly, they know that when they greet the school principal, ask a question in science class, or speak with the piano teacher after school that the nicknames, *you know*'s, *like*'s, *sure*'s, and *yeah*'s are no longer appropriate. Later in the day they will revert to other language choices when they talk to an intimate friend on the telephone before going to bed. They know that each of these circumstances requires another language choice, each different but pointedly suitable and appropriate. They typically aren't aware of all the overt changes they're making; unconsciously, they shift linguistic gears because the social avenue demands it. They know how their society comes to terms with rule violators, and they do not want to be reassigned, ignored, or left out. They want to remain in good social standing with their friends.

THE SOCIALNESS OF THE YOUNG ADULT WORLD

As almost any teacher or parent can attest, most students do not think of school as an academic institution; most learners regard their school as a social organization, the center of their social lives. Ask ten students, "What happened at school today?" and nine of them will either tell you what Tammy said to Nicole about Jason, what Sean said to Jason about Tammy, who's "going with" whom (at this moment, that is), or some similar report on the social goings on. This is a fact of adolescent development.

Since social ties, identification, groups, and networks are of central importance to school-age learners, there is logic behind a decision to focus more language study on its use in society, in real life. Throughout the school years, students increasingly come into greater contact with wider ranges of social classes and have more contact with adults; their language networks grow and become increasingly more socially sensitive and perceptive.[1] A social perspective on language addresses students' natural and developmental interests.

LANGUAGE AS A SOCIAL PHENOMENON

Approaching language study as a social activity, a view that recognizes the importance of authentic discourse in real circumstances seems a natural choice for schools. Much of our language behavior is *social* and emerges from "social facts."

Some social facts shape our personal attire. For example, when I gather my pens, pencils, car and office keys, insurance forms, football ticket order blanks, checkbook, appointment book, and any other paraphernalia I'll need for a trip to campus, I might discover I have more "stuff" than I can put in my pockets. What will I do? I probably won't borrow my wife's purse, which would have more than enough room for my various articles, because of the social fact that in our culture men do not carry purses. A few men in our culture carry a small clutch-bag, it is true, but this item is made in such a fashion that it is unlikely to be mistaken for a woman's handbag or purse.[2]

Some social facts determine where and how we stand when we are in public. For example, in the United States, a social fact determines that we stand in line at a crowded water fountain in school or at a busy ticket window at the theater. In neither case does U.S. society expect the waiting crowd to flit about like nervous tadpoles.

Similarly, there is a social fact governing how people stand in elevators. You can test its strength the next time you step into an elevator: Instead of facing the sliding doors at the *front* of the elevator, face the *back wall* and note the reactions of the other passengers!

Social facts like these are not written down anywhere and are seldom taught directly, but are learned by everyone. The facts are in the collective mind of society and exist over and above the society's individual members.[3]

FOR YOUR INQUIRY AND PRACTICE:

In the United States there is a social fact that requires the person who answers a ringing telephone to initiate the conversation by saying "Hello" or, if it's a business telephone, by identifying the organization or firm. What happens when social facts like these are violated? Test it out the next time your home telephone rings: Lift the handset and *say nothing*. Or, offer a different greeting, like "Who?" What happens?

In the realm of linguistic social facts, too, there are social rules the successful language user must learn: how to ask questions politely, ask directions, use appropriate terms of address (sir, madam, doctor, pastor, aunt, nickname, first names, last names), and so on.

Another reason to study language in authentic social circumstances is found in the observation that most of the "errors" native speakers make in language violate social facts and are, consequently, *social* errors, not grammatical or linguistic errors.

For the most part, native speakers already know how to pronounce words as other members of their language community do, and they also know how to put words together to form meaningful sentences and other utterances. Under normal circumstances, the speaker whose language of nurture is English will never say, *live United the States in I.* Instead of learning only the basic syntactical patterns of the language, the school student also needs to learn about the social facts that affect his or her language options. Parents of younger language learners know, for example, that "Please" or "Thank you" are relatively simple terms to teach children to say; the hard part is helping them realize the social facts that indicate *when* the terms are appropriate and, then, *remember* to use them.[4]

TEACHING THE ENGLISH LANGUAGE AS A SOCIAL ACTIVITY

How to teach the English language as a social activity that is governed by social rules and facts can be illustrated by the following examples, all of which were used in classrooms.

For our first example, let's consider the recurring linguistic questions of where language comes from and how people learn to use it. These are significant issues in an individual's awareness and sensitivity to the power of language. Sue Spilker, a teacher friend of mine, tried to help one of her classes understand these concepts better by helping them *create* a word. All the members of the class were first sworn to secrecy about the creation of the word; then they were told to use it around the school when its use would seem normal and appropriate. Within five school days, members of the class reported that their "word" had been used in gym class, in the cafeteria, and in the corridor one morning before classes began.

"What does this tell us," Mrs. Spilker asked, "about where language comes from? Or about how people learn language?" The resulting discussion was perceptive, lively, and based upon the students' real observations and experiences; it also helped them better understand two basic issues about language.

Another teacher, Paula Cvitek, uses role-playing with her classes. Based upon her observations of her students' recent writing or speaking, she selects a usage item such as *ain't/isn't* or *them/those*. Then, she frames for the class a social setting in which a conversation will take place:

> You are at an awards dinner ceremony in the school cafeteria and there's something wrong with the scalloped potatoes. Four of you are sitting at a table with the school principal, who asks how you're enjoying the meal. What will you say?

After this role-play has run its course, another scene is set, substituting a popular teacher for the principal. A third option might be to substitute a student who is known to all the members of the class, instead of the principal or the popular teacher. Another scenario might take place in a local fast-food restaurant.

Following these brief conversations, Mrs. Cvitek helps the class make observations about the influences the social setting and just one person can have on a conversation, and how the person's age, sex, and social standing help shape the kind of language used; then she includes observations about *ain't/isn't, them/those* as they might be used in varying contexts. The question of "good" versus "bad" English is seen from a different, perhaps more difficult but more genuine perspective when approached in this manner.

Students studying language as a social activity can correspond with students of the same age in a school in another state, in order to observe the similarities and differences in their language. Through these exchanges they learn that one language is not necessarily "better" than the other. The languages may reflect some differences, but they both *work*. They're both "good English."

Or they can consider the language (use of adjectives, pronouns, simple versus complex sentences, active versus passive sentences, etc.) used in the daily announcements they receive at school and compare and contrast it with the language used in the school or local newspaper. How can they explain the differences? Which is "good English?" Why?

These examples are presented as illustrations. You will observe in Section II that language as it is found in real society is at the center of all of the recommended classroom activities.

Two or three English language arts teachers could expand this list of illustrations tenfold over one pot of coffee and with thirty uninterrupted minutes in the staff lounge. Their efforts would be received enthusiastically by their students. And in time, possibly not until the latter part of the school year, the students will have gained insights into the authentic nature of *their* language and the rigorous demands of multiple criteria of "correctness."

THE INSEPARABILITY OF LANGUAGE AND SITUATION

LEA teachers recognize that the language people use—including, of course, children and young adults in our classrooms—varies from situation to situation throughout the day. Language and situation are generally inseparable.

Postman expands on this idea in his description of the "semantic environment." While a semantic environment is complex, it possesses at least four elements:

1. People (their formal and informal relationships)
2. Their purposes (to convince, describe, apologize, please, flatter, obscure, etc.)
3. The general discourse rules through which the purposes operate
4. The particular speech being used (intimate, informal, formal)[5]

For example, the settings of a witness box, a batter's box, and a confessional box are three different semantic environments, each with definite purposes and rules implicitly understood by the respective participants.

As we observed in Chapter 1, participants who disrupt a semantic environment by making inappropriate language choices suffer serious consequences. For example, a batter who turns to an umpire and says, "Father, I have sinned . . ." is either making a tasteless joke or is flirting with ejection from the game and a subsequent referral for professional help! Similarly, people in a witness box are not likely to remain in the courtroom long if they promise to tell the truth, the whole truth, and nothing but the truth, at least, mostly.[6]

Postman calls these violations of semantic environments either "crazy" or "stupid" talk. As another example, he suggests that we imagine a young woman on a beach in Waikiki who is beginning to experience romantic feelings. She turns to her boyfriend and sighs, "Isn't that a gorgeous sunset?" What if the boyfriend earnestly and seriously replies: "Well, strictly speaking, the sun is not setting. Nor does it ever do so. The sun, you see, is in a relatively fixed position in relation to the earth. So, to speak precisely, one ought to say that the earth is rising."[7]

The boyfriend's comments are accurate enough from a scientific point of view, but *in this context* they are oafish and moronic, clearly violating the semantic environment. He has misunderstood the relationship between language and situation, and is revealing himself as either crazy or stupid.[8]

LEA emphasizes the relationships between language and situation, given the learners' present stage of development and heightened awareness of the processes of socialization. Quite unlike the traditional list of isolated, decontextualized, and anonymous sentences just waiting to be parsed, this approach is built upon the commonsense view that language is used by real people who don't just *talk,* they actually talk *to each other.*[9] The traditional language program has seldom reflected this view of language and people.

The traditional approach seems to operate from the fixed-code belief that language wasn't made for people, people were made for language; if people would only roll up their sleeves, grit their teeth and try harder, their language would be "good English."

Language, however, exists for people and their multiple uses of it. Language as a real activity, used in society by real people for authentic purposes, is a necessary foundation for LEA. Language study in the classroom should not be reduced to rudimentary analyses of the structure of isolated, decontextualized and made-up sentences. Rather, language study should approach language as a complex, multidimensional activity.

REMEMBERING PAIN, BOREDOM OR NOTHING

In some cases, however, language study is decontextualized and reduced to a list of inchoate "Do say" and "Don't say" directives in textbooks. The results of this approach have not been satisfactory. In his cogent and witty book, *Who Cares about English Usage?*, David Crystal observes, "Something has gone seriously wrong when so many people find themselves looking back at their English grammar lessons at school remembering only the pain, the boredom— or nothing."[10] I believe this is a frustrating irony. Learners, who are developing levels of social, psychological, and linguistic sensitivity naturally, ought to find language study one of their favorite school activities. It is not. Goodlad's research indicates that English is the subject the fewest junior and senior high school students around the country rate as interesting.[11]

To illustrate Crystal's observation and Goodlad's research, any English teacher can recall instances when the person sitting next to you in an airplane or a new acquaintance at a social gathering has asked, "And what do you do for a living?" When teachers reply, "I'm an English teacher," the next line in the conversation is predictable: "An English teacher, eh? Well, I'd better watch what I say [in your presence]!" While math and science teachers may suffer similarly, I've never heard comments like, "Oh, you're a home ec teacher? I'd better watch what I eat [in front of you]," or, "You teach history, huh? Well, I'd better be careful with my dates."

Elbow says, "For an explanation [of this public response] we need only look to our tradition. English has tended to stand for two things: the teaching of grammar and the teaching of literature." Elbow suggests that grammar and literature lessons bore students with details they consider insignificant, models of civility they believe unattainable, and leave them feeling incompetent, "unwashed, not right."[12]

Our professional pride might tempt us to discount the negative and, we would like to believe, isolated results reported by Goodlad and described by Elbow. Well, I'm sorry to say you can forget the temptation. Elbow makes us face the issue when he points out that the public's pessimistic assessments do not come from an angry few. He reminds us that the public has taken more English in school than *any other* subject.[13] You can verify this by reviewing your own K–12 school experiences and the subjects you studied.

English as a subject came into the school curriculum using a model and method of *correcting* students' native language. Unfortunately, despite some notable exceptions, over the years many have continued to believe that students' language is imperfect, and requires austere remediation. Thus, the public's perception of who English teachers are and what they do: They repair learners' language. That our students' language is imperfect is, however, debatable.

LANGUAGE LEARNING GOES ON . . . AND ON

It is important for us as professional English language teachers to remember that one of the most important "givens" for the school language arts curriculum is that language learning and development *continue* well into adolescence and young adulthood. Mike Stubbs emphasized this point several years ago with a characteristically sage subtitle which bears repeating here: "Why Children Aren't Adults."[14]

Competence in the language is not acquired by some arbitrary age, whether it be age eleven, fourteen, or seventeen. Adolescent learners, therefore, still have much to learn about how to use the language with precision, for different purposes, and in numerous contexts and circumstances.

Indeed, adults continue to learn about language. When an adult is in a new context—joins a new organization, takes a new job, visits a new church, travels to another city, or watches the evening news on television and learns about the events in another part of the world—he or she needs new words, expressions, terms, and ways of behaving, linguistically. In these examples, as the adult's universe expands, the adult's language expands to assimilate or accommodate the newness. If this is true for adults, who have had more practice with language and are more experienced language users, it would seem obvious that it's also true for young people in school.

Nevertheless, there is a persistent tendency among adults to expect young people to possess a completed language which reflects adult mastery. As an example, consider how adults respond in confounding ways to young people who are learning language. On the one hand, we hear a two-year-old exclaim, "Daddy goed to work!" and we smile, nod approval, and encourage the speaker of this overgeneralized verb form; it's cute. On the other hand, the thirteen- or sixteen-year-old who injects "like," "I mean," or "ya know" into statements is scolded for being slangy, imprecise, lazy, or all three.

Actually, the thirteen-year-old who uses "I mean" is including it in sentences for a variety of reasons: The other speakers in his or her speech network probably use it, and one way to be identified with any group—a prepotent need for all school learners (and adults)—is to talk the way the members of that group talk. "Ya know," "I mean," "doncha know," and similar expressions may be either linguistic *fillers*, used to maintain social bridges between the speaker and listener(s), or as conversational *turn-holders*.

Syntactically, "I mean" and "ya know" are used in fairly predictable positions in sentences in order to introduce a justification for a previous claim or to connect two propositions included in the sentence,[15] as in two sentences I heard this morning: "That's a neat song, ya know; don't you love it!" and "I'm not riding in his car; I mean, he's crazy!"

We also hear young speakers consistently use "one" as a vague, generic adjective, as in "Do you know that *one* guy?" or, "Where is that *one* book?" This is a speech pattern teachers frequently decry, but it results from two interrelated causes: The young speaker hasn't yet learned more precise alternatives or options, and hasn't had sufficient practice speaking in contexts where those options might be required and used.

These examples are used to demonstrate a few features of normal usage by adolescents whose language is still developing and growing. It is within the context of this development that language curricula become operational. The classroom is an ideal setting for both *exploring* those options, and *practicing* their use.

SOME ESSENTIAL LANGUAGE OBJECTIVES

Any curriculum follows some kind of design. While I do not pretend to know all of the precise objectives, goals, or outcomes a school curriculum might establish for its diverse K–12 learners, I propose at least three essential long-term goals that have major applications in language competence. They are: spontaneity, precision, and elaboration.

Spontaneity refers to one's ability to speak freely and confidently, so that the speaker can allocate more attention to *what* is being said, the shared communication. The spontaneous user of language engages comfortably in social conversation and classroom discussions and presentations, and can be poised and assured when speaking before an audience. For these purposes, the opposite of *spontaneous* might be *reluctant*. Reluctant language users do not use language freely, are embarrassed and self-conscious, and demonstrate— both verbally and non-verbally—uncertainties about themselves and their abilities.

Precision describes the quality of exactness. The precise language user demonstrates the ability to utilize an expanded repertoire of words in order to speak more directly and cogently. The precise language user might be described as facile. The opposite of *precision*, at least in this discussion, could be *vagueness*. The vague language user overuses words devoid of real meaning, like "thing," "that one," "doohickey," and "whatchmacallit." The vague language user frequently stops in the middle of a deeply-felt expression and says, as if in surrender, "Oh, you know what I mean."

Elaboration refers to the ability to use more complex language structures, weaving phrases that provide support, subordination, clarification, and greater specificity into the natural fabric of a sentence and sequences of sentences. An elaborative language user demonstrates the ability to combine and coordinate several ideas and propositions coherently and cohesively, and automatically uses the larger frames of discourse.

As used in this book, the opposite of *elaboration* is *fragmentation*. A language user whose speech is fragmented utilizes chains of simple subject-verb sentences which appear to have no relationship to each other, or are presented in a boring, tedious, incoherent, and inarticulate manner. Instead of presenting an elaborated idea, these simpler sentence-chains are characterized by "mentioning" where one idea is mentioned, then another is mentioned, another, and so on, as if to say: "There's this, and there's this, and there's this . . . and so on." The larger frames for language structure are missing.

These objectives clearly relate to each other. For example, language users who demonstrate *elaboration* do so, at least in part, because they command a sufficiently large word pool (*precision*) and they feel confident (*spontaneity*) about their language abilities.

These objectives relate to each other in a broader way, as well. Before language users can control precision, spontaneity, and elaboration, they must first become aware of, reflective about, and sensitive to the roles language plays in their daily routines.

LANGUAGE LEARNING REQUIRES PRACTICE

Spontaneity, precision, and elaboration are long-term goals and they, like all other language abilities, need time to develop. These abilities will not be fixated just because one forty-five-minute class period is devoted to one of them. Time alone, however, is not enough. The time spent in language learning must be invested with numerous opportunities to experience and use language, and to do so in ways they judge as meaningful. One of the simplest ways to surround learners with meaningful language is to provide more opportunities for student talk in the classroom.

There is a fairly common assumption that if a speaker is articulate in one dimension of spoken language (the social, for example), that ability will automatically transfer to other language domains, and the speaker will be similarly facile in another sphere (a more formal context, perhaps). As Brown points out, however, any teacher knows that this simply isn't true. Students who carry on invigorated and impassioned conversations with their peers in the corridor can be reduced to discombobulated inarticulacy when they are expected to speak before the class or when they are asked to justify or explain an answer.[16]

One obvious reason for this dichotomy is that students have more opportunities to explore and to practice the talk that goes on in the social register of corridor-talk than they have for practicing the precise and elaborated talk expected in nonsocial settings. *Speaking* is one of the four traditional language arts, but reading and writing have all but crowded it out of most K–12 curricula. This is unfortunate, given the fact that throughout our lives most of our communicating is *oral*.

Recommending more student talk in any classroom may sound muddle-headed to teachers who believe they already spend more time than they want to trying to redirect the focus and attention of a rowdy or boisterous class of adolescents: surely, if students know anything at all, it's how to talk! "Talkers," after all, are frequently seen as troublemakers.

The student talk I recommend, let me hasten to clarify, is not a verbal free-for-all in which students are either allowed or directed "to talk" or "to visit" about whatever their fancies lead them to discuss. Quite to the contrary, regularly scheduled small-group talk activities ought to have two important distinctions:

1. They should have a definite purpose or direction
2. The effectiveness of the discussion should be assessed

First, the direction or purpose should be established by selecting an issue *the students* see as meaningful, if not urgent, such as the surprise cancellation of a school dance, the midterm announcement of a dress code, new school regulations, or whatever a local "hot" topic might be at the moment. These illustrations are merely examples and should not be used unless they represent current issues in a school. *Every* school has similarly controversial issues readily available.

Initially, the teacher can select the topic. The responsibility for its identification should gradually be shifted to the class as soon as feasible in order to ensure its authenticity.

Secondly, following the small-group talk activity the class should be helped to become amateur linguists who carefully observe specific matters:

1. *What* topic was discussed
2. *By whom*
3. *To whom*
4. *For what purposes*
5. With *what effectiveness*

Using these or similar criteria to interpret their observations of their own small-group discussions might cause the students, for example, to recommend to David that he stick to the point; or, Linda to speak more, because she has good ideas; or, Steve to try to include more people in the discussion and dominate it less; or Mary's position might be stronger if she gave an example, and so on.

A representative from each group might report back to the entire class, then recommend a course of action, a summary, or a conclusion on the topic discussed, and make a statement on the *effectiveness* of the group's talk. On this latter point, it is important to establish a ground rule: There may be no public negative comments about individual participants.

A substantial amount of information is available that tells us that students in an average or typical classroom participate very little. For example, Jackson reports that young people spend over 1,000 hours a year in school, which amounts to 10,000 to 12,000 hours by the time they graduate or leave.[17] When talk is going on in classrooms, 70 percent of the time, according to one estimate, *the teacher* is doing the talking.[18] Among the several outcomes or observations of this participatory imbalance is the implicit assumption that the most important student role is *passivity*, and that it is, ironically, the teacher's job to be at the center of situations in which student learning is supposed to take place.[19]

Students should talk more, in small groups of three or four, or five or six, sometimes in same-sex groups and sometimes in mixed groups, with opportunities to explore language and discuss important issues in a classroom environment. They should then receive immediate feedback from their peers concerning their individual contributions.

These talk groups might be convened once or twice a week for no more than fifteen to twenty minutes initially. An alert teacher will take advantage of a "topic of the moment," realizing both its authenticity and the students' desire to talk it through.

Group size and task assignment can change throughout the year. In addition to the fifteen-minute small-group discussions there can be brief debates; or more carefully prepared oral editorials; or role-playing, casting students in the parts of Building Principal, Hot-headed Student, Mediating Student, Concerned Parent, and the like. Whatever the group size, composition or assignment, it is important that members of the class assess its effectiveness:

1. *What* topic was discussed
2. *By whom*
3. *To whom*
4. *For what purposes*
5. With *what effectiveness*

By varying both the topics and the contexts in which the topics are discussed, argued, and expanded, the teacher is giving the language learners opportunities to hone their language skills through *practice*; thus they become more spontaneous, more precise, and more elaborative. It is less likely that pain or boredom will result from authentic classroom talk activities such as these, and the students will have enjoyed, perhaps unknowingly, the opportunity to explore issues and language, and to practice in the flesh (as opposed to a worksheet) important language abilities that will help them become more competent language users.

Finally, Nancie Atwell points out that classroom teaching must be organized in ways that help our students understand and participate in adult realities.[20] Few adults carefully underline subjects and predicates and draw circles around direct objects when they read the morning paper. They do *talk* about issues, which demonstrates the importance of language in their daily lives. Establishing talk-groups in the classroom will not be students' ultimate initiation into adulthood, but it's a step in that direction.

Section II of this book gives numerous classroom activities. These activities will focus on one aspect of language—dialectology—properties of language, discourse conventions, and the like—but all of the activities meet the Chapter 1 criteria for explorations and all require student talk in the classroom.

Further, two recent National Council of Teachers of English publications are especially germane here. *Talking to Learn*, edited by Patricia Phelan, and *Perspectives on Talk and Learning*, edited by Susan Hynds and Donald Rubin, present many additional classroom talk activities that have been used in classrooms from the elementary school grades through high school.[21]

ENHANCING LINGUISTIC AWARENESS

Student talk is important to the student's growth in language awareness and linguistic maturity, owing to the experience and practice with language that talking provides. All too often the language arts curriculum—whether a planned course of study prepared by the local school district or a "curriculum by default"—a textbook series adopted for classroom use—is prepared with the implicit view that the students already know the central role of language in life. The official curriculum leads the students and their teachers through exercises and activities designed to shape the learners' language control and competence. I contend that until the learners are more *linguistically aware*, even the best-written (and certainly well-intentioned) language curricula are premature.

Give students the opportunities to actively participate in language lessons while they explore the uses of language in real-life settings. Hold serious discussion groups on how language varies by region, age, education, and the like; how the languages of radio, television, newspapers and magazines are similar and dissimilar, and why; and examine the implicit languages of uniforms, dress, and hairstyles. Through these the teacher helps students become aware of the complexity of language options, uses, and patterns. These are legitimate learning experiences, and prerequisites to continued language growth. Instead of remembering language learning as painful, boring, or, worse yet, remembering nothing, students who engage in exploration and awareness activities will remember the power and joy of learning language as it is used in real life.

NOTES

1. William Labov, "Stages in the Acquisition of Standard English," in Harold Hungerford, Jay Robinson, and James Sledd (eds.), *English Linguistics* (Glenview, IL: Scott Foresman, 1970), 275–302.
2. The discussion of "social fact" is based upon Geoffrey Sampson, *Schools of Linguistics: Competition and Evolution* (London: Century Hutchinson, 1987), 43–44.
3. Ibid., 44.
4. Gordon Wells, *The Meaning Makers: Children Learning Language and Using Language to Learn* (London: Hoder & Stoughton, 1986), 15.
5. Neil Postman, *Crazy Talk, Stupid Talk* (New York: Delacorte Press, 1976), 9–11.
6. Ibid.
7. Ibid.
8. Ibid.
9. M. A. K. Halliday, "Linguistics in Teacher Education," in Ronald Carter (ed.), *Linguistics and the Teacher* (London: Routledge & Kegan Paul, 1982), 11.
10. David Crystal, *Who Cares About English Usage?* (London: Penguin Books, 1984), 10.
11. John Goodlad, *A Place Called School* (New York: McGraw-Hill, 1984), 120.
12. Peter Elbow, *What Is English?* (New York: The Modern Language Association of America and Urbana, IL: the National Council of Teachers of English, 1990), 111.
13. Ibid., 112.
14. Michael Stubbs, "The Sociolinguistics of the English Writing System: Or, Why Children Aren't Adults," in Michael Stubbs and Hillary Hiller (eds.), *Readings on Language, Schools and Classrooms* (London and New York: Methuen & Company, 1983), 279.
15. Brit Erman, *Pragmatic Expressions in English: A Study of "You know", "You see" and "I mean" in Face-to-face Conversation* (University of Stockholm: Stockholm Studies in English, 1987), 206–207.
16. Gillian Brown, "The Spoken Language," in Ronald Carter (ed.), *Linguistics and the Teacher* (London: Routledge & Kegan Paul, 1982), 75–86.
17. Philip W. Jackson, *Life in Classrooms* (New York: Holt, Rinehart and Winston, 1968), 70.
18. Ned A. Flanders, *Analyzing Teaching Behavior* (Reading, MA: Addison-Wesley, 1970), 89–90.
19. Michael Stubbs, *Discourse Analysis* (Oxford: Basil Blackwell, 1983), 64.
20. Nancie Atwell, *In the Middle: Writing, Reading and Learning with Adolescents* (Upper Montclair, N.J.: Boynton/Cook, 1987), 26.
21. Patricia Phelan, *Talking to Learn* (Urbana, IL: National Council of Teachers of English, 1989); Susan Hynds and Donald L. Rubin, *Perspectives on Talk and Learning* (Urbana, IL: National Council of Teachers of English, 1990).

SECTION II

Language Exploration and Awareness: The Elements

CHAPTER **4**

Properties of Communication and Language

Language study is not a subject, but a process.
—Peter Trudgill, *Accent, Dialect and the School*

WHERE, WHEN, AND HOW DID IT BEGIN? WHY?

People have long been interested in beginnings. Beginnings are observed annually in the forms of birthday celebrations and wedding anniversaries. Presidents give inaugural addresses. A high school graduation is usually referred to as a "commencement," a word intended to symbolize the new opportunities and beginnings on the graduates' horizons. "Where did I come from?" is one of the earliest and most frequently recurring questions children ask. What was on Earth before there were dinosaurs? Do you think Adam and Eve were really the first people? What language did they speak? Where did language come from, anyway?

Answers to the latter questions have been offered by parents, scientists, theologians, and linguists and the replies are a curious mixture of opinion, fact, theory, speculation, and creed. Whenever our available knowledge seems to falter, speculation becomes a ready reference, as any conversation at a family reunion or in the teachers' lounge will attest! As to questions about the origin of language, there has been as much speculation as fact.

The simplest answer to the question of the origin of language is: We don't know. There are no video or audio tapes of the first utterance in the Smithsonian archives. *The National Enquirer* has not published an article, "Here! For the First Time! Language!" Neither Geraldo Rivera nor Phil Donahue has scheduled televised interviews with "Urg and Ylms." We can almost hear the announcer intone, ". . . those wonderful folks who created language!"

The popular arts have made their unique contributions to the question of language origin. In the novels of Jean Auel (see *Clan of the Cave Bear, The Valley of Horses, The Plains of Passage*), Ayla and the other characters speak—in modern English—with what can only be described as prodigious linguistic repertoires, given the fact that the novels are set in the Pleistocene epoch when humans first appeared. For example, in *The Valley of Horses* there is this exchange, initiated when Ayla asks: "What are counting words?" Jondalar replies: "They are names for the marks on your sticks, for one thing, for other things too. They are used to say the number of . . . anything." Seeing that Ayla is close to understanding the concept he is describing, Jondalar elaborates: " 'Let me show you,' he said. He lined [the stones] up in a row, and, pointing to each in turn, began to count, 'One, two, three, four, five, six, seven' "[1]

Some popular movies, on the other hand, have reflected quite an opposite view in terms of the linguistic development of its characters. Raquel Welch (*1,000,000 B.C.*), Shelly Long, Ringo Starr, and John Matuszak (*Prehistoric Women*) stumble around bushes and piles of rocks alternatingly muttering either gritty and guttural "Argghs" or suggestive and sensuous "Ummms."

Neither the novels nor the movies are serious attempts at linguistic scholarship, but they do help to illustrate the diverse myths and notions about the beginnings of language. With both the novels and the movies set in roughly the same time-periods, on one hand we see linguistic development generally equivalent to what we in the twentieth century are accustomed to, while on the other hand we hear only bestial rumblings and murmurings.

There have been other attempts to account for the beginning of language, and we'll examine just of few of them here. What they lack in accuracy is more than compensated for in good humor.

THE ORIGIN OF LANGUAGE: SOME SPECULATIONS

According to the Judeo-Christian view, God created Adam and language at the same time. In Genesis 2:19 (RSV), we read:

> God formed every beast of the field and every bird of the air, and brought them to the man to see what he would call them; and whatever the man called every living creature, that was its name.

The precise language spoken by the man (In Hebrew *Adam* means "man") has received its share of attention, too. Andreas Kemke, a Swedish philologist who can be described as a flag-waving, patriotic polyglot, claimed that God spoke Swedish in the Garden of Eden, Adam spoke Danish, and the serpent spoke French.[2] Clearly, Kemke had higher regard for his Danish neighbors than for the French!

While in the Hindu tradition language comes from Sarasvati, wife of Brahma, the creator of the universe,[3] *The Holy Qur'an* gives the Muslim account:

> And among His Signs
> Is the creation of the heavens
> And the earth, and the variations
> In your languages[4]

Similar accounts of the Divine Origin theory of language appear in American Indian beliefs. It is probably safe to say that each religious tradition in the world asserts that language came from a divine source, inasmuch as the Divine Creator created everything else.[5]

Another view of the origin of language is referred to as the Natural Sounds Source, the Bow-wow Theory, or the Echoic Theory. This belief holds that the first words were actually human imitations or pantomimes of sounds the cave people heard in the natural world. For example, when Pleistocene Peter observed a creature flying overhead making a "caw-caw" sound, he would imitate that naturally occurring sound in "naming" the bird. Similarly, when Pleistocene Paula walked by a stream and heard what she interpreted as "ripple" or "babble," she used those words to describe to Peter what she had seen. Little by little, as a "bow-wow," a "hiss," a "boom," and other sounds were encountered, these natural sounds became words and the lexicon grew.[6]

Of course, every language has a fairly full range of onomotopoetic words like these. For example, the English "boom" is "bum" in Spanish, and "krawomms" in German. Nevertheless, how abstract words (peace, love, justice) might have come into the language according to this theory is not explained.

Similar to the Natural Sounds Theory is the Yo-Heave-Ho Theory of language origin. It goes something like this: When Pleistocene Peter was attempting to move a large boulder or a fallen tree from the path, he strained hard, expelling a burst of air through his lips. Unable to budge the heavy object, he went for help and tried to explain the nature of his request for assistance. The result was another expulsion of air like the first, thus creating the word "push!" As more boulders were rolled away from more paths, heavy trees felled and moved, boats launched and beached, and as other heavy objects were moved, the sounds made by the workers became prototype expressions for words.[7]

Although each of us has grunted and groaned during periods of physical exertion—mowing the lawn, playing tennis, or lifting heavy objects—this theory has more than a few limitations. An obvious one is a limitation cited earlier for Natural Sounds: Try to explain "life, liberty, and the pursuit of happiness" using Yo-Heave-Ho talk!

SOME PROPERTIES OF COMMUNICATION

Certain features of these theories seem downright ludicrous today, but at one time each of them enjoyed some degree and period of acceptance and popularity, no matter how brief. Further, there are some aspects of these theories that most linguists would accept today as linguistic principles. For instance, when people need a language feature, whether a term or phrase, they create it. Furthermore, when people need to cooperate, coax, encourage, scold, warn, explain, exclaim, or celebrate, they most often use the language of their society. Language is a cooperative, collaborative, social-communication activity, an idea reflected in these theories.

Much of the human talk represented in these theories seems to exhibit what Yule calls the interactional function of language, which is contrasted with the transactional use.[8] **Interactional language** is the language used when we interact with others socially, showing friendliness, hostility, cooperation, pain, or pleasure. Interactional language is frequently listener-oriented and intends to maintain effective relationships and social bridges. The purpose of **transactional language**, on the other hand, is to transmit knowledge, skills, and information. Brown describes it as message-oriented, since its intention is to bring about a change in the listener's state of knowledge.[9]

We have good reason to suspect that our earliest ancestors used whatever language was available to them for both of these general functions. The very survival of humanity from its Pleistocene beginnings is concrete evidence that there was both transactional language (as in, "Stay away from steep cliffs" or, "Do not eat bushes with purple berries"), as well as interactional language (as in, "Hey! Don't point that sharp stick at me!" or, "May I put my arms around you while we sit here in this cozy cave beside this romantic fire?").

Human communication can also be described as either direct or inferential. **Direct, intentional communication** results when the "meaning potential" of an expression offers a smaller range of alternative understandings or messages.[10]

Direct communication is illustrated in statements such as, "I want the red sweater," "Don't run in the halls," "Tell me the answer," and, "Let me explain." There are not many alternative meanings in these statements.

When the meaning potential offers more alternatives, on the other hand, communication is more likely to be **inferential**. For example, you observe a friend in the aisle following church services or a colleague in the parking lot. The friend's characteristic smile is missing or the colleague's typical bounce is replaced with a weary plod. In either case, what you observe is counter to what you expect, so you make an inference. You needn't ask your friend or colleague, "Is something the matter?" Instead, you skip that part of the discourse, infer that there obviously is something the matter, and say: "Tell me what's bothering you."

Inferences are very common but are also challenges to accurate communication. A tourist from the United States, for example, may drive a rental car along the M4 or any of the other major motorways in Britain and observe a road sign bearing the words "Lay By." Having observed other vehicles pull off the M4 at earlier Lay By exits, and further observing that this type of exit does not appear to lead to a village, city or petrol station, the tourist infers that the Lay By must be like a Rest Area one finds at intervals beside a United States interstate highway, and infers moreover that the Lay By will provide toilets, picnic areas, a public telephone, and an area for exercising pets.

On the other hand, the tourist can enter a public house in Wales and notice a door displaying the sign "rest room." With no small measure of relief, the tourist (having enjoyed four cups of tea at breakfast) hurries to the door and opens it, only to find a small room containing two overstuffed sitting chairs and a small sofa. It isn't a rest room; it's a resting room. Wrong inference!

SOME PROPERTIES OF LANGUAGE

Humans are not the only earthly creatures capable of communicating. Animals communicate with others of their species, and there is extensive testimony that pets communicate with their owners. Animal communication is largely direct, and there are fewer alternatives in the meaning potential of its signals; which is to say, when my Maltese dog barks to signal an urgent need to go to the backyard, there's no mistaking what he wants and needs!

Human language differs from animal signals in other, possibly more important, aspects as well. For example, we know that a hungry animal will bark, whine, or meow to signal that it wants food. If you ask your pet, "Do you want the same thing I gave you last night?" you'll most likely get the same bark, whine, or meow. The latter will be accompanied by either a disinterested or imperious yawn, no doubt.

The response to your question will be identical because animals communicate in the here and now. They do not understand "last night's dinner" or "next week." A dog's bark cannot communicate, "Last week in Central Park we really rock and rolled!"

Human language, on the other hand, can transcend time and space. Humans can refer to past or future time, events, or other places. This transcendent property is called **Displacement**.

It appears that only humans have the capacity to talk about things other than the present, thus transcending *this* place and *this* time.[11] Bees apparently have some ability to return to the hive and communicate—through a "dance"—the location of nectar; this indicates some degree of Displacement, but the word "degree" must be emphasized. Scientists believe bees refer only to the *most recent* source of nectar,[12] not a source located three weeks ago or a source at First Avenue and Maple Street.

Displacement enables humans to talk about things, places, people, and events not only removed from the here and now, but also those whose existence we're not sure of. Displacement enables humans to talk of the past and the future, to articulate hopes and wishes and other structures contrary to fact, to create fiction and science fiction, and to write interpretations of history or predictions for the future. Animal signals do not have this property.

The property of displacement suggests that one reason human language can transcend space and time is that human language is more symbolic than animal signals. Given this symbolic quality, human language is, therefore, also characterized by the property of being **Arbitrary**, in that there is no direct relationship between an object (a tree, for example) and the word *tree* used to symbolize the object. The relationship is arbitrary.[13] Both *tree* and either *arbol* or *arbre*, can signify the same physical object.

Similarly, the word *dog* has no iconic relationship to the Maltese member of my family. If there were an iconic relationship, then all languages in the world would use the same symbol, the same word *dog*. They do not, which everyone knows. Either a *dog*, a *perro*, a *chien* or a *hund* can be a family pet.

Since symbols and meanings (senses) are arbitrary in human language, we know that words do not "fit" the objects, the referents they denote. Animals, on the other hand, have a set and fixed sound for signaling conditions like pain, pleasure, or hunger.

This arbitrary property is important in human language because it enables another property of language used by humans, that of **Productivity**. Humans can manipulate their linguistic resources to create new statements, expressions, words and figures of speech.[14] The degree to which the property of productivity is evident in human language is clear when one considers the staggering numbers of new words entering the vocabulary. These processes are described in some detail in Chapter 5 in the discussion of word-formation.

Animal signals lack this property. A cicada, for example, has four relatively immutable signals, not three and not five. A vervet monkey has thirty-six vocal signals, not thirty-five and not thirty-seven.[15] Given the permanency of their signaling sounds, these creatures cannot alter their communication systems.

Neither the cicada, the vervet monkey, nor any other animal has the capacity to create either a new sound or new strings of sound combinations. Humans, however, can and do. Human language is anything but fixed; it is astonishingly productive.

There are those, of course, who decry the process of change in language. As Aitchison observes, significant numbers of intelligent people resent and condemn changes in the language; they regard alterations as examples of sloppiness, laziness, or ignorance.[16] Attitudes toward language change will be examined in more detail in Chapter 8. For the purposes here, however, it needs to be stressed that human language is unique precisely because it is so productive. When humans have a need or desire to produce a new linguistic construction, they can and will do so.

Not only are most animal signals permanent, they are also universal signals within each species. This is not the case with human language because of the property of **Cultural Transmission**. To illustrate the feature of Cultural Transmission, consider the biological fact that humans inherit the color of their hair, eyes, and skin pigmentation from their parents, grandparents, great-grandparents, and so on. Regardless of where you choose or happen to spend your adult life, your physical characteristics are shaped by the genes you inherit from your parents. While this is a biological fact, it is not a linguistic fact. Language is not inherited; it is learned and transmitted through one's culture.[17]

Animals of the same species, on the other hand, make the same sounds throughout the world. A German shepherd in Bonn makes the same sounds as a German shepherd tending a herd of sheep in Australia. A Manx cat in Moscow makes sounds just like a Manx in Madrid. On the other hand, a newborn Nigerian infant adopted immediately after its birth by a New York family grows up speaking Long Island or Brooklyn English, not Ibo. Language is transmitted and acquired through one's culture, not through the genes.[18]

FOR YOUR INQUIRY AND PRACTICE:

Charles Berlitz has collected the representations different languages use to describe sounds made by some animals. Among them are:[19]

	English	**Japanese**	**Russian**
Dog	bow-wow	wau-wau	gaf-gaf
Cat	meow	n'yao	myaou-myaou
Pig	oink-oink	bu-bu	kroo-kroo
Bird	chirp-chirp	pi-pi	tyu-tyu

Do these examples support or refute the claim that animal sounds are species-specific and not culture-specific?

Some speakers of American English *wash* the dishes while others *warsh* them. Similarly, some speakers of American English place pieces of chicken in a *fry pan*, some use a *frying pan*, and others a *skillet* or a *spider*. Further, other speakers of American English say, "We are going to the movies; do you want *to go?*" while others say, "We are going to the movies; do you want *to go with?*"

The particular uses of individual sounds, words, or syntactical arrangements in a human being's first language, one's language of nurture, are learned from the culture in which the first language is acquired. Animal signals, on the other hand, are not culture-determined but are species-specific.

It is possible to distinguish between the sounds in *wash* and *warsh* because the sounds in human language are meaningfully distinct, exemplifying the property of **Discreteness**. The sounds utilized in creating human language are discrete and, therefore, separable.[20]

For example, the aural differences between the spoken /p/ and the spoken /b/ are not great, but they are extremely meaningful differences in *pack* or *back* or in *bit* or *pit*. The differences in these four words are due to the difference between the /p/ and the /b/ sounds. Animal sounds, however, do not appear to be separable.

The aspect of discreteness helps when examining the final property of human language to be considered here: **duality**. Human language is organized not only at the discrete sound level, but simultaneously at the level of *word*. By manipulating the discrete sounds of /r/, /d/ /a/ and /e/, for example, a speaker of American English can generate "read," "dear," and "dare." The sound-symbol duality is unique to human language.

When a dog hears a noise—the doorbell, the arrival of the morning mail, or the screech of automobile tires—it may "yip." However, the same dog can not rearrange its signals to form "piy." Similarly, contented cows always make a "moooo" and never an "oomoo." Duality is not a feature of animal sounds.

A TENTATIVE SUMMARY

Communication and language are patently important. Through language we are able to shape and express ideas, plans, dreams, and emotions for ourselves and others. Through language we become who we are; one's language is a large and inseparable part of one's personal and social identity.

Some attempts at communication are relatively clear and easy to understand; others are more obscure, depending on the nature of the message, the ability of the sender to present it effectively, and the ability of the receiver to understand it within the range of its potential meanings.

One purpose of this chapter is to demonstrate partially that language is a complex system. The study of language in a class that reduces the range of linguistic inquiry to a series of isolated and decontextualized choices between "who" or "whom," "lie" or "lay," either assumes that the learners already understand the complexity of language, or ignores and denies the complexity.

LEA provides opportunities for both the teacher and the school-age language learner to explore various aspects of language and communication. Language may be complex, but it is complex because it is a human activity and humans are complex.

In studying a wider range of aspects of language, school-age learners become more familiar with the intricacies of language use. The remaining chapters discuss additional features of language and provide several learning explorations which will help your students understand language and use it more clearly.

Explorations

STUDENT EXPLORATIONS FOR PROPERTIES OF COMMUNICATION AND LANGUAGE

Exploration: Uniforms

DIRECTIONS: Prepare a collage of photographs taken from magazines, newspapers, or your own collection of photos, which shows people dressed in a variety of formal and informal "uniforms." Then, be prepared to discuss answers to the following questions when you bring your collage to class:

1. Why do people wear uniforms?
2. What happens when someone is "out of uniform" when that person is expected to be wearing it?
3. How many uniforms do you wear, and for what purposes or activities?
4. Why are the uniforms designed as they are? What "statement" is the uniform attempting to make?
5. Based upon your study of uniforms, how would you describe the language(s) of uniforms? How is this language similar to or different from the language we typically speak?

[TO THE TEACHER: Vary this activity by asking different groups to focus on hairstyles, shoes, hats, shirts, blouses, sweaters, etc.]

Exploration: Signs

DIRECTIONS: Collect from newspapers, magazines, and other publications illustrations of at least ten interstate road or street signs. Explain what each sign means.

1. How do you know what each sign means? How did you learn this?
2. Who decided what these signs would "mean"? How were the signs' designs and meanings agreed upon?
3. Prepare an alternate sign for each one in your collection and explain why you think yours is better.
4. Why do you think different states in the United States use the same interstate and other road signs?

Exploration: Keep Off the Grass

DIRECTIONS: Regulatory signs like "Keep off the grass," "Stop," or "No running" were created by *someone* who thought that the actions of other people needed to be changed or directed. Think of a change you'd like to see in other people; then create a sign with a shape, color scheme, and wording that tells them what to do. Draw the sign.

1. Hang all the signs on the classroom walls. Which do you especially like, and why?
2. Which signs will attract attention? Which are more likely to be ignored? What's the difference?
3. How do signs fit into the discussion of "good" or "bad" English? Which signs are good or bad?
4. What are the chances that one of the better signs will be adopted by your school?

Exploration: Codes

DIRECTIONS: Using the Morse code shown below, encode the following sentences:

Meet me after school.

Are you busy Friday night?

1. Perhaps you are familiar with *semaphore code*. The braille system is a code, too. What are some of the differences between an *alphabet* and a *code*?
2. Why are codes used?
3. Can you think of any special languages that resemble codes?

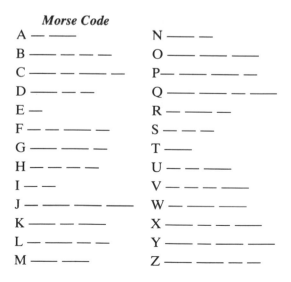

Morse Code

A — —	N — —
B — — — —	O — — —
C — — — —	P— — — —
D — — —	Q — — — —
E —	R — — —
F — — — —	S — — —
G — — —	T —
H — — — —	U — — —
I — —	V — — — —
J — — — —	W — — —
K — — —	X — — — —
L — — — —	Y — — — —
M — — —	Z — — — —

Exploration: Wordless "Talk"

DIRECTIONS: Prepare a short skit in which you and the members of your group conduct a conversation *without words*, using gestures, body language, hand-clapping, finger-snapping, and pointing, etc. The entire class should agree upon the topics of the conversations beforehand (titles of songs, famous Americans, and the like). The success of your skit will be determined when you ask the class if it understood your conversation.

1. How do these "wordless" statements communicate?
2. How do we *know* what the gestures mean?
3. Are some people better than others at "wordless" talk?
4. Based upon the skits you've seen, do you think "wordless" communication is as effective as speaking or writing?

Exploration: Faces

DIRECTIONS: From newspapers, magazines, or your own collection of photos, bring to class at least seven photographs of people's faces, each demonstrating a different *mood* or *emotion*.

1. How do we *know* which mood or emotion is being communicated?
2. How might these faces be related to common phrases like "two-faced," "evil eye," and the like?
3. How is your face part of your general language system?

Exploration: Einbahnstrasse

DIRECTIONS: An American traveler in Germany once commented that "Einbahnstrasse" must be a popular street name in Germany because *every* town had one, and sometimes *two*! Later he learned that "Einbahnstrasse" meant "one way street."

How many *regulatory* signs do you see every day? You know, signs telling you things like: No exit, no running, keep off the grass, entrance, drive thru. Pick out one regulatory sign; then translate it to another language. Your school or public library, or a teacher of a foreign language, or a speaker of another language who lives in your community may help you. Prepare a copy of the sign, with the conventional shape and color scheme, using the alternate language. Post the signs in your classroom, in the corridors, or any other place where they'll be seen. Then observe how others respond to these new versions of old signs.

1. Why do some regulatory signs tell people, in very direct and clear language, what *not* to do, then add "please" as an add-on?

2. What do the translations mean in the other language? Do they mean *exactly* the same thing as the English words?
3. When you observe other people reading your signs, how do they respond to a familiar shape bearing *new* language?

Exploration: Do Clothes Make the Person?

DIRECTIONS: At one time or another we all make snap decisions about other persons based upon inferences we make about their clothing, shoes, hair style, and the like. Some people decide what they will wear with the deliberate intention of making a statement through their attire; using clothes to make an intentional statement can be called a *specifically communicative signal.* On the other hand, some people don't. We still might make inferences about them, however, by interpreting the *unintentionally informative signals* their clothing sends. Using the chart on the next page, record information you gain—whether you think it's specifically or unintentionally informative—as you observe people you encounter during the course of one day. (A sample entry is included as an example.) After you've completed your people-watching log, answer the questions that follow.

People-watching Log

Person Observed	Social Role	Signals	Interpretation
Mr. Sims	10th grade teacher	Tie askew	Preoccupied with other things?

(Specify whether in your judgment a signal is *specifically communicative* or *unintentionally informative.*)

1. Share your interpretations of signals with members of your small group. Remember, these are *interpretations* and do not necessarily represent absolute or accurate statements.
2. If someone were observing *you* today, what interpretations might that person make about you, based upon your clothing?
3. Invite members of your group to help you arrive at alternate interpretations of the signals you've recorded in your log.
4. What can you conclude about the distinctions between intentional and unintentional signals? How accurate are they? How permanent are they? How much of the observer is included in the interpretations?

Exploration: Creating Dialogue

DIRECTIONS: The teacher will have a supply of wordless picture books available for your use. Select one of the books, then read the wordless story. After you decide on a narrative to fit the pictures, write appropriate dialog for each page.

1. Reread your completed story, satisfying yourself that your dialog is faithful to what you believe the author/illustrator is trying to convey.
2. Find another person in the class who used the same wordless picture book and trade dialogs. Discuss how your versions are similar. In what respects are they different?
3. Based upon your conclusions in item two, what generalizations can you make about the information the illustrations in children's books convey? What is the purpose of dialog in children's books?

A Sampling of Wordless Picture Books

Martha Alexander (1970). *Bobo's Dream*. Dial.

Mitsumasa Anno (1982). *Anno's Britain*. Philomel.

―――― (1984). *Anno's Flea Market*. The Bodley Head.

―――― (1980). *Anno's Italy*. Collins.

Edward Ardizzone (1970). *The Wrong Side of the Bed*. Doubleday.

Raymond Briggs (1978). *The Snowman*. Random House.

Eric Carle (1971). *Do You Want to Be My Friend?* T. Crowell.

Tomie de Paola (1981). *The Hunter and the Animals*. Holiday House.

―――― (1978). *Pancakes for Breakfast*. Harcourt.

John Goodall (1977). *The Surprise Picnic*. Atheneum.

John Hamburger (1971). *The Lazy Dog*. Four Winds.

Iela Mari (1969). *The Magic Balloon*. Phillips.

Mercer and Marianna Meyer (1971). *A Boy, a Dog, a Frog and a Friend*. Dial.

Mercer Meyer (1976). *Ah-choo*. Dial.

―――― (1974). *The Great Cat Chase*. Four Winds.

―――― (1976). *Hiccup*. Dial.

Ellie Simmons (1970). *Family*. McKay.

Chris Van Allsburg (1984). *The Mysteries of Harris Burdick*. Houghton Mifflin.

Lynd Ward (1973). *The Silver Pony*. Houghton Mifflin.

David Wiesner (1988). *Free Fall*. Lothrop, Lee & Shepard.

Exploration: These Boots Were Made for . . .

DIRECTIONS: It is not unusual for people to be evaluated on first sight, based on their looks, clothes, hair style, and the like. A single feature like shoes can say something to others about the wearer. These images are often stereotypical and can be either fair or unfair.

1. What type of person do you think is most likely to wear the following?

Hush Puppies	Spiked high heels
Converse (canvas) sneakers	Saddle shoes
Air Jordans	Birkenstock sandals
Vans	Platform shoes
Western boots	Biker boots
Work boots	Oxfords
Wingtips	Penny loafers

   Can you think of additions to this list?
2. What kind of shoes do you wear? Do your shoes "say" anything about you?
3. Can we always depend upon judgments we make about others based upon their shoes or their other clothes? When is it helpful to use nonverbal clues? When might it be harmful?

Exploration: Give Me a Sign

DIRECTIONS: At every sporting event the officials—umpires, referees—use hand signals so that they can communicate to the timer, starter, scorekeeper, and the viewers. The baseball umpire jerks a thumb over his shoulder to communicate "You're out!" or, the umpire crosses his hands horizontally to communicate "Safe!" Not only are signals like these used at sports events, they're also used by members of the ground crew at airports, and by drivers of large, tractor-trailer rigs as they pass each other on the road.

1. Consider the various signals mentioned in the directions. Where do you think these signals came from?
2. Interview a number of people who are employed and ask them about signals they use on the job. You can record the results of your interviews on the form found on the following page. Discuss your findings with others in your class.
3. How universal are the signals you learned about in your interviews? Would people from other *jobs* and in other *parts of the country* understand these signals? Why or why not?
4. Are these signals *language*?

SIGNALS: INTERVIEW LOG

Description of signal: _____

_____

_____

Signal given by: _____

Signal given to: _____

Intended meaning of signal: _____

_____

_____

Description of signal: _____

_____

_____

Signal given by: _____

Signal given to: _____

Intended meaning of signal: _____

_____

_____

Description of signal: _____

_____

_____

Signal given by: _____

Signal given to: _____

Intended meaning of signal: _____

_____

_____

Description of signal: _____

_____

_____

Signal given by: _____

Signal given to: _____

Intended meaning of signal: _____

_____

_____

NOTES

1. Jean Auel, *The Valley of Horses* (New York: Bantam Books, 1982), 466–467.
2. Fred West, *The Way of Language* (New York: Harcourt Brace Jovanovich, Inc., 1975), 4.
3. George Yule, *The Study of Language* (Cambridge: Cambridge University Press, 1985), 1.
4. *The Holy Qur'an*, S.xxx.22.
5. West, *Way of Language,* 5.
6. Ibid., 9.
7. Yule, *Study of Language,* 3.
8. Ibid., 5–6.
9. The distinctions between listener- and message-oriented talk are based on Gillian Brown, "The Spoken Language," in Ronald Carter (ed.), *Linguistics and the Teacher* (London: Routledge & Kegan Paul, 1982), 75–87.
10. M. A. K. Halliday, *Learning How to Mean: Explorations in the Development of Language* (London: Edward Arnold, 1975), 37.
11. Charles F. Hockett, "Logical Considerations in the Study of Animal Communication," in Charles F. Hockett (ed.), *The View from Language* (Athens, GA: University of Georgia Press, 1977), 147.
12. Yule, *Study of Language,* 18.
13. Hockett, "Animal Communication," 142–143.

14. Yule, *Study of Language,* 19–20.
15. Ibid., 20.
16. Jean Aitchison, *Language Change: Progress or Decay?* (New York: Universe Books, 1985), 16.
17. Hockett, "Animal Communication," 155.
18. Yule, *Study of Language,* 21.
19. Charles Berlitz, *Native Tongues* (New York: Grosset & Dunlap, 1982), 146.
20. Hockett, "Animal Communication," 145.

CHAPTER **5**

Words and Lexicography

> *Dictionopolis is the place where all the words in the world come from. They're grown right here in our orchards.*
> —Norton Juster, *The Phantom Tollbooth*

WHERE DO WORDS COME FROM?

As we saw in Chapter 4, the origin of language has been a fertile field for speculation. The subdisciplines of historical linguistics and comparative linguistics, as well as studies in language acquisition and development, are helping us to understand more about how it originated, from a scholarly point of view. Nevertheless, the question of where words come from can be answered simply: Words, being an essential part of language, come from people.

When people need a new term or word, they come up with one. Sometimes an existing word is used in a new context with a newer meaning. Or a prefix or suffix is added to an existing word, thereby altering the first and older meaning. Sometimes people borrow terms from other languages if they lack an equivalent term in their own language. For example, what are the English equivalents to *pizza* or *taco*?

Not only do we borrow names of foods from other languages, but we can reach into other available word collections to name important elements of our lives. For example, consider where the names of the days of the week originated. Sunday, the first day of the week, got its name from Old English *sunnan daeg*, "sun day," or "the sun's day"; Monday is Sunday's Old English opposite, formed by *monan daeg*, "moon day," or "the moon's day"; Tuesday has both Old English and Old Norse roots, being derived from *Tiwes daeg*, Tiw being the name of the Norse god of war. A quick consultation with your dictionary will give you the derivations of the other days of the week.

The names of the months show similar influences. The name *January* comes from the fact that the Romans dedicated the first month of the year to the god Janus. March is the month of the god of war, Mars. The month of May commemorates Maia, the mother of the god Mercury. Again, I invite you to use a quality dictionary, one with word histories, for the names of the rest of the months. Most come from Roman mythology.

While some myths played a constructive role in applications of language, others caused confusions. For example, among the myths surrounding language in general and **lexicography** (the creation of dictionaries) in particular is the mistaken notion that words, definitions, and pronunciations "come from" the dictionary in sacred, **immutable** form. Indeed, some people seem to believe that when Moses descended Mt. Sinai it was not The Law which he brought to the people, but it was the dictionary!

There is another belief, that every word has *one* correct meaning and that this meaning is maintained for reference, whenever a question might arise, in the dictionary. The dictionary is, after all, the final arbiter in questions of

word use and meaning, or so some think and would have others believe. These persons seem to believe that "the meaning" a dictionary provides for a word is as firmly fixed as the Ten Commandments or any other religious laws.

It is more accurate to say that words come from people. Dictionaries are not law books but are history books that explain how the words have been used and are being used at the time of publication. The job of the **lexicographer**, a professional linguist who creates dictionaries, is to record information, not regulate, command, or control.

Words enter the language as people need and create them, then are modified during the time they remain in use. Some words are sustained in the language for a long time, but some of them aren't and will leave the language. Dictionaries record this history of usage.

WORD FORMATION PROCESSES

If words come from people, then what is it, exactly, that people do when they create or form a new word? Except for those persons who are employed as speech writers or advertising executives, few people actually sit down and decide, "We need a new word!" As we'll see later in this chapter, the sources of new words vary, but the basic word-building processes have been identified. Keep in mind that these processes have been identified descriptively, ex post facto, after the fact. That is to say, word-formation processes were not established beforehand so that people would understand how to go about adding new words to the **lexicon**, the stock of words in a language available to speakers and writers. To the contrary, the processes have been derived from analyses of new words and their histories.

Coinage

While coinages are among the least common formation processes, they are the only ones representing entirely new, previously nonexistent words.[1] *Aspirin* is an example of a coinage. Aspirin was initially a trade or brand name, but it has become a generic term.[2] Anytime a person undergoes a physical or emotional shock or trauma and then suffers from a headache and says something like, "What? Grades are due tomorrow? Gimme an aspirin," any brand of aspirin will do, whether it is Bayer, Anacin, or St. Joseph's; I have observed some people calling nonaspirins (Tylenol) "aspirin." Another example of a coinage is the brand-name *Kleenex*, coined by a specific company for a specific product, but now a generalized word denoting any and all facial tissues, whether *Kleenex*, *Puffs*, or any other trade name. *Xerox* is another example of a coinage, functioning today as a general word, and used either as a noun or a verb. In my office it is commonplace for people to go to the Mita electronic duplicating machine *to xerox* a letter. Other examples of coinages are *victrola*, *frigidaire*, and *scotch tape*.

Derivation

Derivation may be the most common method of forming newer words, inasmuch as it builds on existing words and expands to create newer meanings. The derivation process uses a large number of smaller bits and pieces of the language, which carry lexical rather than inflectional meanings.[3] Derivational word parts include **affixes** like *un-*, *mis-*, *pre-*, *-ful*, *-less*, *-ish*, *-ism*, and *-ness*. Examples of words created through the process of derivation include *unhook*, *misapply*, *prejudge*, *joyful*, *careless*, *boyish*, *terrorism*, and *sadness*.

One of the more ubiquitous and senior affixes is found in words such as attend*ee*, examin*ee*, employ*ee* or refug*ee*. The sense of the *-ee* suffix is mainly passive, indicating a receiver or a sufferer of an action. Although the use of *-ee* can be traced back to fifteenth-century legal language (*assignee* is recorded in 1467, *grantee* in 1491 and *lessee* in 1495), it is sometimes disparaged.[4]

Language prescriptivists often flinch when some derivations enter the language. It is not unusual to hear people complain not only about the use of *-ee*, but also the *-ize* affix in *prioritize* or *hospitalize*. Another derivation which has received comments in the complaint tradition is the *-ish* form, as in "Let's do lunch, say, around noonish." The other affixes of derived words (-less or -ful) seldom receive as much negative attention. Regardless of our personal feelings about *-ee*, *-ish* or *-ize*, derivation is, nevertheless, a common route for new words to enter the language. To paraphrase Chapman, purism usually gives way to utility in most language matters.[5]

Borrowing

Another common word-formation activity is borrowing a complete word from another language.[6] Sometimes borrowings are called "loan-words," but *adopted* might be more accurate. It is doubtful, for example, that anyone ever asked the Italian government whether English speakers could borrow the words *piano* or *pizza*. We simply adopted them and they are now as much a part of the American English lexicon as are our words of Anglo-Saxon origin. Borrowings are common in English, as a glance at almost any page in a dictionary containing etymologies (word histories) will demonstrate. American English has borrowed thousands of words from other language families. Just a few examples of borrowings include *alcohol* (Arabic), *boss* (Dutch), *croissant* (French), *numero uno* (Spanish), *pretzel* (German), *yogurt* (Turkish) and *zebra* (Bantu). An extensive list of borrowings is available in Robert Hendrickson's very readable and recent book *American Talk*.[7]

Compounding

English is not the only language that creates new words by joining existing words. The new word (the compound) will be used as the same part of speech as the rightmost member of the newly compounded word. Consequently, *highchair* becomes a new noun (high and chair, a noun) and *overdo* becomes a new verb (over and do, a verb).[8] Some common examples of compounds are *bookcase, sunburn, baseball, textbook, classroom*, and *waterbed*.

There is some controversy about the use of hyphens in compound words, because the conventions governing the use of hyphens are inconsistent. Generally, however, new compounds are hyphenated; if and as they become sustained entries in the lexicon, they seem to lose their hyphen. This is what happened with *baseball*; originally, it was two words, *base ball*; then it was written *base-ball*; not until the 1930s was it written as *baseball*, a one-word, fully joined compound.[9]

Blending

Blending is a word-formation process similar to compounding, but with a major difference: Compound words retain all parts of the original words; blends, on the other hand, use only parts of separate words.[10] For example, a recent word, *infomercial* (*info*rmation + com*mercial*), has emerged to denote those thirty-minute programs on television that look like normal programs. Infomercials have a jovial host, "guests," and enthusiastic audiences, but are really half-hour commercials for woks, heated sandwich makers, tabletop hot-air bread bakers, beauty products, exercise machines, and financial success strategies, to name a few.

Another recent example, *chunnel*, is a word created to describe the recently completed underwater *tunnel* spanning the English *Channel*, thus linking Great Britain and France. *Irangate* (Iran and Watergate), *smog* (smoke and fog), *brunch* (breakfast and lunch), *motel* (motor and hotel) are older and more established blends.

Clipping

People will frequently reduce some words of two or more syllables, especially in informal, casual speech or in newspaper headlines, by "clipping" off one of more of the syllables in a word.[11] This is what happened to the word *gasoline* as it was clipped to form the word *gas*. Some additional examples of clippings are *ad* from *advertisement*, *fan* from *fanatic*, *frat* from *fraternity*, and *bus* from *omnibus*.

Acronym

Creating new words which are acronyms is another reduction process; acronyms usually take the first letters in a sequence of words (*l*ight *a*mplification by *s*timulated *e*mission of *r*adiation) and form a new word (*laser*). Acronyms often are printed in capital letters, as in NCAA, NATO, AWOL, NASA, but sometimes are written in lower case, as in the examples of *laser* or *radar*.

Conversion

This word-formation process does not actually create a new form of a word, but it changes the function; for example, taking a word that was previously a noun and using it as a verb is a conversion. Conversion is sometimes called "functional shift" or "zero-derivation."[13] (See "Derivation," above.) Numerous words in the English lexicon initially were used as verbs but have come to be used as nouns: *walk, laugh, run, guess, must, spy* are a few examples. Conversely, some words originally used as nouns have come to be used as verbs:

> They *papered* the bedroom.
>
> Please *butter* the toast.
>
> We *vacation* in July.

Adjectives can also be converted to verbs, as in *to dirty*, *to empty*, or *to total*.

Backformation

A specialized form of reduction, backformation, typically alters a noun (*television*) and converts it to a verb (*televise*).[14] Some additional examples of backformations are *edit* (editor), *opt* (option), and *emote* (emotion).

ATTITUDES TOWARD NEW WORDS

Chapter 4 described the property of productivity as a characteristic of human languages. As these word-formation processes demonstrate, the relative ease with which new words can be created certainly makes English a productive language.

The relative ease of creating new words and the linguistic principle that whenever there's a need for a new word or form, a speech community creates one, lead to a recurring paradox in language: New words are frequently controversial, and general or widespread acceptance of a new word is often slower than its creation. In fact, some new words generate active opposition.

John Simon, William Safire, Edwin Newman, and Charles, Prince of

Wales and are just four examples of a larger group of people who have written and spoken out in opposition to words and usages they consider bloated, obscure, imprecise, sloppy, or inaccurate. Language critics make statements about current language usage because they understand and appreciate the intricacies of language and its relationships to the thoughts that language attempts to convey. They speak from firmly held convictions that language, like any other tool, ought to be used properly.

I do not believe language critics are malcontents. On the other hand, I do believe that they do not fully understand or appreciate a language universal: A language still in use will change. Stuart Berg Flexner, editor of the *Dictionary of American Slang*, points out: "It is impossible for any living vocabulary to be static."[15]

After examining changes in English over several centuries, Aitchison concludes that "language change is natural, inevitable, and continuous." Further, she points out that whether or not one considers these changes disruptive or signs of progress or decay, "it is in no sense wrong for human language to change."[16] She might have said, but did not, so I will: Changes in language are neither *right* nor *wrong*. They simply *are*. They are inevitable.

As long as there are people using a language, the language will change. This evolutionary process is as natural, normal, and inevitable as the growth of an acorn into an oak or a tadpole into a frog.

THE ROAD TO THE LEXICON

We know, on the other hand, that not all acorns or tadpoles achieve maturity. The same is true for language changes generally, and for new words in particular.

As people use language to respond to new concepts, new social and technological developments, and any and all other new aspects of living, new words may enter the language at the level of **slang**. Flexner defines slang as "words and expressions frequently used by or intelligible to a rather large portion of the general American public, but not accepted as good, formal usage by the majority."[17] As slang words and expressions are used with more or less frequency by a growing or diminishing number of people, they either enter the lexicon or perish from disuse.

A recent example of a slang term's "field test" is the use of *bad* to signify something *good*, a reversal of meaning originating among speakers in the African-American community. For example, an attractive and desirable automobile might be called "a *bad* ride."

A national fried chicken franchise company launched a television advertising campaign several months ago stressing the use of the word *bad* by several musicians who are shown enjoying some *bad* (meaning *good*) fried chicken during a lunch break. A square, un-hip member of the advertising cast of characters says, with the deadpan expression of a comic foil, "I don't think this chicken is bad; I think it's good." Much of the intended humor in the ad is lost, however, since *bad* signifying *good* seems to have been dropped as a slang term before the ad was aired!

From observations I've made in school corridors, *bad* meaning *good* has been replaced, however temporarily in our city, by *stupid*, as in "Hey, girl! I love your new hair. It's really *stupid*!" Who knows how long this usage will survive?

Several words first that appeared as slang terms, however, have enjoyed greater popularity and longevity. Some examples of slang now accepted in the lexicon are: redcoats, greenhorn, fink, split-level (house), yankee, veep, and ponytail.[18] You might contrast your understanding of these terms as they are currently used with their etymologies in a dictionary.

DEMYSTIFYING AND DEMYTHOLOGIZING DICTIONARIES

It is as common as the air we breath to hear people say, "Let's look it up in the dictionary." The use of the definite article is significant in this sample sentence because it seems to signify that there is, after all, *one* dictionary published in varying shapes, colors, and bindings by different publishers.

Alternatively, another common expression is, "Let's look it up in Webster's." Noah Webster was the first major lexicographer in the United States. Using *Webster's* and *dictionary* as synonyms is a classic example of an **eponym**, a word that was created from someone's name. (Our use of the word *sandwich* is another example of an eponymic word, in this case derived from John Montagu, the Fourth Earl of Sandwich—1718–1792—who once spent twenty-four hours at a gaming table eating only two slices of bread with cold meat between.)

The dictionary is a misnomer. There are several versions of American English dictionaries, each with its own set of editorial policies guiding the selection of entry-words and the information describing each entry. Obviously, since book-publishing is a highly competitive enterprise, policies, and therefore published texts, will differ.

The contents of dictionaries have evolved over the years, and clearly not all dictionaries contain identical information. There are, nevertheless, some features most dictionaries have in common. Most dictionaries, except for pictionaries and other types of dictionaries prepared for use in the primary grades, will include:

1. Head words or main entries, called **lemmata** by professional lexicographers, printed in boldface and arranged strictly in alphabetical order. The main entry provides the word's conventional spelling and also includes a **variant spelling**, an acceptable option, when appropriate. Both *meager* and

meagre, for example, are included in one of my dictionaries since the dictionary's editorial staff considers both spellings acceptable and conventional.

2. A guide to the entry's pronunciation(s), usually using a respelling system based on the International Phonetic Alphabet. The pronunciation guide(s) usually include the more frequently heard pronunciation, but also include optional or regional **variant pronunciations**. The first pronunciation is *not* preferred or more accurate; it simply is more frequent, in the publisher's judgment.

3. The etymology, or history, of the word. Sometimes the etymology appears at the beginning of the entry, and sometimes at the end. Where it appears should be of less interest to language teachers than the fact that the etymology is present. The etymology explains how the word came into English. The word "dictionary," for example, comes to English from medieval Latin (*dictionarium*) in the early sixteenth century. "Red-coat," on the other hand, an example cited earlier in this chapter, grew out of a description of British soldiers in the United States during the Revolutionary War.

4. Each head word is also given several definitions or **senses** according to the publisher's policies. Sometimes the definitions are listed in the chronological order in which they entered the language; sometimes frequency of use is the order of presentation. It should be clear that the first sense, like the first pronunciation, is *not* the correct or preferred definition. Only by reading the front matter in a dictionary will the rationale be known. The myths surrounding the first pronunciation or definition as somehow being better and preferred over those that follow are persistent, but they are, nevertheless, plain wrong.

In some dictionaries, entries include illustrative quotations. The quotations illuminate and clarify the different meanings or senses of the main entry as it is used in various contexts.

5. Finally, the more complete dictionaries also include **labels of convenience** or **usage notes** indicating, when germane, whether the editors consider the entry, its pronunciation, or definition "archaic," "obsolete," "slang," or representative of a particular geographic region.[19]

FOR YOUR INQUIRY AND PRACTICE:

What labels of convenience does your dictionary use for the *italicized* words in the following sentences?

A. I'm *agin* it!
B. Do you feel *alright*?
C. Jim *busted* his watch.
D. Don't *argufy* with the preacher.
E. Goshen is a *thorp* near Brandon, VT.

F.   For *supper* we had beans and *light bread*.
G.   That place is nothing but a *clip joint*!
H.   *Irregardless*, we'll just have to go.
I.   *Ain't* she a piece of work?

Not all dictionaries have all of these features. Only the *Oxford English Dictionary* has consistently aimed to present all of them.[20] On the other hand, one of the college dictionaries in my office lists some forty-six separate explanatory notes for main entries, including all of the items listed above and inflections, synonyms, dates of the word's entry into the lexicon, and so on.

Similarly, some dictionaries have precious little information. The relatively inexpensive paperback dictionaries at supermarket and discount store check-out counters have only the most spartan entries. These dictionaries are little more than word-lists and are not sufficient for classroom use.

As you can see, a modern dictionary can contain copious information about a main entry that goes far beyond the incorrect limitations of "preferred" meanings or definitions. The myth of one correct or one preferred definition or pronunciation ignores how dictionaries are written, ignores the information in them, and ignores the essential fact of English, which is that it varies across time, regions, and social classes, as well as from one sentence-context to another; a word's use in context will determine, for example whether *conduct* is being used as a noun or a verb. This seems simple enough, but it is an example of basic language knowledge some people forget when they use dictionaries.

The greatest activity in American lexicography in the past forty or fifty years has been the development of the college or desk dictionary. These desk-sized, one-volume dictionaries are peculiarly American and possess a number of attractive features: They are relatively inexpensive, portable, and current.[21] The typical unabridged dictionary has been published in a twenty- to thirty-year cycle, whereas the publishing cycle for the collegiates is approximately every ten years. Obviously, the collegiates are able to reflect language change more rapidly.

MULTIPLE USES OF DICTIONARIES

Given the vast array of information in a modern dictionary, its uses are multiple. Unfortunately, dictionaries, like other tools, can be misused. Some people use them as bookends, because of their size and weight. I have an aunt who uses a dictionary as a doorstop. In the junior high school where I began my teaching career, a science-teaching colleague used a dictionary to dole out punishment to rambunctious fourteen-year-olds by making them copy a page or more of the dictionary. Guilty of a purposeful lie, I told him I used the students' science text for the same purpose; he roared "Why on earth would you do that? They'll learn to hate their science book!" I'm still not sure he understood my point.

There are better uses for dictionaries. They can help with spellings when students edit their written work. Students can learn more about the *several* pronunciations and meanings many words have, thus making the dictionary an indispensable aid in the study of dialects. Further, some of the history of the language is told through the histories of words, which makes the diction-ary a prime source for exploring language change. The student activities at the end of this chapter will enable learners to explore many of these aspects of language.

FOR YOUR INQUIRY AND PRACTICE:

You'll need your dictionary to answer these questions.

1. What do the words *saxophone, diesel,* and *cardigan* have in common?
2. What information does your dictionary provide about the spellings of *theater* versus *theatre, center* versus *centre* or *pajamas* versus *pyjamas*?
3. Is *bye-bye* considered Standard English in your dictionary?
4. One of the terms in the following word pairs is usually considered more prestigious than its partner. Look at their etymologies and see if you can determine a possible reason for this.

hut : cottage

aubergine : egg plant

fat : corpulent

5. What pronunciations does your dictionary offer for the following terms?

creek garage orange white

Explorations

STUDENT EXPLORATIONS FOR
WORDS AND LEXICOGRAPHY

Exploration: Make-a-Word

DIRECTIONS: With the cooperation of everyone in your class, create a new word for something all of you know or have experienced (perhaps a new adjective meaning "good," or a new noun meaning "textbook"). Do not tell anyone outside your class about the new word, but use it freely around school whenever you have a chance.

1. How long does it take for people *outside* your class to begin using your word?
2. What does this tell you about where words come from? About how people learn language? About how people react to new and different words?

Exploration: Launching New Words

DIRECTIONS: After you've created a word and observed its degree of use and acceptance by those outside your English class, try creating *several* words. You might, for example, create another adjective for "good," and another new adjective to describe something "boring" or "bad." Similarly, create another noun to denote "textbook," "teacher," or "student." Ultimately, select three or four new words, swearing everyone to secrecy, of course; then use this set of new words around school whenever you have an opportunity.

1. Again, observe how long it takes for people *outside* your class to begin using one or more of your set of new words.
2. From the complete set of new words, which one(s) catch on? Which words do not get used?
3. Are there any similarities between the accepted words? Do the unused/unaccepted words have similar characteristics?
4. After you have analyzed the "successful" and "unsuccessful" words, consider again what your analyses lead you to generalize about *where* words come from, *how* people learn language, and *why* people react to new and different words the way(s) they do

Exploration: Interview

DIRECTIONS: Schedule a visit with an older relative or a person in a retirement or rest home. Talk with this person about language use. You should prepare a list of questions before the interview, including the following:

80

1. What words did the person use at your age that are no longer in use today?
2. What happened to these words?
3. What words are being used today on radio or television or in the newspapers which the person considers "new" words? Where did these words come from?
4. How does this person feel about these particular language changes, or any other language changes he or she has observed?
5. What do the results of your interview make you think about language change: Why does it change, how does it change, and who changes it?

Exploration: Variant Stress

DIRECTIONS: You have heard a number of words pronounced in different ways. However, these words have alternate pronunciations for completely different reasons. Using your dictionary again, learn the reasons for the differences in the pronunciation for the following pairs of words:

CONduct/conDUCT	conTENT/CONtent
conTRACT/CONtract	subJECT/SUBject
PERfume/perFUME	PREsent/preSENT
conVICT/CONvict	EXploit/exPLOIT

Write a generalization or a "rule" describing what is happening with the pairs of words when you pronounce them differently.

Exploration: Holiday Meals

DIRECTIONS: Which foods that you eat at holiday meals are your favorites? Roast turkey and stuffing (or dressing, as it is sometimes called) at Thanksgiving? Cranberry sauce? Fourth of July hot dogs? New Year's Day black-eyed peas? Make a list of four or five of your favorites. After you complete your list, look up each name in a dictionary, then discuss your findings in a small group.

1. How many of the foods originated in another country?
2. How can you account for the inclusion of "foreign" foods on the menus of "American" holidays?
3. How do holiday meal traditions start? How and why are these traditions maintained from year to year?
4. Are the *names* of these foods "American" words?

Exploration: Chocolate Moose

DIRECTIONS: Homonyms are words with different spellings but identical pronunciations, like "boar" and "bore" or "hall" and "haul." Fred Gwynne uses homonyms in his book, *A Chocolate Moose for Dinner*. Before enjoying a dessert of chocolate moose, what meat would you want to eat: stake?

1. Can you plan a complete menu using homonyms?
2. When you *hear* a homonym used in a conversation, how do you know which word the speaker is using?

Exploration: Television Talk

DIRECTIONS: New words come into the vocabulary almost every day, frequently without our being aware of their entry. Some of these new words originate as names for household products. Frequently, television gives us new words and expressions. Brainstorm with your class, listing on the chalkboard as many phrases you can that are related to television ("boob tube," "tune in," "tune out," "wrong channel") but are used in other contexts as well.

1. Look up in at least two dictionaries—one older dictionary, and one newer—some of the words on the list. Some of the words are likely to be in the newer dictionary but not in the older one. Why?
2. Ask your school librarian or media specialist to help you with some word research. When did the words or phrases from television first enter the language? Are there television expressions you're hearing today that you think might enter the general vocabulary?
3. Given your findings in this activity, be prepared to hypothesize why some words and expressions used on television enter our general vocabulary but others do not.

Exploration: Lexicography Legwork

DIRECTIONS: Lexicographers, the special group of linguists who create dictionaries, are constantly "tracking" words, collecting evidence of new words and how they are used, and observing newer uses and meanings for existing words. They use this evidence of how people use words when the information for a dictionary entry word is prepared. Here are six commonly used words:

run   walk   sleep   car   ball   type

1. Based upon examples of each word's use in speech or print, have your group write as many different definitions as you can think of for these

six words. Remember to include both the *noun* and the *verb* functions where appropriate.
2. How did your group decide which meanings or definitions to use? Which meanings were used first? Second? Third? Is one meaning "more correct" or "preferred"?
3. Explain how lexicographers arrive at the definitions and meanings they include in dictionaries. Where do the meanings and definitions come from?

Exploration: Whoville

DIRECTIONS: Columbus, Ohio, was named after Christopher Columbus. Cambridge, England, got its name because it was the site of the *bridge* crossing the *Cam* river. Some places are named after nearby landforms, like Council Bluffs, Iowa. Knowing how places got their names can help us better understand the history of the region and the people who settled there.

1. What do these suffixes mean when they are added to the name of a place? ;
   -ville   -mont
   -ton   -burg (or bury)
   -cester (or chester)
2. Using a map or atlas, find an example of each of the suffixes shown above.
3. Can you think of places whose names end with the following?
   -ford   -land
   -field   -haven
   -port   -hill
   What do these suffixes mean?
4. Can you think of five cities named for people? For other countries? With descriptive names?
5. For whom or what were the thirteen original colonies in the United States named? (The *World Almanac* can help you answer this question.)
6. What conclusion can you draw about how people name the places where they live?[22]

Exploration: Give Me Some Good Old American Pizza

DIRECTIONS: Write the name of the country or the national group from whom we get the following *italicized* foods.

1. An *eclair* is a _____ pastry.
2. The word *tortilla* is _____ for "pancake."
3. *Zwieback* (bread "baked twice") got its name from _____.

4. Cookies known to us as *macaroons* were first baked by
   _____.
5. Beaten egg whites baked on top of a pie are called *meringue*, which is
   a _____ word.
6. The word *chowder* means "thick soup." We got this word from the
   _____ people.

Exploration: Tracking New Terms

DIRECTIONS: Look up the following items in your dictionary; then answer
the questions below.

minivan	word processor
microwave	VCR
fax	camcorder

1. Are all of these terms listed in your dictionary? If not, why not? If
   they are, do the meanings in the dictionary agree with the way(s) you
   use the terms?
2. Do the spellings in your dictionary agree with the spellings used here?
3. From what other words do *fax*, *VCR*, and *camcorder* come? How
   were these three words created?
4. Do you agree or disagree with the statement: "Words come from
   people, not from dictionaries."

NOTES

1. Jeffrey Kaplan, *English Grammar: Principles and Facts* (Englewood Cliffs, N.J.:
   Prentice-Hall, 1989), 21.
2. George Yule, *The Study of Language* (Cambridge: Cambridge University Press,
   1985), 51–52.
3. Kaplan, *English Grammar,* 87.
4. Raymond Chapman, "A Versatile Suffix," *English Today* 7 (1991): 39.
5. Ibid., 41.
6. Yule, *Study of Language,* 52.
7. Robert Hendrickson, *American Talk: The Words and Ways of American Dialects*
   (New York: Penguin Books, 1986), 25–34.
8. Adrian Akmajian, Richard D. Demers, Ann K. Farmer, and Robert M. Harnish,
   Linguistics: An Introduction to Language and Communication, 3rd ed. (Cambridge: Massachusetts Institute of Technology Press, 1990): 24.
9. Gerald Astor, *The Baseball Hall of Fame 50th Anniversary Book* (New York:
   Prentice-Hall, 1988), 7.
10. Yule, *Study of Language,* 53.

11. Albert C. Baugh and Thomas Cable, *A History of the English Language*, 3rd ed. (Englewood Cliffs, N.J.: Prentice-Hall, 1978), p. 257.
12. Yule, *Study of Language,* 53.
13. Kaplan, *English Grammar,* 86.
14. Akmajian, et al., *Linguistics,* 14.
15. Stuart B. Flexner, "Preface to *The Dictionary of American Slang,*" in Paul Escholz et al. (eds.), *Language Awareness*, 4th ed. (New York: St. Martin's Press, 1986), 182.
16. Jean Aitchison, *Language Change: Progress or Decay?* (New York: Universe Books, 1981), 222.
17. Flexner, "Preface," 180.
18. Ibid., 183.
19. Robert Burchfield, "The Oxford English Dictionary," in Robert Ilson (ed.), *Lexicography: an Emerging International Profession* (Manchester: Manchester University Press, 1986), 19.
20. Ibid.
21. Kenneth G. Wilson, *Van Winkle's Return: Change in American English, 1966–1986* (Hanover, N.H.: University Press of New England, 1987), 18.
22. For additional resources on place names see: Kelsie B. Harder, *Illustrated Dictionary of Place Names, United States and Canada* (New York: Van Nostrand Reinhold Co., 1976); George R. Stewart, *American Place Names* (New York: Oxford University Press, 1970); Allan Wolk, *The Naming of America* (Nashville, TN: Nelson Publishing, 1977); and, *The United States Dictionary of Places* (New York: Somerset Publishers, 1988).

CHAPTER **6**

Syntax, Spelling, and Good English

When you're lying awake with a dismal headache, and repose is tabooed by anxiety,
I conceive you may use any language you choose to indulge in, without impropriety.

—W.S. Gilbert, *Iolanthe*

For a variety of reasons, the English program in most schools in the United States has emphasized syntax, to the virtual exclusion of all of the other aspects of language and linguistics. Syntax is the most difficult and abstract, as well as the least productive aspect of school language study (in terms of student growth in either oral or written performance). The empirical evidence demonstrating the ineffectiveness of traditional grammar instruction in classrooms is reasonably conclusive.

Traditional grammar instruction, with its goal of increased explicit knowledge of syntactical terminology to achieve increased performance in oral and written language, has been ineffective in improving students' writing or speaking competence.[1] Teaching students the names of the traditional parts of speech and the rules of "correct" usage ("Do not split infinitives") may help them learn the names of the traditional parts of speech; or rules of a grammar that do not pertain to English (the split infinitive being a classic example); or something about social etiquette or social classism; but they will not learn to be better writers or speakers.

Other language conventions have been included in school curricula in a similarly ill-begotten manner. Within the optional varieties of punctuation, for example, *one* choice will be selected as the *correct* or *preferred* choice. Similarly, spelling is too-often emphasized either by testing students each week on twenty to twenty-five words selected by a committee or a textbook, or by the teacher's putting a circle around the student's unconventional spelling of a word used in a piece of writing.

We can distill the several shortcomings of the traditional approach to language study, already cited both here and in Chapter 1, and group them into one broader issue: the erroneous belief in a single standard of what some people believe is language correctness, known alternatively as "Standard English," "good grammar," "correct grammar," and "proper mechanics," which also includes "correct spelling."

SOME IGNOTIONS ABOUT "CORRECT" GRAMMAR

The traditional insistence that people adhere to the "correct rules" of grammar is simply a false issue. Native speakers of any language do, in fact, speak and write in accord with the grammar of their native language, similar to the unthinking and automatic way they follow the other customs of their social communities and networks. Native language users may not be able to articulate precisely why they drive on either the right- or left-hand side of the road, other than to explain, "that's the way we do it"; why they hold a knife in their right hand and a fork in the left, shifting the fork to the right hand after the meat has been cut; or name the parts of speech in a sentence. The native speakers will, however, create sentences that conform to the syntactical patterns used in their culture or network.

To illustrate, a native speaker of American English might say, "My mother is a housewife." On the other hand, a Latino who has learned English as a second language might render the same thought, "My mother is the wife of the house." In terms of overall meaning, the sentences are clearly related, but the *structure* of the second sentence is built on Spanish syntax. The native English speaker, on the other hand, shapes the sentence according to the structure she learned: English syntax. Both speakers in these illustrations are using their implicit knowledge of syntax which was learned indirectly and incidentally years ago.

The fact is, no one directly teaches infants how the structure of their language of nurture actually works. Infants learn native language structure through language immersion, observation, testing and trying, and through active participation and practice.

When a young speaker of American English who is learning the language utters a construction like "the house white," the parents or care-givers usually do not correct the language learner by saying, "No, darling, in English the adjective comes *before* the noun. In Romance languages it comes *after* the noun."

To the contrary, the adult is more likely to say, "Yes, that's a white house," thus presenting the *conventional* structure through typical adult modeling.

Nevertheless, when a child enters school there is an odd transcendental assumption that children either have no understanding of language structure, or the language they believe they understand is somehow incomplete or incorrect. Consequently, an English language curriculum has been devised to remedy the language of children.

This attempt at remediation assumes that in order to discover how American English works, one must look in a textbook, or look to logic or look to some other language—like Latin—rather than examine how people actually use the language. This misguided thinking seems to conclude that the language is pure; the people who use language, however, are corrupt.[2]

Among the further problems with traditional language study is the fact that several rules of Latin syntax have been imposed on English, creating, at least by those with one-eyed views of the world (see Chapter 2), all kinds of grammar and/or usage problems among the unwashed, the lazy, the untutored, and the uninformed.

WHERE YOU CAN PUT YOUR PREPOSITIONS

Many of the traditional rules of classroom syntax, having been borrowed from Latin, simply are not valid descriptions of the syntactical arrangements possible in English. For example, "Do not end a sentence with a preposition" is a threadbare caution that mature and "proper" English users are expected to observe. Where did this rule come from? Latin.

In Latin, it is physically impossible for a preposition to appear at the end of a sentence. (Is this why we don't call them *post*positions?) It is possible, however, as everyone knows, that in English a preposition is a word a sentence can end with.

Telling students to avoid placing prepositions at the end of a sentence is not a rule of English syntax. It may be a usage rule of social class, however, which is no justification for its being advocated in a classroom.

Similarly, students in U.S. classrooms have been told for generations, "Do not split infinitives." Now, this is an accurate syntactical statement for Latin, French, or Spanish or any other dialect of a Romance language. An infinitive in Latin, or either Spanish or French for that matter, is a single word! It is physically impossible to insert another word between the parts of the infinitive in these languages because the infinitives are inseparable and cannot be divided into "parts"; English infinitives, on the other hand, come in two components (to run, to read, etc.).

HOW YOU CAN SPLIT YOUR INFINITIVES

For example, the two-component English infinitive *to read* appears in Spanish as the one-word *leer*. In order to achieve special emphasis, a teacher in an English-speaking classroom might exhort a class ". . . *to* carefully *read* . . ." the next assignment, but a teacher in a Spanish-speaking classroom will never be able to say the equivalent, which might look like ". . . *le* con cuidado *er* . . ." Anyone hearing this latter construction would recognize it as noise; it will have no meaning.

Like the preposition-final rule, the split-infinitive rule is *not* an accurate description of how English sentences can be constructed. Syntactically, they are nonrules. They are not linguistic statements, but are statements of personal or social class preference.

We know these rules are invalid. "Where are you *from*?" is one of the more common questions I hear my students asking each other, and no one raises an eyebrow or claims not to understand when the question is posed.

I suggest further that those who observe these pseudorules are welcome to their opinions, but they have no authority to claim that *all* language users should adhere to them. Many of the distinctions pseudorule followers adhere to are *not* linguistic statements but represent either personal dialect preferences or unexamined assertions that have been passed down from one generation of school teachers to the next.

LANGUAGE ERRORS PEOPLE MAKE

It might be helpful at this point to examine the issues of natural language use, school curricula, and society's expectations for good English from a slightly different perspective. Let's entertain for the moment the notion of "error." For example, when I recently reached for a text on the bookshelf beside my desk and did not grab the book I intended to reach for but another, that was a *mistake*. Inadvertence. No big deal.

When I was entertaining a widely known and recognized scholar on my patio several years ago and I unthinkingly made a satirical comment (one I believed extremely clever, of course) about a statement I'd read recently, forgetting it was a statement from one of *his* books that was a *blunder*! Blunders sometimes are arrogant, frequently are stupid, and almost always are ignorant actions. They are also embarrassing!

In a softball game last summer a fly ball came soaring out to me in center field. Instead of catching the ball in my glove, I misjudged it. The ball hit my wrist and fell to the ground. What should have been an easy out was properly recorded in the scorebook as an *error*. Errors are sometimes stupid, ignorant, or embarrassing, but they also imply a standard of more correct behavior. The standard and correct behavior expected of a center fielder is to catch a reachable fly ball. If the ball is within reach but is booted, the player is guilty of incorrect behavior, a variation from the standard, an error.

Let's take these notions of mistake, blunder, and error and apply them to language use. Some are popularly called slips-of-the-tongue or Freudian slips, as in the case of a speaker saying, "I wonder who invented *crosswords* (meaning jigsaw puzzles)?" or, "Look at the fuzzy *patter-killer*" for caterpillar.[3] Other examples are, "I believe the capitol of Texas is in Houston," or, "I said, PASS THE DAMN SALT!" at a church potluck supper, or, "Hopefully, it won't rain today." Which of these statements would you classify as a mistake, a blunder, or an error?

THE LINGUISTIC LEECH

Why school curricula have emphasized instruction in the overt knowledge of traditional grammar terminology and with sentence parsing is somewhat mystifying. I have some conjectures and they are described in Chapters 1 through 3 of this book. Those earlier comments are my speculations, resulting from several years of teaching, reading, doing research, and observing schools. They are not, however, certainties.

On the other hand, I do know and am certain of this: If I suffered from chronic headaches for several weeks and went to a physician seeking relief, I would scramble out of the physician's office as fast as possible if he or she started to apply a leech to my arm, telling me that a good leeching would cure my headaches. Leeching was believed to be a curative at the same time Robert Lowth published *A Short Introduction to English Grammar*.[4] Medical science and practice, at least, have made significant progress since then. It is time for our profession to advance beyond the equivalent practice of linguistic leeching. Parsing and related practices are not cures for any known linguistic or other social diseases.

DE-LEECHING: A MODERN ATTITUDE TOWARD LANGUAGE STUDY

In the LEA approach to language study, we substitute the terms **conventional** or **appropriate** for the false notion of a single standard, "correct." In keeping with modern linguistic theory, determining conventional or appropriate language use (and their counterparts, unconventional or inappropriate) can be done only by *observing* language as it is used in varying contexts. Consequently, LEA substitutes *information* about language for either misinformation or for statements of someone's personal preference. Further, this approach will accomplish another substitution: replacing a single standard of correctness by *multiple* standards, which requires much more linguistic sensitivity and awareness by the user.

Lowth's *A Short Introduction to English Grammar* is one of the most influential grammar texts ever published. Lowth theorized about how people *ought* to use the language; then he wrote his grammar text; and then he demonstrated how people were not meeting his linguistic standards.

This approach can be described as a **theory-to-practice model** of language. In terms of a description of human behavior, this model is as useful as a model which would theorize that all thirteen-year-old eighth graders ought to be five feet tall. By examining the actual height of eighth graders anyone would conclude that the model is based on an arbitrary and unusable theory.

Lowth's prescriptions about English grammar were popularized in the United States by Johannis Wallis in 1764. Using Lowth's content and method, Wallis set forth any number of theory-to-practice "rules" about the language and how people should talk and write if they want to talk and write correctly. The *shall-will* rule and the *lie-lay* distinctions, both of which are still found in schoolroom grammars but seldom if ever appear in the language of people, are only two examples of Wallis's legacy.

Modern linguists, on the other hand, follow a **practice-to-theory model**. The basic questions they ask are more in the manner of: How does the language actually work? How do users of English arrange their language? How can we describe it? After observing English as it is practiced and used, modern linguists create descriptive theories that account for the usages they have observed.

This approach to linguistics does not suggest that one way of behaving linguistically is inherently superior to another. A linguist does not explain what ought to be, but explains what is.

WHAT IS "GOOD ENGLISH"?

Nevertheless, what is good English?, that is, which usages of English are superior to others is a recurring question. Sampson claims that the issue identified in this text as "good English" is of particular importance in the United States. Speakers and writers of American English seem to lack linguistic self-confidence, possibly because of the large proportion of English speakers whose command of English is only a couple of generations old.[5] Carlson, on the other hand, describes a long-lived fear of any form of heterogeneity in the United States, and a resulting quest for homogeneity, doctrinal conformity, and orthodoxy in high visibility areas like personal habits, personal appearance, and language.[6]

What is good English?' is also an important question for classroom inquiry because of its relationship to social status. Language use is generally regarded as one of the more reliable predictors of the speaker/writer's social position. Why and how this is so is an important sociological matter deserving attention in any classroom.

At a more applied level, what is good English? is a recurring question asked by parents, teachers, prospective employers, and students. The answer that is closest to the approach to language learning advocated in LEA is the one suggested by Pooley:

> "Good English" is marked by success in making language choices so that the fewest number of persons will be distracted by the choices.[7]

This definition means that good English is:

Appropriate to Speaker/Writer's Purpose

Our purposes in using language range from the highly formal to the extremely informal. According to this definition, users of good English are aware, for example, of the differences between a lecture and a casual conversation. They are able to shift from a language style of intimate informality when asking a close friend about the status of her father's health, to a more formal style when addressing a local civic club on the need for the community to support the school bond issue in next spring's election. Confusing the purposes of language in these two examples might result in either hurt feelings, astonished surprise or disappointment, or lost voter support.

Similarly, to return to the lecture/conversation dichotomy, persons who consistently conduct their language affairs in either a formal or an informal chatty style, making no allowances for purposes, will be judged either as boors or as clowns who are never serious. Either case is distracting and is an example of bad English.

Appropriate to the Context

If you're chairing a meeting of teachers in your building, but continue to talk to your colleagues the way you talk to the third or tenth graders you teach during the day, you're clearly using language inappropriate to a meeting of professional educators. Similarly, if you are asked to give a brief report to the local school board and you do so using the same style of language you use with your bridge club or golf foursome, then another context has been violated and the language is distracting.

Comfortable to Both Speaker and Listener

Perhaps the best way to describe this criterion is by way of an analogy. If you're having guests for dinner and you know that burning incense will cause one of them to sneeze, or that one of them is allergic to strawberries, you'll be courteous to your guest and won't burn incense or serve strawberries. Users of good English are sensitive not only to their purposes of communicating and the context in which they find themselves, but are also sensitive to how their conversational partners are responding to what is being said and how it is being delivered.

When people are comfortable with our language choices, effective communication is more likely. Conversely, if our language use makes people uncomfortable—for whatever reason—distraction and, therefore, miscommunication can be predicted. In our definition, this illustrates bad English.

Some audiences or conversational partners will be distracted, for example, by the use of male pronouns in the generic sense of "All men are created equal" or "Each person will bring his own book." Regardless of one's personal feelings about language that some consider sexist, knowing that others will be distracted by a usage but stubbornly insisting upon using it is bad English. Similarly, some conversational partners and audiences will be distracted by a usage that treats *data* as a singular noun ("the data is conclusive"), or a pronunciation that renders *nuclear* as *new-kya-ler*, or a spelling of *a lot* as *alot*. (I have heard or read each of these illustrations within the past week. While they distract me, I also recognize them as candidates for language change. Given the current ubiquity of these illustrations, I suspect they might become widely recognized as more "standard" usages within the next twenty to twenty-five years.)

If participants in a language event are distracted, communication will suffer. If the participants are distracted by the features of *how* an idea is being

Alot of people

offered, they will pay less attention to *what* the idea is. Finally, if the participants are distracted by any of these examples or by a host of other possible illustrations, they will discredit the speaker/writer as either unreliable, pretentious, intellectually deficient, or just plain stupid. These judgments may not be accurate, but they'll be made, nevertheless. They represent the assessment of a social tax.

These distinctions between "good" and "bad" English are different from the schoolroom definitions typically used. This is largely because modern linguists do not view language as an *object*, but, rather, as a human *event* that takes place in a particular *context* for a similarly particular *purpose*. This more modern view of language study, then, views participants, intention, purpose, and context as inseparable elements in the use or analysis of language.

Furthermore, this view sees language as inherently social, a point already stressed in Chapter 2. Where language comes from was discussed in Chapter 5, and although there are no conclusions mentioned in that chapter, I can add another social speculation: language began when people needed to communicate either intersocially or intrasocially.

Newer emphases in language study are clearly moving away from studying words or sentences in decontextualized isolation: People simply do not normally use language this way. Those who do are usually diagnosed as schizophrenic. When, for example, did you last hear anyone utter a string of sentences like:

All right. I'm ready for a Scrabble match.

Put that trunk anywhere that it will fit.

Aren't you interested in this drawing, Stan?[8]

Each of these sentences—presented in numbered isolation and devoid of any real context—is used in a recent handbook to illustrate what the handbook offers as examples of acceptable and unacceptable expressions.

No, thank you, normal people just don't talk in or write isolated sentences. They use language in connected and responsive discourse, with real purposes in mind and in an authentic context. Clearly, as the contexts change, all the other features will change, which leaves us with the inevitable conclusion that any definition of "good" or "bad" English must be determined case by case.

The previous sentence does not mean that anything goes! Rather, it means that issues of good or bad English must be considered in a broader view, which includes multiple criteria—intention, purpose, participants, context—instead of a single standard.

We do not, for example, purchase a pair of shoes according to an immutable criterion. Are ballet slippers "good"? Of course they are, but probably not for a fishing trip to Lake Barbara in Wisconsin. Is a hammer a "good" tool?

	Spoken	Written
Productive	speaking	writing
Receptive	listening	reading

Figure 6.1 The Four Traditional Language Arts

Yes, but probably not for opening a can of paint. The use of a single criterion ignores the fact that language varies according to intention, purpose, use, context, and the participants.

The older paradigm used to plan language arts curricula consisted of a rather simple listing of the four traditional language arts. Experienced classroom teachers will recognize the four-way division in Figure 6.1.

DIALECT AND DIATYPE

As helpful as the model in Figure 6.1 might be, it leaves unexplained as much as it illustrates. It cannot account for the essential principle of *language variation*, already shown as evident in the changing (varying) contexts, purposes, and intentions that affect our language choices. At a broad level, language variation can be described as:

1. **Dialect**, the term used to denote variation according to the *user* (regional and social variations in pronunciation, word choice, and syntax)
2. **Diatype**, the term used to denote variation according to *use* (field, tenor, and mode, as described in the next paragraph). Diatype is sometimes used synonymously with "register" or "style."

Halliday describes *field*, *tenor*, and *mode* as the environmental determinants of text. **Field** refers to the setting and the subject matter or topic, the field of action (scientific discourse in a scholarly journal describing the behavior of ions and quarks, or casual conversation about knitting or baseball). **Tenor** refers to the relationships between the participants (mother to daughter, principal to teacher, teacher to pupil, or superordinate to subordinate). **Mode** refers to the channel of transmission (written or oral; newspaper or television).[9]

Using these features of diatypes, along with some features of dialects, discussed in greater detail in Chapter 8, Stubbs graphically shows language variations accordingly:

The chart in Figure 6.2 demonstrates that we can think of language use varying across two dimensions—the dialectical and the diatypical—within the more specific aspects or features of language, such as the organization of

	DIALECT		DIATYPE		
	Regional	Social	Field	Tenor	Mode
phonetics/ phonology					
morphology					
lexis					
syntax					
semantics					
discourse					
graphology					

Figure 6.2. Dimensions of language variation[10]

Source: Michael Stubbs, "Dimensions of language variation," *Educational Linguistics,* pp. 20–25, Copyright © 1986 by Basil Publishers. Reprinted with permission.

sounds (**phonetics** and **phonology**), word structure (**morphology**), vocabulary (**lexis**), syntax (grammar or sentence structure), meaning (**semantics**), and the organization of text beyond the level of the single sentence (**discourse**). **Graphology** refers to the organization of writing systems (spelling).

I do not intend for this discussion to become more complex than it already has. My purpose in presenting the Stubbs model of language variation is to show that comments about language being merely "good" or "bad" are too simple. This model of variation can help us to analyze oral and written language to determine whether it is a predicted or unpredicted use, whether it is appropriate or inappropriate or, consequently, an effective or ineffective exchange.

Field, tenor, and mode clearly affect the kind of language used. For example, the question, "What've you been doing?" will require different responses in different situations.

FOR YOUR INQUIRY AND PRACTICE:

What would you predict to be "good English" replies to this question in the following contexts?

What Have You Been Doing?:
1. Professor to student at the library
2. Mother to daughter coming home at 3:00 A.M.
3. Manager to employee at office party
4. Rabbi to congregant who has not been to synagogue for six months
5. Social worker to parolee
6. Father to son coming home from college at semester break
7. Coach to basketball player who just picked up her fifth foul
8. Aunt, to nephew she hasn't seen in three years
9. Building tenant to elevator operator
10. Television news analyst to president of the United States on a Sunday morning newscast following the president's recent trip

When language is viewed as a social process and when learners have repeated opportunities to talk in classrooms, and to explore language events they have observed, they become more adept at describing good and bad uses of English. They do so, however, from a larger, more challenging, interesting, and accurate perspective. Further, as they gain experience with analyses such as these, they rely less on external and arbitrary judgments of language and become more alert observers of language and its uses.

There are several learner activities at the end of this chapter. They can be used as starters in exploring matters of good English. These activities are, however, only illustrative explorations. You and your students can discover better language events as you go through your daily routines of listening to the radio, watching television, reading newspapers, magazines, billboards, menus, and through your participation in hundreds of conversations each day. Analyzing these events will make your students more aware of the power of the languages surrounding them.

WHAT ABOUT THE SPELLING PROBLEM?

What's wrong with spelling? Among language critics, this a familiar cry. They infer that no one cares enough to teach spelling as it was taught twenty-five, thirty, thirty-five years ago, or more, depending upon the age of the critic's memory. The "spelling problem," like the "grammar problem," is a favorite topic of back-to-the-basics people: Nobody cares about correct language anymore; spelling isn't taught anymore; the progressives (liberals, educationists, etc.) have decided that anything goes. Correct spelling, like correct grammar, is often viewed by many people as an indicator of the speller's value system; bad spellers are, it seems to some, indolent, truculent, rebellious, and marginal citizens who could do better if they tried to, or if they had teachers who *made* them try. The simple solution offered most frequently is a written test, complete with national standards for everyone to meet and old-fashioned rigor!

Newspapers routinely run human-interest stories about the results of springtime spelling bees, expressing great pride in the thirteen-year-old who wins because she could accurately spell *sarcophagus*, winning over a young woman who missed on the word *colluvies*.[11] The articles seldom ask when these two young adults might have needed or will need to use and spell these words!

Educators, on the other hand, try to rationalize the charges of poor spelling by suggesting that some kids can spell, some cannot. Or, some claim, we make too much over spelling. The more scholarly may point out that our spelling system is simply too irregular and random for anyone to learn it in a rational way.

It is true that our conventional English spelling is not regular, but neither is it random. The fact is, English spelling does not have a system, but is the result of many systems.

Modern English spelling is the result of many historical influences: the Viking raids on Great Britain, which transplanted numerous Norse words (their spellings as well as meanings); the Angles, Saxons, and Jutes waged similar forays, leaving behind not only the basic grammatical foundation for English, but also orthographical features. In 1066 William the Conqueror won the Battle of Hastings and enthroned Latin as the official language of government, schools, and the church in Great Britain. His orders were carried out in French; consequently, English spelling added several additional squares to its linguistic quilt. Since then, English has freely borrowed words from other languages around the world (see Chapter 5), each with its own spelling patterns of sound-symbol relationships.

To fully appreciate this marvelous admixture of spelling systems, consider the following words, each of which contains a different orthographical representation of the long-*a* sound heard in the word "bay": *ate, rain, gauge, ray, steak, veil,* and *obey.* The etymologies of these words will reflect spelling influences from several languages; it's worth the thirty minutes you'll spend reading the histories of these words to observe the various influences.

Not only are the spellings of vowel sounds the result of numerous influences, but so are the spellings of consonant sounds. Consider these different spellings of the sound heard at the beginning of the word "shut": *shoe, sugar, issue, mission, notion, suspicion, ocean, conscious, chaperon, schist, fuchsia* and *pshaw*! Once again, use your dictionary to study the etymologies of these words, and you'll understand that English spelling is the product of many influences.

What all of this illustrates, of course, is that there is no English system of spelling. There are several systems at work in our spellings. They demonstrate a basic fact: American English spelling is not the simple matter some education critics would have us believe!

On the other hand, the matter of unconventional spelling is too often condoned by too many teachers when they offer, "But, she or he knows the subject matter," or, "Hey, I teach social studies! Spelling's the English teacher's job." In the latter sentence you can substitute math, science, music, or any other content area in place of "social studies."

DOES SPELLING COUNT?

"Does spelling count?" is a question asked innumerable times each day in schools. Usually it's a question asked by a student who is completing a writing assignment for a science, social studies, home economics, or any other content area class. There are many possible answers to this question, but we'll examine only two potential responses.

First, from a sociological perspective, spelling certainly does count! American culture generally places a higher value on the use of written language than any other form, and spelling is written language. Many language teachers believe this emphasis is out of proportion to its long-range communicative value, but it's there, nevertheless. American culture exacts a high social tax on those who do not use conventional spellings.

As for writing in school, spelling counts more or less, depending upon its use, context, and purpose. If a student is drafting a story he or she wants to write, only a foolish adult peeks over the writer's shoulder and says: "Tsk, tsk. You've misspelled 'receive'." The purpose of the draft is to get ideas on paper. If the final version is to become public, spelling and other editing matters can be attended to later. *Writing* and *editing* are different processes. [Only in the final stage of editing should students consult a dictionary to confirm a spelling.]

Usually, spelling is tested more often than it's taught. The most common forms of spelling instruction are circling misspelled words on students' written work, and giving spelling tests on Friday. The two forms of instruction present an irony that teachers must attend to: One source is more authentic than the other!

The Friday spelling test is usually built around a commercial, prepackaged source of words; that is, the editorial staff of a company in Los Angeles, Chicago, or Dallas, for example—has divined a list of twenty words to be assigned each week during the school year. Any relationship between these divinations and the needs, interests, or wants of the student writers in your local school or district usually is random and chance, if not arbitrary. Try to make a list of 20 words all eighth graders in the United States (or fifth graders or tenth graders) *must* know how to spell, ignoring the language networks these young people have either grown up in or will enter as they assume adult roles in society! This is the problem publishers of spelling texts and advocates of national tests ignore.

A newer approach is for a school to create a spelling list of its own, which is a workable idea if spelling must be tested, and *only* if the list is revised annually. Too often these local lists become stagnant and institutionalized, and as phony as the lists commercial publishers create.

Like other aspects of language study, spelling is included in many school curricula in a decontextualized way, without any meaningful contexts. Most spelling word lists are unrelated to what the students are learning, reading, and writing about in the total school curriculum. The LEA approach is built on the belief that spelling, like other aspects of language study, must be *recontextualized*.

For example, all teachers are responsible for teaching the spelling and vocabulary for their respective subjects. The trigonometry teacher, not the English teacher, is responsible for helping students use and spell the word "exponential." The word "cohesion" is spelled the same but has different meanings in music, physics, and English. Words that represent key concepts in a class are the responsibility of the teacher of that subject.

Clearly, developing independence in spelling is a school goal. Students who are sensitive to words in general, how they operate in different contexts, and how they interact with each other will be better spellers.[12] The LEA approach is consistent with this important finding.

In addition to the several Student Explorations throughout Section II of this book, there are additional strategies teachers can utilize to heighten students' interest in words, their meanings, and their conventional spellings.

The first Student Exploration at the end of this chapter describes the use of spelling logs. Let's take two minutes to look at it. As you can see, using spelling logs is an excellent way for your students to establish and maintain their own personal spelling programs. Teachers who use spelling logs in their classrooms are enthusiastic with the results, because their students focus their attention on words they actually use. Further, spelling logs place control and responsibility in the appropriate place: with the language user.

Another approach combines spelling instruction with vocabulary learning. In this approach, which we are currently testing in a pilot project, one member of the faculty (a reading or English teacher, or a volunteer) collects from other faculty members a list of six or seven words each teacher has identified as *key concepts* for the month. The volunteer teacher then assembles these words into lists, according to subject matter area, and has them printed on different colored paper, such as blue for seventh grade, white for eighth, and yellow for ninth.

In the ensuing month all teachers use the words from their respective grade-level lists. These words represent key concepts in the various subject areas. As the words are used in different classrooms in both oral and written work, spellings are being reinforced and repeated. Word meanings are either repeated or are differentiated according to their application in different academic subjects. Built upon the word-learning principles of repetition, reinforcement, and semantic differentiation, this approach has much promise.

There are two more specific curriculum options to suggest, both of which have been effective in spelling and vocabulary learning.

Uninterrupted Time for Reading

This is sometimes called Reading Workshop or Sustained Silent Reading (SSR). If students spent twenty-five minutes per day reading at a rate of 200 words per minute for 200 days a year, they would encounter 15,000 to 30,000 unfamiliar words and learn between 750 and 1,500 of them![13] The research supporting incidental learning from extensive and uninterrupted reading is clear and defensible from several perspectives: Increased word knowledge is only one of them.[14] If school patrons learned about the several positive language learning outcomes resulting from using school time for sustained silent reading—improved attitudes toward reading, increased reading comprehension, increased vocabulary size and generally higher reading achievement—they would clamor for its becoming a *scheduled* and regular part of all school language programs.[15]

Uninterrupted Time for Writing

The Writing Workshop (WR) model described by Atwell,[16] sometimes called the "process approach" to writing, has been shown to be two to four times as effective as the "product-oriented" approach, with its attendant focus on grammar, structure, and mechanics.[17] The better approach enables language learners to improve their attitudes toward writing, to write more and more often, and to make more significant gains in written language use. As was pointed out earlier in this section, the better spellers are students who are sensitive to words in general, and how they operate in different contexts—in different *social* contexts and in *oral and written* contexts—and how words interact with each other.[18]

Writing Workshop often includes short mini-lessons based on the teacher's observations of the writers' needs. Some of these minilessons may focus on selected aspects of syntax.

The traditional approach to grammar study in the classroom has not worked, according to Noguchi, not because teachers have not tried, "but, ultimately, because expectations of grammar were unrealistic."[19] He proposes a sensible "less is more" (less grammar is more effective, more efficient) approach to assisting developing writers with only those aspects of syntax that are closely associated with more common writing problems such as sentence fragments and run-ons, subject-verb agreement, modification, and punctuation.[20]

Uninterrupted time for reading and writing at regularly scheduled periods each week throughout the school year in a supportive and nonthreatening atmosphere is absolutely essential to continued oral and written language development. At present there is no commercially prepared language text, handbook, or set or series of workbooks that can yield the overall language growth that SSR and WR make possible.

This may sound too good to be true; consequently, the primary weaknesses of SSR or WR are:

They appear to be too simple. Passers-by who do not know the results of current educational research are inclined to think the children or young adults are not learning anything when they see them "doing nothing" but reading or writing. It is an ironic assumption that school athletes, debaters, and musicians need to practice and rehearse to develop fluency and performance, but language users don't.

They require patience and trust. Administrators and classroom teachers must be patient and must trust the students. Artificial constraints such as teacher-approved or teacher-assigned writing topics or an approved list of fiction or nonfiction titles destroy either SSR or WR. When teacher-centered and product-anxious educators are extremely nervous and uncomfortable with SSR and WR, it is the learner's loss; students' comfort and growth should take precedence.

Explorations

STUDENT EXPLORATIONS FOR SYNTAX, SPELLING, AND GOOD ENGLISH

Exploration: Keeping a Spelling Log

DIRECTIONS: One of the ways you can take charge of your own spelling growth is to keep a spelling log. Richard VanDeWeghe suggests the use of a log like the one you see here.[21] You can create your own log, or perhaps your teacher will prepare copies for everyone in the class. Keep the log with your writing drafts and make entries in it when you need to. The first entry is an example.

Spelling Log

Conventional spelling	*My spelling*	*Why the word is confusing*	*Helps for remembering*
meant	ment	I spell it like it sounds.	It's the past tense of *mean*.

Exploration: Language Diary

DIRECTIONS: Keep a language diary for one day, recording your language use. You can use the language diary on the following page. When you write your entries in your diary, be as complete as you can be. Bring your completed diary to class and either exchange it with a friend or analyze your own, using the following questions as starters.

1. What observations can you make about who your primary language partners are during a typical day?
2. Is there a relationship between topic and language partner; topic and time of day; language partner and purpose; purpose and time of day?
3. Contrast your languages for getting out of bed, eating breakfast, going to school, attending school, after school, and at home. In how many ways do they differ?

Language Diary
Date _____

Time	*Language partner(s)*	*Purpose of language*	*What was said*

Exploration: Slang

DIRECTIONS: Make a list of your most frequently used slang expressions.

1. Who else uses these expressions? Be specific by listing (1) the names of other people who use them, and (2) their relationship to you (best friend, neighbor next door, cousin).
2. Are there similar phrases you hear every day but would *never* use? Why? Who uses them?
3. Are there times during the day or week when you would not use *any* or *some* of the words on your list?
4. How do people decide when, where, and with whom slang expressions can or should not be used? How do people define "slang?"

Exploration: "Oldies But Goodies" Slang

DIRECTIONS: Share the list of your slang with one or both parents, or with someone the same age as your parents.

1. How many words on your list do they recognize? How many do they *know* and *use*?
2. What terms or phrases did they use to express the same or similar ideas when they were your age?
3. Share your list with a grandparent, asking the same questions.
4. Why do different age groups use different slang expressions? Which terms, do you think, are more accurate or more expressive, the newer or the older slang expressions?
5. How do people decide when, where, and with whom slang expressions can or should not be used?

Exploration: Shifting Gears

DIRECTIONS: You have an article of clothing—a shirt or a blouse, a pair of jeans—you don't like and hardly ever wear. In fact, it looks like new, although it isn't. Nevertheless, you're wearing it on a day when you meet several people. Each of the following persons will say, "Is this a new [*shirt, blouse, etc.*]? What answers are you most likely to give to their question (play fair; be honest), and *why* are your answers different?

A. your best friend
B. your pastor, priest, or rabbi
C. your favorite teacher
D. your father's best friend
E. your favorite aunt or uncle
F. your neighbor

    G. the school principal

    H. someone "hot" you want to impress

    I. someone you don't particularly like

Exploration: Good and Bad English

DIRECTIONS: Here are several conversational exchanges. Which demonstrate, in your view, good English? Which demonstrate bad English? How did you arrive at your answers? Might a "bad" reply sometimes be a "good" reply? Be prepared to defend your position.

  1. A: Do you know what time it is?
     B: Yes, it's 10:30.

  2. A: Do you know what time it is?
     B: Most assuredly; I own a timepiece.

  3. A. Do you know what time it is?
     B. Yes. Do you?

  4. A: Do you know what time it is?
     B: Yeah, Babe. It's time we got it on!

  5. A: Do you know what time it is?
     B: Time . . . It's an abstract and arbitrary idea, over which we are overly concerned, if not obsessed.

Based upon your answers and other answers you've heard, what is your *tentative* definition of "good" or "bad" English?

Exploration: What Is a "Bad Sentence"?

DIRECTIONS: Probably you have heard people complain about the language use of others. Sometimes sentences are described by language critics as using "bad grammar." Sometimes sentences are described as "rude." What, if anything, is "wrong" in the following sentences?

    A. The farmer drove the barn into the cows.

    B. Females dominate conversations.

    C. We was happy to be able to watch the movie.

    D. St. Louis is east of New York.

    E. The lettuce pretended to cry.

    F. Males are more decisive.

    G. Thanksgiving Day always falls on November 24.

    H. Everyone should bring his money tomorrow.

    I. The cow jumped over the moon.

    J. One cannot always beleive everything one hears.

    K. She gave the dog it's food.

1. Analyze the errors you've identified in the sentences and see if they can be grouped into categories or families. How many different types of errors did you identify?
2. Rank the errors you've identified according to their seriousness. Are some more important than others?
3. There are probably differences of opinion among the members of your class concerning what is or is not an error, and how important or unimportant an error might be. Why?

Exploration: How Many Ways Can You Say "I'm sorry, but . . ."

DIRECTIONS: There are several ways we can apologize for something we've done, depending upon the circumstances. Here are some examples. Read the examples, then answer the questions below.

A. You arrive at school thirty minutes late (because the bus was late) and you must report to the principal's office before you may go to class.
B. You are thirty minutes late for a date.
C. You are thirty minutes late for a study session with friends.
D. You are thirty minutes late for work for the second time this week.
E. You are thirty minutes late picking up your mom at the grocery store.

1. Create an apology for each situation.
2. In how many ways are your apologies different? In how many ways are they similar? Can you think of other circumstances that would require apologies in even more different forms?
3. Why did you use different forms of apologies in these situations? How do *situations* affect the language choices we make?

Exploration: Intonations Are Meaningful

DIRECTIONS: Here are five simple sentences.

A. Jeff loves Kate.
B. We beat them.
C. Rambo likes school.
D. Bald is beautiful.
E. Lassie eats chickens.

1. Read each sentence three different ways: stress the first word, the second word, and then the last word. How do the stress patterns affect the meaning?

2. Although intonation is not part of written language, it clearly affects a sentence's meaning. Explain how.

Exploration: "Well, er, like, you know?"

DIRECTIONS: Keep a one-day record of all of the "fillers" you hear people use in their conversations. Fillers are expressions like "um," "er," "well," "like," and so on. Bring your list of observations to class.

1. What are the most common fillers used by speakers your age? Which fillers are more common among older or younger speakers?
2. Based upon your observations, why do you think people use fillers? Do speakers use fillers all the time, or use them in some circumstances but not in others?
3. Based on your one-day research, what functions do fillers provide in oral language?

Exploration: Talking "Right"

DIRECTIONS: Recall the last time someone corrected your use of language. Perhaps a teacher, parent, or friend told you you had misused a word or that something you had written was inaccurate or awkward. Write a paragraph about such an event in which you explain (1) what language usage was "corrected," and (2) how you felt as a result of the correction.

1. Share your paragraphs in a small group and discuss *why* others have attempted to correct your language.
2. Was the attempt to correct your language successful? What do the others in your group report? Did they change their language?
3. Do you think corrections work? When are corrections successful? Unsuccessful? How do we learn different ways of using language?

Exploration: Plain or Special: Both Work

DIRECTIONS: Some words are learned and used in everyday, ordinary conversations. Others are used for special occasions. Here are several word pairs some people consider representative of ordinary/special terms.

fat	overweight	fire	conflagration
skinny	thin	talk	speech
stupid	ignorant	kids	children

1. Would it matter to you whether you use one of these instead of the other? Does it matter to others in your small group?
2. Does your dictionary make any distinction between the meanings and possible uses of these words?
3. Why in your judgment do some people prefer one word in each pair to the other?

NOTES

1. See: Arthur N. Applebee, *Contexts for Learning to Write: Studies in Secondary School Instruction* (Norwood, N.J.: Ablex Publishing Corporation, 1984); Richard C. Braddock, Richard Lloyd-Jones and Lowell Schoer, *Research in Written Composition* (Urbana, IL: National Council of Teachers of English, 1963); Wilbur N. Hatfield, *An Experience Curriculum in English* (New York: Appleton-Century, 1935); George Hillocks, *Research on Written Composition: New Directions for Teaching* (New York: National Conference on Research in English and Urbana, IL: ERIC Clearinghouse on Reading and Communication Skills, 1986); Rei R. Noguchi, *Grammar and the Teaching of Writing: Limits and Possibilities* (Urbana, IL: National Council of Teachers of English, 1991); Stephen Sherwin, *Four Problems in Teaching English: A Critique of Research* (Scranton, PA: International Textbook Company for the National Council of Teachers of English, 1966).
2. James C. Bostain, "The Dream World of English Grammar," *NEA Journal* 55 (September 1966): 20–22.
3. Jean Aitchison, *Words in the Mind* (Oxford: Basil Blackwell, 1987), 18–19.
4. Robert Lowth, *A Short Introduction to English Grammar* (Menston, Yorkshire, U.K.: Scolar Press, facsimile reprint of 1762 first edition, 1967).
5. Geoffrey Sampson, *Schools of Linguistics* (London: Century Hutchinson, 1987), 50.
6. Robert G. Carlson, *The Americanization Syndrome: A Quest for Conformity* (New York: St. Martin's Press, 1987), 2.
7. Robert C. Pooley, *The Teaching of English Usage* (Urbana, IL: National Council of Teachers of English, 1974), 5.
8. Mary Ellen Snodgrass, *The Great American English Handbook* (Jacksonville, IL: Perma-Bound, 1987), 38.
9. M. A. K. Halliday, *Learning How to Mean: Explorations in the Development of Language* (London: Edward Arnold, 1975), 130–132.
10. Michael Stubbs, *Educational Linguistics* (Oxford: Basil Blackwell, 1986), 20–25.
11. "Wrong turn on foul word spells loss," *The Lincoln* (NE) *Star*, 13 March 1991.
12. Richard E. Hodges, *Improving Spelling and Vocabulary in the Secondary School* (Newark, DE: International Reading Association and Urbana, IL: ERIC Clearinghouse on Reading and Communication Skills, 1982), 12–13.
13. William Nagy and Patricia Herman, "Breadth and Depth of Vocabulary Knowledge: Implications for Acquisition and Instruction," in Margaret McKeown and Mary Curtis (eds.), *The Nature of Vocabulary Acquisition* (Hillsdale, N.J.: Lawrence Erlbaum Associates, 1967), 26.
14. William Nagy, *Teaching Vocabulary to Improve Reading Comprehension* (Newark, DE: International Reading Association, 1988), 3.

15. Richard C. Anderson, Elfrieda Hiebert, Judith Scott, and Ian A.G. Wilkinson, *Becoming a Nation of Readers: The Report of the Commission on Reading* (Pittsburgh, PA: National Academy of Education, 1985), 76–77.

16. Nancie Atwell, *In the Middle: Writing, Reading and Learning with Adolescents* (Upper Montclair, N.J.: Boynton/Cook, 1987).

17. George Hillocks, *Research on Written Composition* (Urbana, IL: National Council of Teachers of English, 1986).

18. Hodges, *Improving Spelling and Vocabulary,* 12–13.

19. Noguchi, *Grammar,* 15.

20. Ibid., 33.

21. Richard VanDeWeghe, "Spelling and Grammar Logs," in Candy Carter (ed.), *Non-native and Nonstandard Dialect Students* (Urbana, IL: National Council of Teachers of English, 1982), 101–105.

CHAPTER 7

Discourse Routines and Social Conventions

Whether it's 'Call me Harry' or 'That's Ms. *White,' or an unvoiced understanding that black men are not boys, and women are not girls, we do what we can, often unconsciously, to address people in ways they prefer.*

—Dennis Baron, *Declining Grammar*

RULES AND CONVENTIONS

Recently I rode in a car with three young adults who spent most of the time complaining about one of their teachers. The teacher requires all students to pick up debris from the classroom floor at the beginning and the end of each class period.

"All he cares about," one summarized, "is a clean floor! Like, it's a crime or something to drop one little piece of paper."

Whether you agree or disagree with the teacher's rule or the fifteen-year-olds' reaction to it is irrelevant. The point is, this teacher has a rule against students dropping paper on the floor. Other teachers establish similar classroom rules; some forbid chewing gum; some require that all work must either be written in ink or typed; some have a rule that no one may leave class to go to the bathroom.

Perhaps these are examples of rules in only one or two classrooms. Rules such as these may become institutionalized and become policy throughout a school building, but they are not universal among all schools in the United States. In some schools students are not expected to abide by any of these rules.

All of us probably observe a variety of locally promulgated rules and policies, as well as an assortment of more universal conventions in social behavior. Many of these conventions are tacit, unwritten agreements, social contracts that have evolved over the years by the consensus of members of society. The conventions are similar to the social facts described in Chapter 2.

There are social conventions, using our Chapter 2 example, that determine how we stand in an elevator car. It is also a convention in the United States that we wait our turn; first come, first served. This governs our behavior when we stand in line at the drinking fountain, to buy theater tickets or to check out at the supermarket. Similarly, the location of the red, yellow, and green traffic lights are conventionally arranged in the same order, whether the traffic signal is vertical (the red light is always at the top of the series) or horizontal (the red light is always first on the left).

Restaurants conventionally have a host who seats arriving diners; short-order, take-out, or fast-food eateries do not. To my knowledge, the Food and Drug Administration has not mandated that there be a host in a sit-down restaurant but no host at Burger City. The employment of a host is not determined by law but a social convention.

Similarly, despite what is said about the liberating features of language, there are stringent social language conventions in our society. Those who violate the conventions of social discourse must be prepared to pay the social tax.

For example, conventionally we answer residential telephones in the United States with a simple, "Hello." Sometimes this convention is observed more formally when the answerer says, "the Smith residence." (As relatively uniform as this method of answering the telephone is in the United States, it's just as conventional in England for a residential phone to be answered by giving the last four digits of the telephone number. My British friends answer their telephones with "Hullo. Seven-eight-nine-four.")

We follow different conventions, however, when the telephone we're answering is a business telephone. The name of the business or organization is conventionally identified by the answerer, who will say things like, "South High School," "First Presbyterian Church," "Moore's Market," or the excruciatingly long and synthetically chummy, "Thank you for calling Waldo's, open 24-hours a day for your convenience, now at three locations. This is Jan. How may I help you?"

You can imagine the consternation at the other end if you answered your home telephone with, "The Jacksons: Bill, Betty, Bambi and Bruce. How can we help you?" Or, if you called your bank you'd be taken aback you if you were greeted with, "Yeah? Who is it?" Louis Whitmore, one of my former students who is a banker during the day, says that someone might answer the telephone in this manner at his bank, but they'd do it only once!

In Chapter 6 the diatypic features of field, tenor, and mode were described as environmental determinants of language. It is important to note that the environment shapes and determines the language. The language choices we automatically make are influenced by the field, tenor, and mode. To believe that a participant observes "Let's see, now, I'm only going shopping for a loaf of bread and an onion, so I can leave my telephone voice at home," however, is to misinterpret how field, tenor, and mode exert their influence. It's not that overt.

Discourse and discourse analysis are areas of language study that are the subject of a great deal of recent sociolinguistic research. For the purposes of a school program in Language Exploration and Awareness, however, our focus on discourse is limited to social and primarily oral exchanges and routines.

At the risk of being what one of my daughters teasingly calls "repetitively redundant," I want to help you recall that LEA stresses language as a *social* exploration having to do *with people*. Language in language explorations ought to be authentically human and emerge from real human contexts.

In examining social discourse, it is important to add to this list some other essentials. One of them is **connected language**. Many, but clearly not all, of the language events we experience daily are composed of two or more connected utterances. As a matter of fact, we speak single utterances so infrequently that Hoey has claimed that "in our everyday speech and writing, the sentence is only a small cog in a normally much larger machine."[1]

An exchange might be as simple as one I encountered as I came to my office this morning:

EXCHANGE 1:

(1) SHARON: How's Larry this morning?
(2) LARRY: Fine, thanks. And you?

Or, it might be more involved, like one I participated in on the telephone yesterday:

EXCHANGE 2:

(1) LARRY: This is Larry Andrews. I'm calling about the overdue notice I re-
(2)   ceived in campus mail today.
(3) MARY: What's your I.D. number?
(4) LARRY: 628411
(5) MARY: O.K. Just a minute.
           [*Enters number in library computer and waits . . .*]
(6) MARY: O.K. Here you are. Question?
(7) LARRY: I didn't check out the *Aging in America* book, yet the notice says I
(8)   have it and that it's overdue.
(9) MARY: O.K. I'll mark it returned.
(10) LARRY: Thank you. Is that all?
(11) MARY: Yep.
(12) LARRY: Fine. Bye.

These two examples are ordinary examples of direct speech, and require very little interpretation. Yet, you'll note that each event follows certain "rules." In the first exchange, Sharon offers in (1) an **Opening Sequence**. As Finegan and Besnier point out, conversations are opened in socially recognized ways. A Greeting is one method we have in society of saying "I recognize you. I want to acknowledge you. I want to talk to you."[2]

Since politeness is a trait valued by our society, it is required that the second speaker acknowledge the Opening Sequence Greeting by being courteous and saying something mannerly in reply. Consequently, this social requirement is met by utterance of (2).

The sentences in Exchange 1 are so formulaic that they actually convey little substantive content. They are important, however, for a different reason. They provide some of the paste which helps hold society together.

Another Opening Sequence is shown in Exchange 2. In this case, I identify myself in (1) with a common beginning, Opening Sequence Identification, which is used in hundreds of telephone conversations every day. The identification helps not only to identify the speaker, but also to solicit the answerer's attention, which is indicated in (3), (5), and (6).

ADJACENCY AND UTTERANCE PAIRS

In a similar vein, Finegan and Besnier identify several **adjacency pairs**. Adjacency pairs are structural mechanisms society has found useful in organizing social conversations.[3] Questions are followed by Answers, an Invitation is followed by an Acceptance, and so on.

QUESTION/ANSWER UTTERANCE PAIR
SPEAKER 1: Where's the morning paper?
SPEAKER 2: On the table.

INVITATION/ACCEPTANCE UTTERANCE PAIR
SPEAKER 1: We're having some people for dinner Saturday and hope you can come.
SPEAKER 2: Thanks. We'd like that.

ASSESSMENT/DISAGREEMENT UTTERANCE PAIR
SPEAKER 1: Mr. Wilson is one of the great teachers around here!
SPEAKER 2: Oh? You obviously don't know him very well.

APOLOGY/ACCEPTANCE UTTERANCE PAIR
SPEAKER 1: Sorry I called you so late last night.
SPEAKER 2: That's all right. No bother.

SUMMONS/ACKNOWLEDGMENT UTTERANCE PAIR

SPEAKER 1: Say, Dave!

SPEAKER 2: Yes?

Adjacency pairs follow a prescribed sequence if they are to be successful and, given our definition of good English, if they are to be comfortable to the participants. First, the pairs are contiguous and spoken by two speakers. When a speaker inserts a comment before giving an Answer to a Question, confusion and sometimes anger will result.

SPEAKER 1: Where's the morning paper?

SPEAKER 2: They say it might snow tonight. On the table.

Second, the pairs are ordered. Questions precede Answers, not vice versa (except on television's "Jeopardy"). Acceptances follow Invitations. Apologies cannot be accepted until they are offered.

Third, the pairs must be matched. It would be odd, for example, for the initial part of one adjacency pair to be followed by the second part of another.

SPEAKER 1: We're having some people for dinner Saturday and hope you can come.

SPEAKER 2: That's all right. No bother.

Chaika (1985) examines **utterance pairs,** which are similar to adjacency pairs. Utterance pairs are conversational sequences, too, in which the first utterance elicits a *prescribed* response. Common utterance pairs are:[4]

Greeting : Greeting

Question : Answer

Complaint : Excuse, Apology, or Denial

Request/Command : Acceptance/Rejection

Compliment : Acknowledgment

Farewell : Farewell

An opening sequence Greeting elicits another Greeting in a prescribed reply. A Question prescribes an Answer. A Complaint calls for an Excuse, an Apology, or a Denial.

One of the profound features of oral language in its social uses is that we feel compelled to reply to those who initiate a conversation with us, as an examination of utterance pairs demonstrates. Labov and Fanshell describe preconditions that are at work, for example, when questions are asked: The questioner has a right or duty to ask a question; the one asked has a responsibility or obligation to answer.[5]

This Question:Answer precondition is implicitly understood by everyone in our society. It is the reason that when someone asks a question for which we have no answer we feel uncomfortable: we *must* reply, and we must reply appropriately. An appropriate reply to a yes/no question is either "Yes" or "No" and we must, according to the precondition, use one of the appropriate replies. "Are you still beating your wife/husband?" is an old joke based on these principles. The precondition compels an answer, and it must be either "Yes" or "No."

Chaika extends the Labov-Fanshel precondition of Questions to cover all utterance pairs. Consequently, then, not only does the Questioner have the right or duty to ask a question, but the Greeter has a right or duty to greet, the Complainer a right or duty to complain, and so on.[6] We might summarize these discourse preconditions as follows:

Discourse Routine Preconditions
 I. The first speaker has a right or duty to speak.
 II. The second speaker has a responsibility or obligation to reply.

Closing Sequences are as important as Opening Sequences. A sequence cannot be used until the participants are ready for the conversation to end. Negotiating the timing of the Closing Sequence requires sensitivity: the participants do not want to either appear curt or dawdling. We typically use acceptable code words to indicate that we're about to end a conversation: "Well . . .", "So . . . ." and "O.K." being obvious and frequent examples.

SPEAKER 1: Well, it's been good seeing you.

SPEAKER 2: Yeah! Take care.

SPEAKER A: So, do you think you can make it?

SPEAKER B: Sure! Thanks.

SPEAKER I: O.K., well, I think I'd better . . .

SPEAKER II: Yeah, I need to get going, too.

THE COOPERATIVE PRINCIPLE

The principles governing the conduct and interpretation of conversations are varied and intricate. Describing how speakers cooperate with each other, despite the intricacies in oral communication, Paul Grice defines the **Cooperative Principle**:

> Make your conversational contribution such as is required, at the stage at which it occurs, by the accepted purpose or direction of the talk exchange in which you are engaged.[7]

Grice's Cooperative Principle can be elaborated. The Principle includes the following categories:

Category of Quantity

The Cooperative Principle's Quantity category is relatively simple: speakers are expected (1) to provide as much information as is required (for the purposes of the current exchange), (2) but no more than is required.[8] For example, if we ask Marilyn, "Do you have any pets?" she will reply, "Yes, I have a cat." The category of Quantity allows us to assume that she does not have other pets. She answered our question, we believe, by adhering to this category of the Cooperative Principle. Should we later discover that Marilyn also has a parakeet, a dog and several hamsters, we would feel deceived. By violating the Quantity feature, Marilyn has violated the Cooperative Principle; she hasn't been a cooperative conversational partner.

The category of Quantity can be violated in an opposite manner, as well. Sometimes conversational partners will give more, agonizingly much more, information than was asked for. For example, we might casually ask Mary, "Are you going shopping with us Sunday?" and receive the following tedious reply:

> Shopping? You must be joking. If you had any idea what my calendar looked like for the coming week—which starts with a meeting at 7:00 a.m. Monday—my mother's birthday by the way, and I forgot to call her last year because her birthday was on a Sunday, and we were just swamped! I don't see how I can fit one more thing into my schedule and still have any time to sleep or eat.

About all that can be said about this irksome reply is that if you ask some people what kind of car they drive, they answer with a complete description of how the whole automobile was built! They tell us more than we really want to know. More generously, we can observe that this violation of Quantity makes the speaker an uncooperative conversational partner.

People who consistently violate Quantity by providing too little information are known as secretive, sometimes as liars. Those who tell more than is necessary, on the other hand, are known as blabbermouths, boors, or even demagogues. Society will levy a heavy tax on them over time.

Grice adds an important note to the question of giving more information than is necessary. It might be claimed, for example, that doing so may not be a transgression but merely a waste of time. Grice contends, though, that overinformativeness may be confusing because it is apt to raise side issues and produce an indirect effect: hearers may be misled into believing there is some point to the excess information.[9]

Category of Relation

This category assumes that what is said will be germane and relevant to the ongoing conversation.[10] An example of a relevant reply is shown in the Question/Answer utterance pair. When following the Question "Where's the morning paper?" the Answer, "On the table" is relevant. On the other hand, if we offer an invitation and say, "We're having some people in for dinner Saturday and hope you can come," "On the table" would be irrelevant.

"Do you want to go to a movie next Friday?" is a Question/Invitation that calls for a predictable kind of reply, one which will be relevant. "It's a stormy day and I have to call Uncle Freddy" is an uncooperative and irrelevant response. It is distracting, and could generate frustration or even anger.

Category of Manner

"Organization" might be a term to use in the discussion of this category, which assumes that speakers will be clear and orderly.[11] If speakers and writers are cooperative, they avoid obscure, ambiguous, and disjointed language. George Bush has been identified as one who violates this feature, owing to his syntactic style, which characteristically drops the subject and sometimes the verb in sentences. For example, in his 1990 State of the Union Address President Bush said: "Ambitious aims? Of course. Easy to do? Far from it." Similarly, in an antidrug message to the Academy of Television Arts and Sciences, Bush told the audience: "Twenty million kids. Impressionable. Just waiting to be entertained."[12]

Category of Quality

Normally we expect speakers and writers to say what they believe to be either true or verifiable, or both.[13] Even if a conversation partner observes the categories of Quantity, Relevance and Manner, a Quality violation makes the entire conversation (or writing) worthless, in the judgment of society. This category will not apply, of course, in joke-telling or other humorous talk, but it does apply to most social conversations.

Speakers who violate this category of conversation suffer the consequences. Sometimes they are regarded as the group clowns ("Can't you *ever* be serious?") and are not taken seriously. Sometimes they are recognized as people given to hyperbole ("Well, consider the source.") If their Quality violations are intentional and chronic, these people are avoided; others "know" a liar when they see one!

The Cooperative Principle is routinely violated. Some of the violations come from those we may identify as windbags, unorganized, poor speakers, or liars. Other violations are not as serious or severe, but are simply routine characteristics of oral discourse.

As Chapters 1 and 7 illustrate, structures that ordinarily are classified as interrogatives really aren't interrogatives at all in some oral discourse.

SPEAKER 1: Would you like to have this ticket to the concert?
SPEAKER 2: Is the Pope a Catholic?

Answering a Question with another Question technically violates the Cooperative Principle as it operates in adjacency pairs. In this example, however, speaker 2's reply is not interpreted as a question. Or, using an example of an **indirect speech** act, Widdowson (1979) demonstrates how Relevance is *not* being violated in this exchange:

SPEAKER 1: Phone!
SPEAKER 2: I'm in the bath.
SPEAKER 1: O.K.[14]

Speaker 2's answer makes no relevant response, at least on the surface, to speaker 1's "Phone!" There are no cohesive elements linking speaker 2's reply

to speaker 1's opening. Frequently, however, conversation, and indirect speech acts in particular, require indirect rather than direct or literal interpretation.

Even when it appears that a respondent is being uncooperative, the conversational partners make adjustments and the Cooperative Principle is still at work. One of the reasons indirect speech acts "work" is the degree of personal and cultural knowledge and experience the participants share. It's as though they "talk between the lines."

Indirect speech acts are complicated by the cultural values of the United States, a polite and equal society. Although we may not like being courteous or polite, and may privately believe that some are more equal than others, we know that being courteous and behaving as if all were created equal are rotarian virtues good Americans are supposed to practice.

Consequently, adjacency pairs are frequently altered to adhere to culture values. For example, to establish a more coequal atmosphere in my classrooms, I often avoid initiating a Request/Command:Accept/Reject utterance routine and substitute a Question/Answer pair by asking my students, "Will you please turn to page ninety-nine in our text?" I do this for a simple reason—in our culture it's bad to be dictatorial and give commands; it's good, on the other hand, to phrase questions like invitations, especially in classrooms! Actually, however, I'm telling (dictating to) my students, "Turn now to page ninety-nine," but I'm disguising the Command. The question, "Can you stop on your way home for a loaf of bread, please?" is a Request/Command similarly disguised as a question. You hear similarly disguised Commands all the time: "Will you please close the window?" "Can you close the door?"

Sometimes we disguise Requests, primarily because we don't want to lose face. For example, instead of admitting that we're lost, forgetful, stupid or all three, we'll ask for directions by saying: "Do you know the way to San Jose?" or, "Excuse me, but do you have the time?" Others in our culture implicitly understand this feature of discourse, which is why they do not answer questions like the latter two with a simple Yes or No.

Modesty is another public virtue, regardless of our private feelings about our accomplishments. As proud as we may be about a new promotion, article of clothing, witty remark, and the like, we are told over and over again: "Don't be a braggart!" Consequently, the Compliment:Acknowledgment utterance pair presents us with cultural etiquette problems.

Because of the societal virtue of modesty, some people simply cannot accept and do not otherwise know how to acknowledge a compliment. They do not want to appear boastful. My good friend Martha, for example, is a marvelous cook. (Actually, her name is Betty, but my wife and I have called her Martha for years, after the Martha in the Greek Scriptures who is always, seemingly, toiling in the kitchen.) At the conclusion of a meal she has prepared we always compliment Martha because the food is always superb. In acknowledging our compliments, however, Martha deflects our comments by pointing out a weakness in the menu only she can know about. ("I had to go next door to borrow an egg to fix this." Or, "I do wish our refrigerator made nicer ice cubes.") I'm waiting for the day she acknowledges a compliment by telling us the napkins are the wrong shade of white!

Language users abide by a number of unwritten and silent contracts. The ability to use language with precision, elaboration, and spontaneity clearly has a liberating and enabling effect on us. Nevertheless, competent language users also intuitively know the rules of oral discourse routines, the social facts, and the principles of cooperative communication.

FOR YOUR INQUIRY AND PRACTICE:

1. Has your otherwise peaceful evening been interrupted lately by a telephone solicitor? You know, those people who always call you by your first name with an exaggerated chummy tone? The next time you receive a telephone sales pitch, immediately interrupt the caller by asking, "What is it you are selling?" At this, the caller will frequently pause. Why?
2. Summarize some discourse conventions (tacit rules) observed by the participants in the following language events:
   A. A telephone conversation between friends of the same age and same sex; different ages; different sex
   B. Meeting your major professor, principal, or superintendent at the supermarket
   C. A parent-teacher conference
   D. Sitting beside a nun or clergy person at the movies or on an airplane
   E. An interview with a top-flight school district where you very much want to teach

---

Explorations

STUDENT EXPLORATIONS FOR DISCOURSE ROUTINES AND SOCIAL CONVENTIONS

Exploration: Titles

DIRECTIONS: Watch the 10:00 or 11:00 o'clock news on the same television channel for one week, focusing your attention on one use of language: Under what circumstances and how do the broadcasters and reporters refer to people "in the news?" Do they always call the governor of the state "Governor"? Do they always refer to private citizens as "Mister," "Mrs.," or "Ms.?" Do they sometimes use the first name of the individual being interviewed or spoken of?

1. Are titles used for both males and females?
2. Are titles used for all people, regardless of ethnic background?
3. Who, and under what circumstances, is a person in the news referred to by his or her first name?
4. For which groups are titles most frequently used: elected officials (local, state or national?), representatives of the military, or members of the clergy?
5. What can you conclude from your observations about the station's terms-of-address policy? Does the policy treat all people equally?
6. Since thousands of viewers in your community watch this channel's newscasts nightly, weekly, and monthly, will the newscasters' and reporters' habits affect the viewers' attitudes toward the persons interviewed or talked about, or the groups they represent)?

[Vary this Exploration by substituting a local or state radio or newspaper.]

Exploration: Do You Hear What I Hear?

DIRECTIONS: Have you ever seen an adult walk into a room and ask, "You call this clean?" Or, did you ever see a teacher unexpectedly enter a room full of talking students and ask, "Do I hear noise in this room?" Questions like these really aren't *questions*. What are they?

1. Can you think of several examples similar to those above, which *say* one thing but *mean* another?
2. Why do we sometimes talk indirectly, saying one thing but meaning another?

Exploration: Predicting Language

DIRECTIONS: Have you noticed that you can often predict how a speaker will end a sentence? Because you know the speaker well or because you know a lot about the topic (or both), you *know* how the sentence will end.

Here is a series of statements. For each, identify:

1. *Who* the speaker is (generally, not a specific name)
2. *Where* or *how* the statement was used
3. *Who* is the intended receiver of each statement or message below. Be prepared to defend your answers with specifics.
   a. Ladies and gentlemen of the jury
   b. Roger, Tango 778
   c. This is to certify that
   d. Dearly beloved
   e. Soaring Temperatures to Continue
   f. We'll be back right after this
   g. Final Reduction
   h. May I help you
   i. Drive-thru
   j. Ladies
   k. Beauty tips for cold weather
   l. Off
   m. Narrow ruled with margin
   n. Shake before using
   o. Stir until dissolved

Exploration: Language Strategies

[NOTE TO THE TEACHER: You will need to bring to class a variety of magazines for this activity. The greater the variety, the better.]

DIRECTIONS: Select one of the magazines from the supply available. After you have had an opportunity to study the advertisements in one magazine, respond to the following questions.

1. Is the intended magazine readership primarily male or female? Is the language used in the ads more appealing to male or female readers? How do you know?
2. Share your observations about the ads with a small group. Do others in your group agree with your observations about the language patterns in the ads? Is the agreement or disagreement related to male/ female membership of your group?
3. Do magazines use a particular style of language intended to "speak

to" the intended audience? Is this an appropriate or inappropriate use of language?

Exploration: Telephone Discourse

[NOTE TO THE TEACHER: Task cards will be needed for this activity. Sample tasks might include: (1) ordering pizza for a party, (2) getting a telephone number for L.A. Gear in Los Angeles, (3) calling the state highway patrol for a report on interstate highway conditions, (4) making a call on the 900 "Teen Line", (5) calling your best friend to ask if he or she will call a "special someone" you like to see if that special someone likes you.]

DIRECTIONS: Using the two prop telephones in the class, role-play a telephone conversation in front of the class, using the task card you've drawn at random. You will need a partner to complete this activity. After all of the conversations are finished, let everyone answer the following questions.

1. How would you describe the differences in language in the different telephone conversations? Give specific examples to illustrate your answers.
2. What are the circumstances in the different conversations that affect how language is used?
3. How is appropriate language use determined? What are some of the factors that determine how we speak in different contexts?

Exploration: Magazine Interviews

DIRECTIONS: Either in the school library, the media center, or at a newsstand or drug store, locate a magazine containing an interview with a politician, rock or film star, or athletic celebrity. Read the interview; then answer the questions below.

1. What is the purpose of the interview? Is the interviewer trying to reveal the "real" person behind the famous image? Is the purpose to reveal an aspect of the subject's life that heretofore has not been widely known? Is there some other purpose?
2. What is the role of the interviewer? Does the interviewer use many or few questions? Does the interviewer become a part of the story, or is the interviewer part of the background?
3. What kinds of unstated rules govern how interviews are conducted and published in magazines?

Exploration: Say Again . . .

DIRECTIONS: Watch an episode of Captain Kangaroo, Mister Rogers' Neighborhood or Reading Rainbow. Pay particular attention to the language used by the Captain, Mr. Rogers, and the Rainbow host.

1. How would you describe the speech patterns these speakers use? Considering their audience, do you think their speech patterns are or are not appropriate?
2. What do you think would happen if these speakers would use their television voices in the restaurant where they have lunch? In an automobile garage, explaining to a mechanic what's wrong with their car?
3. When is it either acceptable or unacceptable to change our speaking voices?

Exploration: Find the Catch

DIRECTIONS: Some television ads seem too good to be true. Some ads want you to buy exercise equipment that will change your body structure and shape in 30 days or less! Other ads offer salves, ointments, and pills that will accomplish the same body-building results ("Get rid of ugly cellulite!"). Too good to be true?

1. How would you describe the language in these ads? Is it scientific, medical, or technical, as we might expect?
2. Do you think ads like these tell the whole truth?
3. Do we expect advertisements to tell us the whole truth? The truth, mostly? The truth sometimes? How much truth do we expect?

Exploration: When Is Journalism Yellow or Purple?

DIRECTIONS: Collect and read two or three issues of tabloid newspapers that specialize in writing about fantastic events or secrets of famous people.

1. Do the articles cite sources for the information contained in them? Are the stories based on real evidence?
2. Are the articles telling the whole truth? The truth, mostly? Or, the truth, hardly? How do you know?
3. Point out specific uses of language that would make the unsuspecting reader believe what's being reported.

Exploration: The Three Bears; or, the Trio of Stocky Mammals

DIRECTIONS: After listening to someone read "Goldilocks and the Three Bears," ask for three groups of four people to reenact a scene from the story. The particular scene is left to the group to decide. The element of the story that will be changed, however, is the setting: the time and place. Have one group reenact Goldilocks in the original setting; one group in frontier Oklahoma in 1860; the third group in a posh condominium, today.

1. Discuss how the language used by the characters accurately reflects their ages, locale, and relationships.
2. What seems to affect our language use the strongest: our age, where we are, or the people we're with?

Exploration: It's Complimentary, Thank You

DIRECTIONS: Why do some people find it difficult to accept a compliment? When compliments are offered ("What a neat shirt!"), you sometimes hear anything but a simple Thank You. ("What? This old rag?")

For one day, focus your attention on the language of compliments you observe at school, on the bus, at the mall and any other place you go. After collecting one day's observed compliments, share your answers to the following questions with the class.

1. How many compliments did you observe? Is the number surprisingly large or surprisingly small?
2. Are compliments more common among males or females? Older or younger speakers?
3. How did those receiving the compliments respond? Were they pleased? Uneasy? What were some of their responses?
4. Why do so many people receiving a compliment avoid saying "Thank you"?

NOTES

1. Michael Hoey, *On the Surface of Discourse* (London: George Allen & Unwin, 1983), 1.
2. Edward Finegan and Niko Besnier, *Language: Its Structure and Use* (New York: Harcourt Brace Jovanovich, 1989), 344.
3. Ibid., 341–344.
4. Elaine Chaika, "Discourse Routines," in Virginia P. Clark et al., (eds.), *Language: Introductory Readings* (New York: St. Martin's Press, 1985), 429–455.

5. William Labov and David Fanshel, *Therapeutic Discourse: Psychotherapy as Conversation* (New York: Academic Press, 1977), 81–82.
6. Chaika, "Discourse Routines," 436.
7. Paul Grice, *Studies in the Way of Words* (Cambridge, MA: Harvard University Press, 1989), 26.
8. Ibid.
9. Ibid., 26–27.
10. Ibid., 27.
11. Ibid.
12. "From Our Files: Bushery." *English Today* 6 (October 1990): 6.
13. Grice, *Way of Words*, 27.
14. Henry Widdowson, *Explorations in Applied Linguistics* (Oxford: Oxford University Press), 1979, 138.

CHAPTER **8**

Regional, Social, and Historical Variations

Language doesn't exist in a vacuum. It reflects all the life and variety and change and divisions which exist in society.
—David Crystal, *Who Cares About English Usage?*

WORDS, TOOLS, AND VARIATION

Several years ago Bergen Evans likened words to tools, instruments for accomplishing what the user wants to accomplish.[1] Evans' analogy is useful for several reasons. First, it points out how we create things (ideas, poems, governments, hopes, dreams, novels, reports) with word tools. Second, the analogy reminds us that artisans use tools differently; the way a woodworker realizes his vision by using his tools enables him to create a table or cupboard that bears his artistic signature.

To recall an idea from Chapter 1, we know that people do not really use language homogeneously. Like the woodworker, writers apply their vision through their ability to select and apply tools—words—which enables them to create works that bears their artistic signatures.

Not only poets and novelists use language heterogeneously and uniquely. You and I do, too. Everybody does. The fact that every speaker or writer uses language uniquely is illustrated by the off-hand comments we hear when a description of a recent event is given and one of the conversational participants says, "Ya know, I can just hear Uncle Don saying that!" or "Yes, that sounds exactly like something Mother would say!"

In informal conversations like those, we not only accept but enjoy the uniquely individual uses of language we observe. At other levels, however, many people find language differences unsettling, if not intolerable.

MORE IGNOTIONS ABOUT LANGUAGE

There are many reasons for this intolerance, some of which can be collected under the heading of "More Ignotions about Language." Although there is more widespread acceptance of these ideas than research or current scholarship can support or verify, they continue to represent the language beliefs of many language users of all ages. As I suggest throughout this book, there is a belief among many members of our society that there is a discrete and fixed code of "right" pronunciations, labels for things and ideas, sentence patterns, and punctuation conventions. Gere and Smith have examined this general idea and identified the following more specific language beliefs that describe different notions of Standard English in more detail:

1. Standard English is a clearly definable set of correct pronunciations, grammatical structures, and word choices. It is "standard" because it represents the widest usage and because it has been refined to be the most versatile and acceptable form of English.

2. Standard English is the kind of language people should use for all occasions. "Standard" means most serviceable and negotiable, and therefore most correct.

3. Standard English is necessary for success in school and therefore in employment. One of the principal reasons for having schools is to equip young people with the skills that improve their chances for social and financial rewards. Conformity to certain ways of using language obviously underlies many of those skills.

4. Standard English is the best version of English for the expression of logical and abstract thought. Because all of the great English and American writers use this form of English and because much of the business of our society is conducted in this form, it must be the form best suited to the expression of precise and sophisticated thought.

5. Some people, such as blacks and hillbillies, speak a version of English that is degenerate. Signs of this degeneracy can be found in their sloppy pronunciation, their imprecise vocabulary, and their violation of many grammatical rules. All of these signs point to a form of language that is inadequate for accurate pronunciation.[2]

FOR YOUR INQUIRY AND PRACTICE:

Examine the five belief statements from Gere and Smith. Which of the five state-ments are more acceptable to you? Which are least acceptable? Write a two-sentence statement that describes your beliefs about Standard English.

Some of these beliefs serve as the reason some people offer for linguistic, racial, or religious intolerance. For example, it is generally accepted in the United States, a country where all people are supposed to be created equal, that good citizens should behave democratically and avoid even the appear-ance of prejudice. Consequently, some speakers are criticized for using lan-guage that is so different that effective communication is not possible. Actu-ally, we can usually understand speakers from other areas of the country, even when their speech is filled with pronunciations and words unique to their locales. Nevertheless, prejudiced statements are permitted, provided that they are disguised as comments about effective communication.

BUT, IT'S IN THE BIBLE!

Negative attitudes toward language variation are not new. It seems people have always been sensitive to linguistic differences. One of the earliest exam-ples is found in the Bible. In the Book of Judges there is a description of the Ephraimites trying to cross the River Jordon to flee from the Gileadites:

> And the Gileadites took the fords of the Jordon against the Ephraim-ites. And when any of the fugitives of Ephraim said 'Let me go over,' the men of Gilead said to him 'Then say "shibboleth" 'and he said "sibboleth" because he could not pronounce it right. Then they seized him and slew him at the fords of the Jordon. And there fell at that time 42,000 of the Ephraimites.[3]

The Ephraimites spoke a different dialect of Hebrew and could be recog-nized by their inability to pronounce the initial /sh-/ in *shibboleth* (a shibboleth is an ear of grain). Consequently, instead of pronouncing it with the local dialect-standard *shibboleth*, the Ephraimites pronounced it *sibboleth*.

The phonological difference in this illustration is similar to the different pronunciations of the word *sumac* in the United States, which I first encoun-tered during my college days when I worked for four summers at a summer camp in Vermont. "I imagine the sumac (which I pronounced SUE-mack) is pretty in October," I commented one day to my Vermont-native employer. "Yes," he answered, "the sumac (SHOE-mack as he pronounced it) is colorful." I am gratified that he merely pronounced "sumac" as he customarily did and did not attempt to slay me on the banks of Otter Creek because I used my midwestern pronunciation!

MORE RECENT ATTITUDES

The Standard English described in the five myths is an idealized notion about language. It is the type of language, some believe, used by film star and television host Vincent Price or, even better by Alistair Cooke, the transplanted Brit-cum-American, as he introduces the weekly episodes on Public Television's "Masterpiece Theater." Coming down a notch or two, Standard English may be seen by some as the language spoken by English professors, school teachers, and librarians. One text not only defines Standard English in a similarly operational manner, but also tells students it's *best* for them: "Standard English, like the language used by most television newscasters and newspaper reporters, is the best choice for your purpose."[4]

Standard English is prescribed in the handbooks and grammar texts used in some schools. These texts are filled with "Do say . . ." and "Don't say . . ." admonitions and prescriptions. They include examples of expressions to avoid or sentences that are "weak," "faulty," or "confusing."[5]

I suppose there is some truth in each of the judgments these books offer about language use. The statements about Standard English in most grammar books used in schools, however, violate the Quantity category of the Cooperative Principle (see Chapter 7); they do not give enough information. What they tell may be true, but it isn't the whole truth.

The rules of good English found in most grammar texts and usage handbooks are appropriate *if* the language user is *writing* and if the written product is to be a formal or a literary piece like those published by professional writers and publishers. This is an important use of language, but it is only one, and ignores too many other aspects of language and communication!

LANGUAGE VARIES

Most people grow up with the ethnolinguistic attitude that their native language is best. Cruz humorously describes this attitude as laying claim to "the birthright of every native speaker of every language in the world—that of thinking that my language is better than anybody else's."[6]

It is commonplace for people (not you, of course, or I, but they) to hear other speakers use "strange" terms and pronounce some words in "weird" if not "wacky" ways. As an encore, Cruz delightfully captures this attitude:

Like everyone else, I do not think of myself as having an accent, although all my American friends think I speak English with a heavy Philippine accent and all my "pure" Tagalog friends think I have a Manileño accent. Like American southerners who think that Jimmy Carter was the only recent president who did not have and accent, or like American fans of the Beatles who thought they [the Beatles] had a funny accent when the Beatles themselves thought they were affecting an American accent, I am completely deaf to my own idiolectal idiosyncrasies.[7]

Nevertheless, we recognize that the Chinese speak Chinese, Germans speak German, the French speak French, and Spaniards speak Spanish. So it goes around the globe from one language family to another. The existence of language families demonstrates that people who speak *with* one another speak *like* one another.[8] The opposite of this principle ought to be fairly obvious: People who do not regularly speak with one another do not speak like them. Consequently, there are similar usages among those who associate with each other and differences between those groups with few or no associations.

As Finegan and Besnier further illustrate, even the most casual observers of language in the United States are aware that language varies in this country; some speak with Boston accents, southern drawls, or in Brooklynese. These comments denote an awareness that language has *regional* variations,[9] sometimes rather loosely called *accents* or *dialects*.

One of the universally accepted linguistic principles is the tenet that everyone speaks with an accent, and in a dialect that is a subset of their larger language. *Accent* and *dialect*, however, are not synonymous.

LINGUISTIC FEATURES OF DIALECTS: PHONOLOGICAL, SYNTACTICAL, AND LEXICAL VARIATIONS

Dialects usually are characterized by three basic linguistic variations:

1. *lexical* (vocabulary)
2. *phonological* (accent)
3. *grammatical*

Using Trudgill's definition, for any dialect to gain the full status of a dialect it must have unique grammatical features. According to Trudgill, then, *dialect* refers to any language variety that is *grammatically* different from any other.[10]

Phonological differences are illustrated by the variant pronunciations you've heard for words, such as idea/idear; wash/warsh; dinner/dinna; humor/

yumar; human/yuman; toosday/tyusday; white/wite; or, duty/dyuty. Linguistically speaking, any of these pronunciations is as good as another. A *Toosday* deadline is certainly as final as one on *Tyusday*. Anyone who performs a *duty* is obviously as responsible as one who does a *dyuty*. At the level of meaning, the pronunciations are equals.

Syntactical differences are evident, for example, in the use of the second person pronoun. In the United States, it is a characteristic of the Southern dialect for a speaker to ask, "Are y'all ready?" In the North Midland dialect area where I live, speakers are more likely to ask the same question, but in a different syntactic form: "Are you ready?"

Another example of a syntactical difference was illustrated on television last night when the Canadian-born newscaster (who speaks more British English than American English) reported that the "injured persons were taken to hospital." In American English one would say that the injured were taken "to *the* hospital." Quite simply, the syntax of British English does not ordinarily require the definite article in a phrase denoting location in time or space. American English does. The only conclusion one can draw from this difference has already been suggested: people who speak *with* one another speak *like* one another. One syntactical pattern is linguistically neither superior nor inferior to another. Some patterns may, it is clear, become socially stigmatized, but that is a social and not a linguistic feature.

Dialects are also characterized by different lexical options. For example, a heavy pan used for frying chicken may be called a *frying pan*, a *fry pan*, or a *skillet*. At the meaning level, the terms are equal; the chicken will taste just as good, regardless of the term used for the container it is fried in. Further, whether you use an *earthworm*, an *angleworm*, or a fishing (or *fish*) *worm*, at the meaning level your chances of catching a five-pound bass are the same.

REGIONAL AND SOCIOLOGICAL FEATURES OF DIALECTS

There are hundreds of additional examples of syntactic, phonological, and lexical variations such as these, which are illustrative of dialects. In fact, the patterns of regional variation are so identifiable that they can be mapped. There are numerous examples of how linguistic variations become regional clusters and can be represented on language maps.[11]

The regional variations represent legitimate, alternative ways to pronounce words, put sentences together syntactically, or name or identify referents. As I noted earlier, however, there is still a degree of intolerance toward persons who speak a different dialect, which is ironic, since any dialect may be regarded as different. Remove yourself to another part of the country, and you're the speaker with a different dialect!

You can observe this intolerance even without leaving for another part of the country. Simply recall the last time you were in a group and one of its members pronounced a word a little differently. The variant pronunciation most likely caused some members of the group either to glance knowingly at others or laugh overtly.

Linguistically, any regional choice is as functional as another. Nevertheless, some of the choices are favored and others stigmatized. These value judgments are sociological comments, however, and not linguistic assessments. Just as dialects vary from one region of the country to another, they also vary from one level of society to another. This is true where I live, and I am reasonably confident it holds true in your city.

Labov made one of the earliest studies of language variation across social lines. Knowing that some New Yorkers pronounce the /r/ at the ends of words like *car*, *far*, and *jar* and that some do not, Labov investigated the presence or absence of the postvocalic /r/ among a number of New York speakers. Collecting data in three department stores—an expensive upper-middle class store, a medium-priced middle-class store, and a discount store patronized mostly by working-class shoppers—Labov discovered that the presence or absence of post-vocalic /r/ was, in fact, remarkably related to the social standing of the shoppers at the three stores: the higher class store employee's more consistently pronounced the /r/. The employees at the lower-class store hardly ever pronounced it. The middle-class store employees fell somewhere between the higher- and lower-class in pronuncing the /r/.[12]

In the United States postvocalic r-dropping has been associated with lower-class speakers for some time. People in the United States who enjoy higher social status, on the other hand, usually pronounce the /r/. Labov's data confirmed these social practices and attitudes.

In the United Kingdom, the general social opinion is just the opposite. More "refined" people, those from the higher social classes, do not pronounce postvocalic /r/, while those considered crude, rude, or uneducated (euphemisms for lower social classes) do pronounce it. These reversals of the pronunciation of postvocalic /r/ across social class divisions are very dramatic, according to Trudgill's data:

TABLE 8.1. Percentage of Postvocalic /r/ Pronunciations in New York and Reading[13]

	UMC	LMC	UWC	LWC
New York, N.Y.	32	20	12	10
Reading, U.K.	0	28	44	49

UMC = upper middle class; LMC = lower middle class; UWC = upper working class; LWC = lower working class.

The presence or absence of postvocalic /r/ is only one example of how language varies according to social class. You are doubtless aware of the judgments people in the United States make about others according to whether they pronounce, for instance, the /th-/ as in "this" or "dis" or the /-ing/ in "running" or "runnin' ".

Social differences emerge in other linguistic features, too, not just the phonological. For example, what are the differences in your community between the lexical choices of *lunch* or *dinner*, or of *supper* or *dinner*, or the pronunciation of the initial vowel in the word *either*: Is it EEE-ther or EYE-ther? Unless your community is different from others in the United States, different social levels will utilize one of these illustrative options and not the other.

The reason for this is that some dialects have greater prestige than others. Broadly speaking, Americans in the midwest assume that New Englanders in general, and Bostonians in particular, are better educated, more urbane, and more genteel and refined, so the midwesterner invests heightened prestige into the New Englanders' speech. Some midwesterners may even copy it by adopting a pronunciation they believe is indicative of New Englanders' urbanity and refinement, such as NIGH-thur instead of the more locally common NEE-thur.

Further, Americans in general assume that British English is somehow more proper. A cosmopolitan character in a film or TV production takes on even more prestige and glamour if he or she has a British English accent. By way of contrast, the simplest way to characterize "the fool"—evident not only in the old black-and-white movies on television, but also in current programs—is as a slow-moving, dim-witted person with either a "southern" drawl or "hillbilly" speech. Many of those stereotypes still survive.

SOCIAL NETWORK FEATURES OF DIALECTS

Our dialects are the product of several influences. Initially, we are born into a language, the style used by our family. The immediate speech network—mother, father, older sibling, or other care-giver—provides our first language model. And, as I said before, people who speak *with* one another speak *like* one another.

Very few people, though, spend their entire lives with their social contacts limited to the close-knit home circle. As one's social environment expands, language networks usually increase in number. Our language is affected, subsequently, by our contact with a larger circle of friends and colleagues at school and worship, work and play. These relationships create our social networks, which in turn shape language—phonological, lexical, and syntactical—to resemble that of a particular network.

A dialect can be viewed as any variety of a language spoken by a given network or community of people, or by a regional, ethnic, or social group. While Hendrickson describes three main dialect areas in the United States, Kurath accounts for many more.[14] The actual number, of course, depends upon how finely the definitions are drawn.

The fact is, at least for the more general language student, the discrete number of regional dialects is unimportant. As a matter of fact, every city, town, and village has its unique language forms. I grew up in central Missouri, and my best friend in high school lived on Again Street (pronounced A-gun). Thirty miles down the highway from where I live today you'll find the town of Beatrice (pronounced Bee-AT-truss). Some upstate New Yorkers do not tell a meddlesome soul, "You're driving me crazy." Instead, they say, "You're driving me to Poughkeepsie." That's where the mental hospital is.[15] With minimal fieldwork you can identify similar language uses unique to your locality.

Actually, one dialect is no better or worse than another. It is people who ascribe social prestige to some varieties and stigmatize others. Why this occurs is an important area for inquiry in classrooms.

VARIATION ACROSS TIME

Just as language varies from one country to another, from one region of a country to another, and from one social group or class to another, it also changes from one age to another. The regional variances are relatively easier to detect; language changes over the years are not as discernible. They are like the changes in a growing human; only by stopping to examine a photograph, for example, or to measure a child with a yardstick do we notice that changes have occurred.

Changes occur in language because people create them. It is a linguist's axiom that whenever a new linguistic form is needed, society creates it. Conversely, when a linguistic form is no longer needed, society stops using it.

For example, about forty or forty-five years ago, *victrolas* were replaced by *record players* in homes where people enjoyed playing recorded music. The record player was replaced by a *hi-fi*, which in turn was replaced by a *stereo*, then a *boom box* and finally a *C.D.* Within the same time frame, the *icebox* was replaced by a *frigidaire*, which was subsequently replaced by a *refrigerator*.

These are obvious examples of word changes over generations. However, individual words aren't the only linguistic features subject to change. Another aspect of time-change can be observed in pronunciations. I have a friend who goes cross-eyed and stiff-legged whenever he hears someone say "NUKE-kya-ler" for "NUKE-leear." The former pronunciation can be heard with increasing regularity and may become a standard pronunciation. Another test item in this category is "realtor." Are you hearing it pronounced in your community as a two- or a three-syllable word?

Not only do pronunciations change over time, but *spellings* change, as well. Greenbaum, for example, analyzes the increasing use of a newly spelled form: *could-be*, as in, "Could-be, he smokes a pipe."[16] *Could-be* is a fairly common informal utterance and with increased use its spelling could become more widely accepted. This use of *could-be* seems to be a forerunner of the fairly widespread *wanna-be*, which no longer causes heads to turn when it's used. The same can be said of *alot*, as we observed in Chapter 6. Is this a new spelling in the making?

Sometimes society ascribes a new meaning to an existing word. If the new meaning catches on, after a period of time we have yet another time-variation. For example, in the pre-radio United States, the word "broadcast" was largely limited to agricultural uses. Post-radio, the existing word took on a newer meaning. "Crash" has a similar history revolving around the advent of computers.

Changes such as these are recorded in the *Oxford English Dictionary* (OED), the largest dictionary of the English language. The *OED* records the meanings that have developed century by century for English words. Etymologies in some desk dictionaries provide more limited word histories.

These etymologies will reveal that many words have changed significantly over the years. Some changes in meaning have been so widespread that they can be described as follows:

A. *Elevation*: The meaning has become more elevated, more prestigious. "Nice" once meant "ignorant" or "not knowing." An "economist" was a "housekeeper" or "house manager."
B. *Degradation*: The meaning has degraded into a more pejorative, disparaging, or negative sense. "Smirk" once meant "smile"; a "gossip" was originally a "godparent"; and anything "awful" once was "awe-inspiring."
C. *Generalization*: A specific meaning becomes more general. The word "butcher" was once limited to mean "slayer of goats." A "zone" was once a "belt."
D. *Specialization*: A general word becomes more specific or specialized in meaning. The word "starve" originally meant "to die." An "angel" was simply a "messenger."[17]

The language you and I speak today has been changed over the years by an enormous amount of *borrowings* (see Chapter 5). English has grown and expanded as a result of these "loan words" from Afrikaans (veldt, commando), American Indian (totem, caucus, raccoon), Arabic (algebra), Sumerian (acre, Eden), and Turkish (tulip, yogurt).[18]

Perhaps the most significant change in the English language took place after the Battle of Hastings in the year 1066. When William the Conqueror defeated the Anglo-Saxons, he established his own county and municipal system of government by naming fellow Norman-French to the positions. Similarly, the church, court system, and schools were administered by William's French appointees, most of whom spoke French as their first language. French quickly became, therefore, the undeclared but nevertheless official language in England.

To make a long and very interesting story disappointingly short, the Battle of Hastings is the reason English has such an astonishing array of Anglo-Saxon, Germanic, French, Greek, and Latin language features today. The linguistic shotgun wedding brought about by William the Conqueror engendered the use of Romance language counterparts for existing Anglo-Saxon words like loving (amorous), cow (beef), deep (profound), sharp (poignant) and hut (cottage).[19]

Inasmuch as the French language became the language of official England, it is no surprise that it also became the language of social England, especially higher society. This is why the terms in parentheses above have higher prestige than their Anglo-Saxon synonyms: They were, and are, more "refined" words because they were used by the "better" folk. Even today, if speakers wish to demonstrate they possess a degree of *savoir faire*, they insert French expressions into their language.

ATTITUDES TOWARD LANGUAGE VARIATION AND CHANGE

People's responses to variations and changes in the language could probably be placed along a bi-polar scale ranging from "positive" at one end to "negative" at the other. Aitchison captures the essence of the two views in the title as well as the content of her book *Language Change: Progress or Decay?*[20]

Language change is inevitable and normal, regardless of how you or I may feel about it personally. We may judge language change as progress if we like the change, or as decay if we don't.

The relatively recent spelling of *lite* for *light* may cause some to grumble; and there is a sharp generational division between younger language users who effortlessly use the word *shit* and older speaker-writers who consider it a four-letter taboo word, to be avoided by all except the morally bankrupt.

The much more public use today of the word "condom" is readily accepted by some, but is objectionable to others. Nevertheless, as several TV comedians have observed, "You want evidence that language changes? Did you ever think you'd walk into a drugstore and say in a normal voice, 'I want some condoms,' and then add with a whisper, 'And a pack of cigarettes'?"

We may call these changes in the language, but I suspect it's actually not the language, per se, that changes. More accurately, people (communities, networks, or generations) change their use of, responses to, and attitudes toward language.

Lite Bulb

LANGUAGE IN LITERATURE

As the divisions in oral and written language learning become more indistinct in school curricula, literature texts can contribute much to the students' meta-linguistic awareness. Teachers will be familiar with the attempts of Charles Dickens, Josh Billings, and Mark Twain, to cite a few classic examples, to depict the regional and social speech patterns of their characters. These speech patterns help to establish and maintain the readers' understanding of the characters' contexts, motivations, and ability to resolve the conflicts they face.

A number of more contemporary writers use aspects of linguistics in their novels. I would like to recommend a few.

William Hogan's *The Quartzsite Trip* tells about P. J. Cooper, an English teacher, who selects a seemingly unrelated group of high school seniors to participate in an excursion into the wilderness each year during spring break (Easter vacation in the novel). Students' "good works" do not assure an invitation; the invitation is "given." The language of the novel supports these religious themes through repetition of place names and the characters' names, dates, and the like. Similarly, the novel assumes verse-like structure in its paragraphing, producing, in conjunction with the language elements already mentioned, a biblical tone. The religious themes are artfully developed through Hogan's language.[21]

A similar response can be made about Margaret Atwood's *The Hand-maid's Tale*. This speculative fiction is set in the future and is narrated by a female character, Offred, a handmaid whose "job" is bearing children for the Republic of Gilead. Women in Gilead no longer use their birthnames but are defeminized and rechristened: Offred, Ofwarren, Ofglen, and the like. Service women who cook and clean the dormitories are referred to only as "the Marthas" (see the New Testament). Public discourse among the handmaids is liturgical:

> " 'The war is going well, I hear," she says.
> " 'Praise be," I reply.
> " 'We've been sent good weather."
> " 'Which I receive with joy."
> " 'They've defeated more of the rebels since yesterday."
> " 'Praise be," I say."[22]

Blitzcat, by Robert Westall, offers readers both a heroic story of a cat attempting to find her way home during World War II and an opportunity to observe a number of language usages which show how British English varies from American English. Westall is a "Brit" and uses the standard British English spellings of: defenceless, learnt, favour, pyjamas and paralysed, to name a few. Lexical variations are also apparent: windscreen, fortnight, potty (crazy, dotty, daft) and sods (as in "poor sods").[23] Other British English usages appear throughout the book, enabling readers to make linguistic observations through "field work" without leaving the reading table or desk.

A Day No Pigs Would Die, by Robert Newton Peck continues to be read and loved by every class who "discovers" the novel. The book enables readers to observe several aspects of language, especially how the language of younger speakers differs from that of older ones. Rob, the narrator and son of Haven Peck, uses language and slang (heck, damn, darn) far removed from the more traditional language of his Quaker father.[24]

This discussion could extend indefinitely, but available space allows me to mention only one more writer. Consequently, I'll invite you to read and share one of my personal favorites: Molly Ivins. In her collection of newspaper and magazine articles, *Molly Ivins Can't Say That, Can She?*, Ivins's wit and perspicacity are made sharper as she describes the goings-on of state and national politics by adopting the persona and voice of a native Texan. She renders her

Texas dialect through respellings like: Meskin, bidness, lookahere, bob war, gennlemen, wimmin, how yew, and hail fahr.[25]

These books are good reads. They also present us and our students with opportunities to see perfectly normal language variations at work in literature.

FOR YOUR INQUIRY AND PRACTICE:

After finishing this chapter, review the two-sentence statement you prepared earlier regarding your beliefs about Standard English. Do you want or need to revise the statement?

Explorations

STUDENT EXPLORATIONS FOR REGIONAL, SOCIAL, AND HISTORICAL VARIATIONS

Exploration: What's in a Name?

DIRECTIONS: A dictionary can reveal interesting facts about languages. Using either the dictionary you normally use or one from the media center or a foreign language teacher, what do you think some of these family names meant originally?

Armstrong, Abbot, Aguilar, Armour, Arrowsmith

Baker, Brewer, Brewster, Barber

Chen, Cooper, Carter, Cutler, Carpenter, Chandler, Cook

Dale, de Leon

Elder

Flores, Fischer, Fuller, For(r)ester, Fletcher

Goldschmidt, Garland, Granger

Hidalgo, Hunter, Huerta

Issacson

Jardine

Kaplan, Kaiser, Knox, Knight, Kaufmann

Lansberg, Laine, Li

Miller, Merchant, Mason, Masterson

Nelson

O'Donald

Palmer, Pei

Quentin

Rodriguez, Radcliffe, Roth, Rosenberg

Schneider, Silverberg, Schwarz, Skinner, Smith, Santos

Tanner, Tailor (Taylor)

Underhill

Vintner

Wheeler, Wu, Wright, Warden

Xavier

Yates, Yin, Young (Younger)

Zimmer

What is the story of *your* family name?

Exploration: The Water River

DIRECTIONS: The word "avon" is a Celtic word meaning "water." William Shakespeare was born in Stratford, England, which is located on the Avon River, or the River Avon, as speakers in England would say it. Does this mean that the Celts called this river "the Water River?"

Examine a highway map for your state, looking especially at the names of the towns and cities. You'll probably find several place names with similar endings, like -polis, -ton, -ham, -ley, -field, -worth, and -ing, to name a few.

1. What are the place names used most often in your county or state?
2. According to your dictionary and your own speculation, what did (do) these names mean?
3. Were these towns and cities named after people, places, or events?
4. Are there any remaining ethnic relationships between the names of these towns and their current residents?
5. Given your research findings, what can you conclude about the place names you've studied and the people who originally settled these areas in your state?

Exploration: TV Homework

DIRECTIONS: For a period of one week try to watch as many episodes as you can of one *type* of television program: mysteries, medical programs, programs about attorneys, families, fishing, sit-coms, and so on. Regardless of which type of program you select, you'll find they all contain similar characters: the stern judge, the hostile witness; the gruff doctor, the kindly nurse (or vice versa); the heroic or the humorous detective. These characters frequently share several language characteristics, regardless of the particular program.

1. What are some of those characteristics?
2. Why do "all" characters of a certain type use these language features?
3. What is the effect of these repeating language features on the other characters? On the viewer?
4. What does this Exploration lead you to believe about language stereotypes? Or, language groups or communities?

Exploration: Pen Pals (1)

DIRECTIONS: With the help of your teacher, principal, or school superintendent, locate pen pals in another state (as far away as possible) who are in the same grade as you. Send them your list of slang terms with your definitions.

1. Which terms or phrases on your list do they recognize? How many do they actually use?
2. Ask them to send you their own lists of slang, with definitions; then analyze theirs. How many of their words do you recognize? How many do you actually use?
3. Why, do you think, are the lists different?

Exploration: Pen Pals (2)

DIRECTIONS: Select three or four poems your class has read; then send copies of the poems and an audiotape to your pen pals. Ask them to tape-record themselves as they read your poems. (You might send them a recording of people in your class reading the poems, too.)

1. When you listen to your pen pals reading the poems, do you notice any differences in the way they read the poem? Do they stress different words?
2. Do they use different intonations at the end of a line or sentence?
3. Do they pronounce individual words differently? Why?
4. Do the varying pronunciations mean that they're wrong and you're right in the way the words are pronounced, or that they're right and you're wrong? Or, do the variations signify something else?

Exploration: Pen Pals (3)

DIRECTIONS: Send your pen pal class another audiotape and ask them to talk informally as they answer several questions you send them on a brief questionnaire. For example, you might write questions that ask them to describe their school, favorite teachers, favorite songs and rock groups, best movies, and so on. When the tape is returned, analyze their speech as you did in Exploration No. 9, above.

1. Do they stress different words?
2. Do they use different intonations at the end of a line or sentence?
3. Do they pronounce individual words differently? Why?
4. Do the varying pronunciations mean that they're wrong and you're right in the way the words are pronounced, or that they're right and you're wrong? Or, do the variations signify something else?

Exploration: Variant Pronunciations

DIRECTIONS: Your dictionary includes a lot of information about words: different meanings people use for a word, the different pronunciations a word may have, and from which language the word originally came. What pronunciations does your dictionary include for these words:

again

garage

orange

roof

strength

tower

wash

1. Which dictionary pronunciation is closest to how you normally pronounce each word?
2. Why does the dictionary include more than one pronunciation for these words?
3. How would you respond to the statement, "The first pronunciation is the preferred pronunciation"?

Exploration: New Ways for Old Words

DIRECTIONS: Sometimes people give a familiar word a new spelling, a new pronunciation, or even a new meaning. For one day keep a record of the new ways people are using old words (using the word *lite* instead of *light*, for example) by using the New Language Log that follows. When your day of language observation is finished, bring your completed log to class and answer the questions below.

1. What was the most frequent *type* of new language use you observed (spelling, pronunciation, or meaning)?
2. What do you suppose there were more examples of this type than the others?
3. What would happen if you used any of the new language forms in your written work at school? Would it matter? Would your grade be lowered?
4. Based upon your observations of new language uses and your discussions of them with your friends, how would you describe the reactions of people to changes in the language? Who are the ones who seem to care most about the changes? Or, who seems to care the least?

New Language Log
Date of observations: _____

New Language Example	Where Observed	Used by Whom?	Why was it used?

Exploration: " . . . them that speak leasing . . . "*

DIRECTIONS: Changes in language are not limited just to slang or to our general vocabulary; the Bible demonstrates language change, too. Here are five sentences taken from the King James version of The Bible; note especially the underlined words.

A. I would not have you ignorant, brethren, that oftentimes I purposed to come unto you, (but was <u>let</u> thereto), that I might have some fruit among you also, even as among other Gentiles. (Romans 1:13)

B. Let them wander up and down for meat, and <u>grudge</u> if they be not satisfied. (Psalms 59:15)

C. And he will appoint him captains over thousands, and captains over fifties; and he will set them to <u>ear</u> his ground, and to reap his harvest, and to make his instruments of war, and his instruments of his chariots. (1 Samuel 8:12)

D. Thou shalt destroy them that speak leasing: the Lord will abhor the bloody and deceitful man. (Psalms 5:6)

E. But their eyes were <u>holden</u> that they should not know him. (Luke 24:16)

1. What do you think the underlined word means in the context of each of these sentences?

2. Locate each of these passages in another Bible translation (New English, Jerusalem, Revised Standard Version, Philips, etc.) and see if the alternate version helps your understanding of the underlined words.

3. Finally, consult your dictionary. Look up the underlined words and see if you can determine how they have changed in meaning over the years and taken on the meanings you are more familiar with today.

---

* From *The SHALOM Leader's Guide* by The Kerygma Program. Reprinted with permission.

Exploration: Invited Variation

DIRECTIONS: Invite to your class someone who came from a different part of the country. Explain to your guest that the class is studying normal language variations. You can decide how to best elicit oral language from your guest: Ask your guest to describe his or her extended family, a special hobby, or his or her job.

1. In what specific ways is the guest's pronunciation or word choices different from yours? Similar to yours?
2. Ask the guest which local pronunciations, word choices, or other expressions used commonly in your community seem "odd" or "different" to him or her.
3. What does this exchange lead you to believe about "standard" or "expected" ways of talking in a particular community?

Exploration: Linguistic Fingerprints

DIRECTIONS: Observing normal and natural language is essential in this Exploration. Without revealing that you are doing so, for one full school day observe one person you know well. Record in a language log what that person says and to whom. Pay particular attention to recurring words, expressions, or pronunciations used consistently throughout the day.

1. Share the final notes in your log with your friend. The contents of the log will help to describe your friend's *ideolect*, the unique way each individual speaks.
2. Discuss the log with your friend. Can your friend describe any influences (other friends, a parent, other relative, a teacher) on his or her ideolect?
3. How do our very personal ways of using language develop? In what ways is our language like that of all people, of some people, and of no other people?

Exploration: You Say Goodbye, and I Say Hello

DIRECTIONS: While expressing similar and related sentiments, our different ways of greeting people can produce special effects or "flavors." Think of the different ways we say "Hello" and "Goodbye." For a day or two, observe the different ways people *greet* you and the ways people indicate they are *leaving*.

1. How often do you hear any of the following expressions:

EXPRESSIONS OF "HELLO"	EXPRESSIONS OF "GOODBYE"
Hi	Bye
Howdy	Bye-bye
How do	See ya
Greetings	Ciao
Hullo	So long
How are you?	Farewell
What's going on?	Adieu
Hey	Toodle-oo
Hola	Cheerio
How's it going?	See you later
What's happening?	Fare you well
What's up?	Good night/evening
Good morning/afternoon	Be seeing you
Hey, dude	Adios

   What hello/goodbye expressions can you add to this list?
2. How many of these expressions have you actually used? Where have you heard them? Which expressions are used by older speakers? Younger speakers?
3. Which expressions are formal? Informal?
4. Some of these terms were borrowed from other languages. Can you identify the original language?
5. Why is it helpful to have so many options available for saying hello and goodbye?

Exploration: The Right or Write Word

DIRECTIONS: Examine this list of words, doing the following:

   a. Circle a word if you usually use it
   b. Put a star (*) beside a word you would think strange for an older person to use
   c. Put an "X" beside those you never use

truant	ditch	hooky	mongo
smidgen	grass widow	humongous	corn
micro	poke	pone	sack
cornbread	snob	bread	squash
hare	uppity	lightbread	jackrabbit

Johnnycake	hollow	feud	booze
divorcee	skunk	reckon	cave
play-pretty	moonshine	redneck	heck
gleek	polecat	guess	rumble
toys	whiskey	figger	bag
cushaw	kinfolk	bunny	fight
conceited			

1. Compare your answers with others in your class. Are there any interesting or surprising differences or similarities in your marked words?
2. Using words from this list, the school principal might report that a student was truant, a parent might say the student played hooky, but the student might say she ditched school. Can you find similar teams of words? Who might use one of the words in the teams you've identified?
3. Why do different speakers select different terms to communicate similar ideas?

Exploration: Some Dialect Fieldwork

DIRECTIONS: Read the following, then select the answer that reflects what you usually and most often say.

1. From what do you get water?
    a. tap
    b. faucet
    c. spigot
2. In what do you fry eggs?
    a. fry pan
    b. skillet
    c. frying pan
3. What do you eat at an athletic contest?
    a. frank
    b. wiener
    c. hot dog
4. What might you eat for breakfast?
    a. hotcakes
    b. flapjacks
    c. pancakes
5. What is a *tavern*?
    a. bar
    b. sandwich
    c. inn

6. What is a *whip*?
   a. licorice
   b. strap
   c. path
7. When do people eat *lunch*?
   a. noon
   b. morning
   c. afternoon

1. Contrast your answers with others' in your class. Discuss why some people might use different terms for the same idea or object.
2. Have you heard members of your family use any of these words? Who? How old are they? Where do they live?
4. Can you add to the sentences above, giving different terms for the same idea or object?
5. How do we decide which word we will use in the sample sentences seen here? How is the decision made?

Exploration: Leave It to Beaver and Bart

DIRECTIONS: Watching television carefully can help us learn a great deal about language. Watch one episode of "Leave It to Beaver" and one episode of "The Simpsons." How many specific differences in language use can you observe? For example, how does Beaver greet his father; how does Bart greet Homer?

1. What slang terms did you hear in the episodes?
2. How do Beaver's conversations with his friends differ from Bart's with his?
3. How do the conversations between Beaver and Wally differ from those between Bart and Lisa?
4. How do the parents on the two programs talk to their children?
5. What are some of the reasons for the language differences you observed in these programs?

NOTES

1. Bergan Evans, *The Word-a-Day Vocabulary Builder* (New York: Random House, 1963).
2. Ann Ruggles Gere and Eugene Smith, *Attitudes, Language and Change* (Urbana, IL: National Council of Teachers of English, 1979), 8–10.
3. Judges, 12:5–6.

4. Mary Ellen Snodgrass, *The Great American English Handbook* (Jacksonville, IL: Perma-Bound, 1987), 92.
5. Mary Ellen Snodgrass and H. Ramsey Fowler, *The Little, Brown Handbook* (Boston: Little, Brown, 1980). Both authors use these terms in their illustrations of preferred usages.
6. Isagani R. Cruz, "A Nation Searching for a Language Finds a Language Searching for a Name," *English Today* 7 (1991): 17.
7. Ibid.
8. Edward Finegan and Niko Besnier, *Language: Its Structure and Use* (New York: Harcourt Brace Jovanovich, 1989), 383.
9. Ibid., 382.
10. Peter Trudgill, *Accent, Dialect and the School* (London: Edward Arnold, 1975), 17.
11. See: Hans Kurath, *A Word Geography of the Eastern United States* (Ann Arbor: University of Michigan Press, 1949); Kurath, *Studies in Area Linguistics* (Bloomington: Indiana University Press, 1972); Kurath and Raven McDavid, *The Pronunciation of English in the Atlantic States* (Ann Arbor: University of Michigan Press, 1961); William Labov, *Language in the Inner City* (Philadelphia: University of Pennsylvania Press, 1972); Roger Shuy, *Discovering American Dialects* (Champaign, IL: National Council of Teachers of English, 1967); Frederick G. Cassidy (ed.), *Dictionary of American Regional English*, vol. I. (Cambridge, MA: Belknap Press of Harvard University Press, 1985); and Craig M. Carver, *American Regional Dialects* (Ann Arbor: University of Michigan Press, 1987).
12. William Labov, *The Social Stratification of English in New York City* (Washington, DC: Center for Applied Linguistics, 1966).
13. Trudgill, *Accent,* 35.
14. Robert Hendrickson, *American Talk: the Words and Ways of American Dialects* (New York: Viking Penguin, 1986), 17; and Kurath, ibid. Hendrickson's text is written more for a general audience while Kurath's reports represent the result of extensive fieldwork of particular interest to linguists.
15. Hendrickson, *American Talk,* 194.
16. Sidney Greenbaum, *Studies in English Adverbial Usage* (Coral Gables, FL: University of Miami Press, 1969), 109.
17. Monica Crabtree and Joyce Powers, *Language Files,* 5th ed. (Columbus: Ohio State University Press, 1991), 327.
18. Hendrickson, *American Talk,* 1–34.
19. Engaging histories of English are available in: Albert C. Baugh and Thomas Cable, *A History of the English Language* 3rd ed. (Englewood Cliffs, N.J.: Prentice-Hall, 1978); and, Robert McCrum, William Cran and Robert MacNeil, *The Story of English* (New York: Elisabeth Sifton Books-Viking, 1986). Of particular interest to the history student is the popular history of the Norman invasion found in David Howarth, *1066 the Year of the Conquest* (New York: Dorset Press by arrangement with Viking-Penguin, 1978).
20. Jean Aitchison, *Language Change: Progress or Decay?* (New York: Universe Books, 1985).
21. William Hogan, *The Quartzsite Trip* (New York: Avon Books, 1980), 13–17.
22. Margaret Atwood, *The Handmaid's Tale* (New York: Ballantine Books, 1985), 26.

23. Robert Westall, *Blitzcat* (New York: Scholastic, 1989), 1–10.
24. Robert Newton Peck, *A Day No Pigs Would Die* (New York: Dell, 1972).
25. Molly Ivins, *Molly Ivins Can't Say That, Can She?* (New York: Random House, 1991).

CHAPTER 9

Meanings and General Semantics

The concepts people live by are derived only from perceptions and from language, and since the perceptions are received and interpreted only in the light of earlier concepts, man comes pretty close to living in a house that language built, located by maps that language drew.

—Russell F.W. Smith, *Linguistics in Theory and Practice*

IT'S ONLY SEMANTICS!

Some of the terminology associated with the study of language is frequently misapplied. For example, the differences between grammar and usage are blurred when a charge is made that someone "doesn't know his grammar." More often than not, those who say this actually are describing their personal preference for a particular *usage*, such as the distinctions some prefer in the uses of lie/lay, fewer/lesser, between/among, avoiding prepositions in sentence-final positions or trying to not split infinitives. These represent usage variations, not errors in grammar. **Usage** denotes the ways people actually perform oral and written language within the range of available options. **Grammar**, on the other hand, usually refers to a description of how words and phrases normally relate to each other in oral or written sentences in a language.

Similarly, the terms *rhetoric* and *semantics* are sometimes misapplied, often used in an unfavorable sense as though the terms themselves were negative labels for bad language usages or habits. Some people might comment, for instance, "If you can cut through his campaign rhetoric, Mr. Smith might be a good candidate for mayor."

Likewise, you may have heard any number of heated discussions brought to an abrupt end by the charge, "Well, that's just a matter of semantics!" This judgment has stopped many conversations. A statement such as that is either an overt or an uninformed attempt to disregard and then dismiss differences of opinion, belief, and perception as insignificant. How *meaning* can be downgraded in this manner is nothing short of pathetic. Usually the person who alleges that a difference of opinion is "just a matter of semantics" is attempting to minimize the different meanings the discussants have ascribed to the words and terms they to define and describe their *beliefs*.

The meanings and beliefs we hold are not, in my view, of little importance. To the contrary, they collectively represent our sense of the universe.

The word "semantic" is derived from the Greek *semantikos*, "significant," from *semainein*, "to signify," "to mean."[1] As practiced by semanticists, semantics is the study of *signification*, the study of the relationship(s) between and among symbol(s) and meaning(s).

As I said in Chapter 1, to most people meaning is the most interesting aspect of language. In this chapter let me elaborate by adding that most people find meaning not only the most interesting but also the most consequential!

SEMANTICS AND LINGUISTICS

The field of general semantics was introduced to United States language scholars by Alfred Korzybski through his book, *Science & Sanity: An Introduction to Non-Aristotelian Systems and General Semantics*. *Science and Sanity* created quite a stir after its publication, and the general semantics movement flourished in the United States in the 1940s and 1950s.[2]

As Hasselriis points out,[3] among the reasons for this burst of interest was the publication of S. I. Hayakawa's *Language in Action*.[4] Still reeling from the successes of Hitler, Mussolini, and others who had perfected the use of "the big lie" and other deliberate misuses of language, the reading public was ready to learn about how *meaning* is perceived, made, received, and filtered and how to detect intentional distortions in language. Hayakawaya's book, and the writings of Stuart Chase, Wendell Johnson, and Irving Lee helped readers look at language use through completely new lenses. Interest in general semantics was keen. In fact, in December of 1941 *Language in Action* was the Book-of-the-Month Club selection, an auspicious achievement for a book about language!

At the same time, however, academic linguistics was undergoing a fundamental paradigm shift. In 1957 Noam Chomsky published *Syntactic Structures*, the first articulation of generative grammar, which de-emphasized semantics.[5]

Since 1957 Chomsky's ideas have been the central, defining force among U.S. linguists in particular, and to some extent among linguists in the larger, global community. Sooner or later in most discussions about language, linguists describe their beliefs in relation to their agreement or disagreement with Chomsky.

Since the late 1950s the field of linguistics in the United States has experienced unprecedented oscillations in the amount of attention paid to meaning, and the status of semantics in general. University students entering programs in language study in the past ten or fifteen years have little understanding or appreciation of the bias against semantics in the 1960s and early 1970s.[6]

Attention to *meaning* has been brought back to a position of importance to U.S. educators largely through the recent writings of British linguists such as M. A. K. Halliday, James Britton, and Michael Stubbs; in the United States, S. I. Hayakawa, Neil Postman, and William Labov have reminded us that meaning is a primary property of language study.

This renewed interest in *meaning* is at the heart of the Whole Language movement that is gaining considerable momentum in U.S. elementary schools. It is also a central feature of the national writing projects. Although I make few claims as a futurist, I see little on the horizon to indicate that these trends will diminish.

Since a number of Korzybski's ideas are helpful in understanding semantics and the processes of *signification*, a review of some of the more salient propositions in *Science and Sanity* will be useful.

ALFRED KORZYBSKI AND GENERAL SEMANTICS

Alfred Korzybski, philosopher, mathematician, and professional engineer, is generally regarded as "the father" of the field of general semantics. As Hasselriis recently observed, Korzybski's *Science and Sanity* is extremely, and possibly unnecessarily, arduous reading![7] Nevertheless, we can glean from it some of the major principles of general semantics. Some of Korzybski's observations and principles of semantics are as follows:

Meaning Is Not in Words, but in People

Meaning is not something to be received, extracted, caught, or gotten from a symbol, a word, or a page, but is what people assign or ascribe to the symbol or the word. In other words, we don't get, but we give, meanings to symbols and words.[8] For example, people are not likely to connect or associate a meaning to a word beyond their experience. Unless you are familiar with the languages in question, the Spanish word *taza* or the Tongan word *ili* will remain only splotches of ink on paper for you. These words do not *tell you* anything. It follows that the same is true for any word from any language we don't know.

That meaning is not in things but in people is not only evident when considering verbal symbols, but is also true for nonverbal, or graphic, symbols. An example of this can be found in the search by traffic engineers for a sign to post at the side of a street to alert motorists that they are nearing a school and should therefore drive with caution. The sign which was first designed used the lamp of knowledge as a symbolic, nonverbal warning meaning, "There's a school ahead and children may be in the street." However, many people did not recognize the lamp of knowledge and obviously did not ascribe any meaning to it at all. Only later was the primitive outline of a school building used; since people could successfully gather meaning from this shape, it replaced the earlier sign.

Words Are Not What They Refer to

An object or a feeling, Korzybski pointed out, is *unspeakable*. A toothache or a chair, for example, may be expressed or described by words, but the expression or the description are *not* the same thing(s) as the *condition*. The condition itself is fundamentally unspeakable and simply *exists*.[9] A word can be a symbol and/or a name for a definition. Whether the word is a symbol or a name, however, it is an *abstraction*, removed from the level of absolute objectivity, which is always unspeakable.[10]

A more familiar paraphrase for this Korzybskian understanding is "the word is not the thing." From the writings of Piaget, for example, we know that children equate names and things. Perhaps you are familiar with the apocryphal comment made by a child: " 'Pig' is a good name for that animal because it's so dirty!" Of course, a statement like this ignores both the symbolic and the arbitrary nature of language. First of all, when we say the word *pig* we've only said a word; we haven't uttered the actual condition or thing. Articulating the word *pig* is to say the name of a definition. Secondly, if pig were the perfect name for the animal in question, every language used on earth would use the word *pig* when referring to the animal in this illustration. Such is clearly not the case, however, since we know that the animal we are discussing may be known only by the name of *cerdo* to some people, as *schwein* to some or as *cochon* to others, to cite but three examples.

Not only does this understanding from Korzybski help to remind us of the arbitrary nature of language, but it also means that even if we are in a community of same-language speakers, saying a word is not the same as "saying" the thing the word refers to, the *referent*. While a word is only a symbol for a referent (thing), it can be, nevertheless, a symbol to which people ascribe a great deal of emotion.

Confusing a word with the word's unspeakable referent results, for example, in cautions to children that they must avoid saying "dirty" words. It is implicitly assumed that having the word in one's mouth is the same as having the actual referent or "thing" in one's mouth: that's why one legendary punishment for using "dirty" language is to wash the culprit's mouth with soap!

One of the reasons people employ euphemisms is to avoid the semantic dilemma of having a dirty, unmentionable, or indelicate word/thing in their mouth. This is one reason why we use terms like "bathroom," "restroom," and "powder room," when, in fact, we go to this room with no intention of taking a bath, resting, or powdering.

I confess that I intentionally exploited this confusion once. Back in my junior high school teaching days I happened one afternoon to come upon some of my students hanging out in the school parking lot. They were using language of the "blue" variety. In fact, their language was bluer . . . No, it was the bluest I had ever heard. My uninvited and unexpected presence startled them; they waited for a dressing-down. Instead of giving them a "You-should-be-ashamed-what-would-your-parents-think" speech, however, or a more academic "Only-those-with-limited-language-or-imagination-use-language-like-that" lecture, all I said was: "Do you eat with those mouths?" They stared back at me in stolid silence, not fully realizing but dimly suspecting what I had accomplished with my brief question. Although they lacked the words to articulate the concept, they realized I was playing some form of word magic. I had turned a taboo event into a "thing," that was lodged in their mouths.

Every society has taboo words. The taboo words, however, are only arbitrary and symbolic referents to other objects or conditions. Remember, a map is only a map, a representation; it is not the actual, objective, and ultimately unspeakable territory. I did not explain this to my students, but I think they were fussing with the general notion.

There is more to be said about euphemisms than has been described here. Euphemisms, which are used for several purposes beyond these illustrations, will be described in more detail later in this chapter.

Language Operates on Varying Levels of Abstraction

This is another Korzybskian notion. Some language, for example, operates at a higher or a lower level of abstraction or concreteness, depending on how "close" the language is to its otherwise unspeakable but verifiable referents.[11] The paragraph below consists of only four sentences, but they progressively change from more abstract and general to more concrete and specific:

> I'm shopping for clothes. I'm looking for a new shirt. I need a new tennis shirt. In fact, I want a white, ribbed-collar knit shirt with a green alligator on the left breast.

It is clearly useful to know whether one is hearing or reading language that is more or less abstract or concrete. Better comprehension and understanding result when we can detect highly abstract claims made about a product being advertised, a candidate running for office, or a vague question asked by a student. In the two former examples we can decide whether we'll purchase the product or vote for the candidate. In the case of the student's question, we'll know whether to ask her to repeat the question, " . . . and please be more specific." When we ask for "more specific" restatements in this manner, I suspect we are usually asking the questioner to be less abstract and to use more specific, more concrete language.

Meaning Has Direction

If you are familiar with the terms connotation and denotation, then you already understand a great deal about Korzybski's observation. He used the terms *intensional* and *extensional* to describe the two directions meaning can take.

The clearest distinctions between intensional and extensional meanings are provided by one of Korzybski's former students, and one of his clearer translators, S.I. Hayakawa. Hayakawa points out that the extensional meaning of an utterance is that which it refers to in the extensional, physical, verifiable but unspeakable state of being. An extensional meaning cannot be expressed in words because it is, fundamentally and essentially, the actual (and unspeakable) territory. We can refer to and illustrate an extensional meaning we may have in mind by putting our hands over our mouths and *pointing* at an extensional meaning, whether it's a tree, a dog, a pencil, or a radio.[12]

Obviously, we can't always point at an object, feeling, or condition. In the real world of authentic language use, we seldom cover our mouths in an attempt to communicate unspeakable actualities. This is why understanding and using the more familiar term, *denotation*, is helpful.

We can use the concept of denotation to refer to that which is being talked about. When I mentioned my Maltese dog in Chapter 4, I could not tell you what I meant by pointing to him, thus communicating to you the extensional meaning, *my dog*. Nevertheless, in the language you and I read, the word *dog* denotes a class of animals in the world, and you easily understood that this word included the pet I referred to.[13]

On the other hand, the intensional meaning of an expression, sentence, phrase, or word is that which is suggested (connoted) inside one's head. Certain words conjure up positive or negative feelings, good or bad connotations that we ascribe to them.[14]

The languages we speak, write, hear, read, and encounter every day sometimes have both extensional (denotational) and intensional (connotational) meaning, and at times one type of meaning predominates. For example, if a report you are reading uses the symbol %, your understanding of its extensional (denotation) meaning, will be free of intensional meanings, or connotations. On the other hand, a statement claiming that one particular make of automobile represents "the heartbeat of America" or that when you drink one brand of beer "it (life) doesn't get any better than this" has no extensional meanings. It is, however, loaded with a variety of intensional meanings and connotations.

Identification

According to Korzybski, *identification* is a "semantic disturbance" consisting of errors in meanings.[15] What I take Korzybski's discussion to mean is that some people cannot or do not distinguish a factual report from an inference, one teenager from another, or one Democrat (or Republican) from another. In the Korzybskian sense, as I understand this concept, identification means something more like *identicalification* because a person who suffers from this "disturbance" identifies similar conditions, events, people, and things as *identical*.

In practice, identification is at work when someone says, "Look at that crazy woman driver! Why can't women learn to drive?" The person who might say this is treating *all* women drivers as *one identical* motorist.

Similarly, we can hear or read related comments about how *all* New Yorkers are pushy and rude, *all* Jews are wealthy because they are shrewd and marginally ethical negotiators, and *all* mothers-in-law are prying and overbearing. Additional examples abound, *identifying*, in the special Korzybskian use of the term, bankers, school administrators, politicians, clergypersons, football players, English teachers, and any other identifiable group you care to name.

Identification can certainly simplify the world we live in, but it's disturbing, inaccurate behavior which results in a faulty map of reality. The fact is, no two instances involving Jews, mothers-in-law, or football players, or any conditions or circumstances are identical.

Korzybski's solution to this circumstance is to suggest the use of index numbers in superscript so that, for example, when we say *dog*, we remind ourselves that we mean dog_1 (my Maltese dog, Christopher Robin), not dog_2 (Rex and Ardis Bevins' Maltese dog, Scruffy), or dog_3 (Jim and Caryl Bryan's dog, Spencer), or dog_4. . . .

As an attempt to deflect semantic disturbance, or *meaning disturbance*, indexing reminds us that when we participate in language events concerning people, objects, conditions, and propositions, we are considering only one case or instance from a larger class of events and objects. Indexing also helps us keep in order the houses our language is building, and makes our maps to those houses more accurate.

EUPHEMISMS AND JARGON

Language critics frequently cite the use of euphemisms and jargon as the chief roadblocks to clear meanings, using them as examples of what Korzybski calls semantic disturbance. Euphemisms and jargon, they maintain, are attempts

Dog₃

to hide true meaning, since the uninitiated listener or reader is misled. Calling a five-year-old automobile with 74,000 miles on the odometer, for example, a "pre-owned," or an "experienced" instead of a "used" car, our examples of this type of misleading language.

Postman defines a euphemism as "an auspicious or exalted term (like 'sanitation engineer') that is used in place of a more down-to-earth term (like 'garbage man')." Euphemizing is, he suggests, an attempt to give a prettier name to an uglier reality.[16] This definition fits the illustration above concerning the pre-owned and experienced, but nevertheless, used car.

It should be pointed out, however, that applying prettier names to uglier realities is not always a deceitful practice. Sometimes we use euphemisms to be sensitive to others' feelings.

For example, Postman terms "Operation Sunshine," the name for a series of hydrogen bomb experiments conducted by the U.S. government in the South Pacific, one of the more detestable euphemisms used in recent years. It is deceitful.[17] More recently, Iraqi civilians who were killed during Operation Desert Storm were referred to by Pentagon sources not as "non-military Iraqi citizens who were killed accidentally" but as "collateral damage."

On the other hand, we may euphemize and substitute *passed away* for *died*. We do this not to be deceitful or hide the truth, but because we are sensitive to the emotional state and needs of those who have experienced a death in their family.[18]

There is nothing inherently wrong with using euphemisms. Euphemisms, like all other aspects of language, are intrinsically neither moral nor immoral in and of themselves. A hammer is an amoral object that can be used to construct a new home or smash automobile headlights. Our judgment should not focus on the tool, but on the user, the intent, and the outcome. So it is with euphemisms. Do they hide the truth, or are they attempts to be considerate? What is the user's intent, and what is the outcome?

Some examples you can examine for your own practice in considering intent and outcome are the following: Internal Revenue Service (tax collector); nervous wetness (sweat); facial blemishes (pimples); convenient terms (20 percent annual interest); full-figured or queen-size (fat, large); shortfall (mistake); cleaning up the historical record (shredding or falsifying official documents); terminate with extreme prejudice (assassinate an enemy agent without a trial).[19]

One way to test language use to determine whether it is or isn't euphemistic doublespeak involves an analysis proposed by Hugh Rank. To analyze the full context in which language, intent, and outcomes occur, Rank asks these questions:

1. Who is saying what to whom?
2. Under what conditions?
3. Under what circumstances?
4. With what intent?
5. With what results?[20]

FOR YOUR INQUIRY AND PRACTICE:

Either observe a televised interview, press conference, or public meeting, or read the account of one of these meetings in your local newspaper. Analyze the questions, answers, and other comments using Rank's doublespeak analysis.

What are your conclusions about the presence or absence of doublespeak in the meeting? Is truth valued?

Studying semantics, euphemisms, or doublespeak in classrooms is not something we do to make our students cynics. We return to Korzybski for one reason for studying semantics.

As early as 1933, Korzybski understood the power and control language can exercise over people. He observed that "The affairs of man are conducted by our own man-made rules and according to man-made theories. Man's achievements rest upon the use of symbols. For this reason, we must consider ourselves as a symbolic, semantic class of life, and those who rule the symbols, rule us."[21]

More recently, Weingartner suggests that the study of semantics "can do more to help students become more perceptive and sophisticated users of language than can any other form of language study" in the school.[22] You may or may not agree with Weingartner's assertion concerning the centrality of semantics in a language curriculum, but there's little doubt about its importance.

The study of meaning and meaning-making is a matter of human interest and consequence. As Caccia suggests, our students will become effective citizens in the world based upon their effectiveness with language. "In saying this," Caccia continues, "I'm not referring to matters of effective usage and style. Competence in these areas may contribute to effective use of language, but dwelling there will never reveal the heart of the matter."[23] Putting semantics to work in the classroom will.

Explorations

STUDENT EXPLORATIONS FOR MEANING AND SEMANTICS

Exploration: Words We Know

DIRECTIONS: Think about a vocation you're interested in, a hobby, or your favorite school subject. Brainstorm by yourself, creating a list of terms used in the vocation, hobby, or subject. Read your list to a partner.

1. How many terms on your partner's list were unknown to you? How many of your terms were unknown to your partner?
2. If a term or word is unknown to you, is the word less real? Where do you locate these terms and words in your sense of reality? Are these words more or less alien to you than words from another language?
3. Where do our words and the concepts they represent come from, especially those used in the special interests we have?

Exploration: The Meaning Is in Here, Somewhere

DIRECTIONS: Almost every word we use can evoke sharp and well-defined images. Here is a short list of common, everyday words. Beside each word make a list of words and terms you associate with that word.

television   dog
cat   mother
spoon   holiday

1. Compare your list with the lists of others in your small group.
2. How can you explain the range of associations attached to each of these rather simple words?
3. Based on the discussions in your group, what can you conclude about meanings and where they come from?

Exploration: Synonyms

DIRECTIONS: For each key word shown in **boldface**, type write several words that are used as synonyms for the key word.

Example:

policeman: officer, buttons, cop, flatfoot

woman:

man:

teacher:

doctor:

actor:

politician:

1. Do all of the synonyms conjure the same meaning as the key word? What additional meanings do each of the synonyms bring?
2. In what contexts might you use one of the synonyms for the key word?
3. Do you find some of the synonyms more powerful than others in evoking more positive or more negative images of each key word?

Exploration: Jargon

DIRECTIONS: Technical magazines abound at newsstands; many are in the library or school media center. Locate three technical magazines—such as *Personal Computing, Modern Aviation,* or *American Cinematographer*—and from each magazine make a list of ten words you may recognize but do not ordinarily use.

1. Examine the sentence from which you took the word and try to explain to a partner what you think the term means. Do this for each of the thirty words.
2. Do you know anyone who uses or might use these terms more often than you do? How did they learn them?
3. Are these special-use terms "jargon"? What purpose is served by using special-use words such as these?

Exploration: Are These Shoes Experienced, Pre-owned, or Used?

DIRECTIONS: After examining a pair of old shoes located in some central spot in the room, brainstorm with a partner as many words as you can think of to describe the shoes.

1. Put your list of words into *categories*, like *size, color,* or *material.*
2. Using the descriptive words, write a limerick or short poem about the shoes using as many words as you can from each category.
3. Now, examine your poem and substitute the *category name* for each *descriptive word* you've used.
4. What has happened to your poem? What was lost in the poem when you used the names of the categories instead of the descriptive words?

Exploration: Word Rainbows

DIRECTIONS: Using color advertisements from catalogs, the Sunday newspaper, or circulars received in the mail, identify the *names* of as many different colors as you can that are either used in an illustration or in the description of an item.

1. List the names of colors with others in its "family" of colors, using the chart on the following page. (For example, "teal" and "eggshell blue" will go with "blue.")
2. How many of the more specific color names come from foods, like "apricot," "olive," "tangerine," or "apple red"? How many of the names come from nature, like "sky" or "dusk"?
3. In your judgment will the choice of color names enhance the product's image for a prospective buyer or shopper?
4. Is there a *logical* connection between the names selected and the objects to which they refer?

Word Rainbows

Using the advertisements available, categorize the color names you've identified with the color groups shown here.

Black: _____

_____

White: _____

_____

Blue: _____

_____

Red: _____

_____

Yellow: _____

_____

Exploration: Nonesuches

DIRECTIONS: In a small group, read Lewis Carroll's "Jabberwocky," Dr. Seuss's *How the Grinch Stole Christmas*, Dr. Seuss's *The Lorax*, or any other selection of literature which uses a relatively large number of nonsense words.

1. Write down at least five of the nonsense words and try to give them definitions, according to how and where they are used in the sentence in which they appear.
2. Discuss your definitions with the meanings other members of your group create. As you compare the several meanings suggested, can your group agree to advocate *one* of the definitions as the best?
3. Reread orally some of the sentences, substituting the created meanings for the original nonsense words. Do the nonsense words or the created definitions add more to, or subtract more from, your enjoyment of the selection?

Exploration: Buffalo Breath

DIRECTIONS: It's very unlikely that you'll ever see an advertisement on television or in your local newspaper for a new cologne called "Buffalo Breath." The names of colognes—for either men or women—more often than not want to connote a different kind of image for the user than "Buffalo Breath" might suggest. Who wants to smell like "Buffalo Breath?" Don't you prefer "Obsession?"

Divide the class into several groups of three or four, and have each group select one family of products: toothpastes, colognes, underarm deodorants, hair lotions and treatments, perfumes, after shave lotions, skin creams and ointments, and the like. Each group should collect as many different ads as possible for its "family" of products from newspapers and magazines; listen for advertisements of your products on the radio and on television.

1. What are the various names used for these products?
2. What features do the names used have in common?
3. Why were these names selected by the manufacturers?
4. Are the names selected because the company wishes to create an image for its *product* or for the *person* who uses the product?
5. What is it that the producer of this product is really trying to sell? The product only?
6. Most of these ads will show people using the product. How are they presented in the ad? How do their physical appearances and actions support the intended image?
7. Based on your observations, what can you conclude about the process of naming a product?

(You might repeat this activity, examining the names of breakfast cereals, cars [family sedans, mid-sized or compacts—be specific], floor waxes and polishes, liquid household cleaners, or any other product line.)

Exploration: Tears in My Ears

DIRECTIONS: Many years ago there was a popular song that included the line: "I've got tears in my ears from lying on my back in the bed while I cry over you." Many disk jockeys used the entire line as the song's title, which meant that it took almost as long to announce the song as it did to play it on the air! Where do song titles come from?

Divide the class into teams of two; then assign each team a year, beginning with the current year and counting back in five-year intervals. (One group will have 1990, another 1985, another 1980, and so on.) Use either back copies (from your local library) of *Billboard* magazine or *Radio and Records* magazine, or interview a disk jockey at your favorite radio station and find out the titles of the most popular song for each month of your assigned year.

1. Are the titles serious or humorous?
2. Are the titles designed to appeal to men or women?
3. What are the basic topics of the most popular songs for your year?
4. If any of the titles seem weird to you, what makes them that way?
5. Based upon what you know about history—or, you might do a little library research—do the song titles reflect what was going on in the world that year?
6. Based on your research, what can you conclude about the relationship between popular music and what is happening in the news? Do songs (as seen from their titles) *reflect* what listeners are interested in and care about? Or, do the songs *shape or determine* what people are interested in and care about?

Exploration: Similar, but Different

DIRECTIONS: Synonyms are usually thought of as words having the same, or nearly the same meaning. It may be more useful for you to emphasize the *nearly* in this definition, since people tend to make very fine distinctions in how they use words. Here is a grid giving you the opportunity to grade some common words. For set 1, put an "X" in the column that best describes each word in relation to the other four. Then do the same for set 2.

	Solemn	*Earnest*	*Sober*	*Serious*	*Intense*
Set 1					
love					

affection _____

adoration _____

devotion _____

passion _____

Set 2 _____

sorrow _____

anguish _____

grief _____

sadness _____

woe _____

1. Compare your rankings of the words in the two sets with those of members of your group. Try to determine on what grounds your rankings are alike or different.
2. Based on your rankings and the subsequent discussions, why do you think people give different shades of meanings to the same words?

Exploration: " 'The time has come,' the walrus said . . . "

DIRECTIONS: You may recall this poem from *Alice in Wonderland*. Walruses are important animals to many Eskimo tribes, just as chickens, steers, fish, and pigs are to other peoples. Eskimos have several names for the walrus:[24]

nutara	baby walrus
ipiksalik	two-year-old walrus
tugar	male or female walrus, with tusks
timartik	big male walrus
aiverk	unaccompanied walrus
naktivilik	mature walrus

1. Can you think of reasons why Eskimos have more names for the walrus than you have in your language?
2. Is there an animal name in your language which has several versions?
3. Predict the number of names an Eskimo might have for "horse."
4. How can you account for the differences in the number of terms your language might have for *dog* or *horse* as compared to the Eskimo's? And, why does an Eskimo have more terms for *walrus*? What does this contrast tell you about how a language portrays the world around us?

Exploration: Tintinnabulatory Effects

DIRECTIONS: Dogs and cats make the same sounds all around the world. The various world languages, however, represent these sounds in different ways. Each language represents the sound of a thunderclap, a gunshot, and a sneeze differently, although the actual noises are probably identical anywhere on Earth. Try to match the following English terms with their French counterparts.

English	*French*
boom	achoum
splash	glouglou
gurgle, glug-glug	badaboum
pooey (stinky)	plouf
achoo	pouah
bang-bang (gun shot)	miam miam
ow, ouch	toc-toc
bang	aie, ouille
knock-knock	boum
yum-yum	pan pan
smack	clac
tickle-tickle	youpi
hurray, goody	oh la la la
Oh dear, oh boy	hic
hiccup	guili guili

(Answers: achoo/achoum;gurgle, glug-glug/glouglou/;boom/badaboum; splash/plouf;pooey (stinky)/pouah; yum-yum/miam miam; knock knock/toc toc;ow, ouch/aie, ouille; bang/boum; bang-bang (gun shot)/ pan pan; smack/ clac; hurray, goody/youpi; Oh dear, oh boy/oh la la la; hiccup/hic; tickle tickle/ guili guili)

1. Given the different spellings for some of the same sounds, do readers of French and readers of English "hear" the same things?
2. Which spellings of these sounds come closer to representing the *real* sound?
3. Do the different spellings for the similar sounds illustrated in this activity carry different *meanings* in either language?

Exploration: Animal Images

DIRECTIONS: When you hear someone say that "It's raining cats and dogs" you are hearing animal imagery. Can you imagine how difficult it would be to explain this image to one who speaks Spanish, German, or any other language? Here are some common animal images from English, with their French counterparts.

English	*French*
to play leapfrog	jouer a saute-mouton (to play leapsheep)
a scaredy-cat	une poule mouillee (a wet hen)
to have goose pimples	avoir la chair de poule (to have hen flesh)
clever as a fox	malin comme un singe (clever as a monkey)
You can't teach an old dog new tricks.	On n'apprend pas a an singe comment la grimace. (You can't teach a monkey how to make faces.)
to open a can of worms	un vrai panier de crabes (a real basket of crabs)
to be hungry as a horse	avoir une faim de loup (to be hungry as a wolf)
to have bats in the belfry	avoir une araignee au plafond (to have a spider on the ceiling)

1. Can you speculate why each language uses the particular animals in its expressions?
2. Do the uses of different animals change the basic meanings of the expressions?
3. Explain why you agree or disagree with the statement, "A language is not right or wrong; it's just different."

Exploration: Birds of a Feather. . . .

DIRECTIONS: Proverbs are universal; all peoples of the world have them in their languages. Here are some proverbs you have probably heard before, with their French counterparts.

English	*French*
When in Rome, do as the Romans (do).	Il faut hurler avec les loups. (You must howl with the wolves.)
Actions speak louder than words.	Faire et dire sont deux. (To say and to do are two.)
Live and let live.	Il faut que tout le monde vive. (All the world must live.)
I'm at my wit's end.	Je suis au bout de mon latin. (I'm at the end of my Latin.)
Out of sight, out of mind.	Loin des yeux, loin du coeur. (Far from the eyes, far from the heart.)
The more, the merrier.	Plus on est de fous, plus on rit. (The more fools there are, the more they laugh.)
Birds of a feather flock together.	Qui se ressemble, s'assemble. (Those who resemble, assemble.)
Put your money where your mouth is.	Selon ta bourse gouverne ta bouche. (According to your purse, govern your mouth.)
Calling a spade a spade.	J'appelle un chat un chat. (I am calling a cat a cat.)
Where there's a will there's a way.	Vouloir, c'est pouvoir. (To want is to be able.)
Nothing ventured, nothing gained.	Qui ne risque rien, n'a rien. (He who risks nothing, has nothing.)

1. Which of these proverbs are most alike? Which are most different?
2. What are the purposes of proverbs? Why do people use them? Do proverbs reveal anything about those who use them?
3. Do you think language shapes the thoughts in proverbs, or do the thoughts shape the language. Or, to ask this question in a more proverbial way, which came first: the chicken (language) or the egg (idea)?

Exploration: Be a Good Sport

DIRECTIONS: Scan the sports section of your local newspaper, read an interview in a sports magazine, or watch a television sportscast and identify three examples of euphemisms. Examples might be calling a bad decision made by a game official or a stupid play by a player a "mental error" or a "judgment call." Or, an athlete who has been arrested for drunken driving, drug use or some other illegal behavior is described as "having off-the-field difficulties."

1. Who used the euphemisms you've identified? The sportswriter? The interviewer? The athlete?
2. In your judgment, what was the user of the euphemism trying to say or *not* say?
3. Why were the euphemisms used? Was effective communication achieved?

Exploration: Are You Sick, or What?

DIRECTIONS: In groups of four or five, brainstorm as many terms or phrases as you can think of that are used in society to describe physical or health-related conditions. Some examples are:

Flu or cold   ". . . under the weather . . ."
                 ". . . have the sniffles . . ."
Pregnancy   ". . . expecting . . ."
                 ". . . blessed event . . ."

Using the list of euphemisms your group has listed, answer the following questions:

1. How do you think these euphemisms originated? Are they harmful to anyone?
2. Compare the terms on your list. Is society more comfortable using euphemisms for certain physical circumstances or conditions?

NOTES

1. Alred Korzybski, *Science and Sanity: An Introduction to Non-Aristotelian Systems and General Semantics*, 4th ed. (Lakeville, CT: International Non-Aristotelian Library Publishing Company, 1958), 19.
2. Ross Evans Paulson, *Language, Science and Action: Korzybski's General Semantics: A Study in Comparative Intellectual History* (Westport, CT: Greenwood Press, 1983), 87–88.
3. Peter Hasselriis, "From Pearl Harbor to Watergate to Kuwait: Language in Thought and Action," *English Journal* 80 (1991): 28.
4. S. I. Hayakawa, *Language in Action* (New York: Harcourt, Brace and Company, 1941).
5. Paulson, *Language, Science and Action,* 87.

6. William Labov, "Preface" in Uriel Weinrich, *On Semantics* (Philadelphia: University of Pennsylvania Press, 1980), vii.
7. Hasselriis, "Language in Thought and Action," 29.
8. Korzybski, *Science and Sanity,* 21–22.
9. Ibid., 34.
10. Ibid., 92.
11. Ibid., 389.
12. S. I. Hayakawa and Alan R. Hayakawa, *Language in Thought and Action* 5th ed. (New York: Harcourt Brace Jovanovich, 1990), 36.
13. Ibid., 36–37.
14. Ibid., 37.
15. Korzybski, *Science and Sanity,* 452.
16. Neil Postman, *Crazy Talk, Stupid Talk* (New York: Delacorte Press, 1976), 208.
17. Ibid.
18. Ibid., 212.
19. William Lutz, "Notes Toward a Definition of Doublespeak," in William Lutz (ed.), *Beyond Nineteen Eighty-Four: Doublespeak in a Post-Orwellian Age* (Urbana, IL: National Council of Teachers of English, 1989), 7.
20. Ibid., 4.
21. Korzybski, *Science and Sanity,* 76.
22. Charles Weingartner, "Semantics: What and Why," *English Journal* 58 (1969): 1214.
23. Paul Caccia, "Getting Grounded: Putting Semantics to Work in the Classroom," *English Journal* 80 (1991): 55.
24. Charles Berlitz, *Native Tongues* (New York: Grosset and Dunlap, 1982), 141.

CHAPTER **10**

The Language of Intolerance and Discrimination

Sticks and stones may break my bones, but words will never hurt me.

—American folk proverb

You probably have heard the proverb quoted at the top of this chapter. It has been in use for well over a century in the United States. Parents and other adult care-givers have taught it to children whose feelings were hurt by others with some well-aimed and generally demeaning or hurtful words.

Typically, proverbs are reserved for resolving conflicts or disputes among children. "Haste makes waste" and "First come, first served" are classic examples.[1]

For those with an interest in language history, the "sticks and stones" proverb can be traced back to the early nineteenth century. Hugh Henry Brackenridge, an early explorer of the Missouri River Valley wrote in his *Gazette* in 1801: "Hard words, and language break nae bane." In 1814 Gouverner Morris, a Philadelphian active in the American Revolutionary War, wrote a strikingly similar idea in his *Diary and Letters*: "These are mere words—hard words if you please, but they break no bones."[2]

These early written uses of this familiar proverb are included here for two reasons: first, the history of language is always interesting. Second, I suspect that from the times of Brackenridge and Morris, to the first time you heard the proverb, and up to the present, the proverbial poultice did not, in fact, actually resolve a dispute or conflict, or make the pain go away. Unquestionably, its use enables a parent or some other care-giver to express nurturing love for the affected child, a linguistic event that needs to occur frequently. Its

173

importance in this respect must not be diminished, but the pain that words can inflict remains. (Can't you recall a time you were the subject of name-calling?) Sticks and stones hurt, as the proverb acknowledges; but, despite the proverb's intent, words hurt, too. And the hurt is frequently more acute and longer lasting than the proverb pronouncers might imagine or prefer.

WHY SOME CHILDREN HAVE MANY NAMES

Peggy Sullivan's novel *Many Names for Eileen* tells the story of a young girl, Eileen, who enjoys a busy Saturday with her mother and father. Throughout the day Eileen meets various people, each of whom calls her by a different name: "Missy," "Curlytop," "Princess," "Little Ella," "Tiger," and "Sport." When Eileen asks her mother why all the people she's met have called her by all of these different names instead of by her real name, her mother replies that although there may be several reasons for the names, the most special reason is that the child who is *loved* has many names.[3]

It is a different matter, on the other hand, for those children who grow up in a more hostile culture, which attaches stereotyped labels, built-in judgments about them, or other assumptions about their personal value: words like *Jewboy, fag, girl, crip, boy, bitch, nigger, queer*, or *spic*. Children who have been called by these labels—often over a period of years—clearly do not believe that they have many names because they are loved!

Most speakers in the United States, however, have learned over the past fifteen or twenty years that using these labels is a cultural taboo in polite society, and they should not be used in public either. Their use violates the rotarian virtues of a democratic society where all people are supposed to have been created equal and enjoy impartial and unrestrained opportunities.

As an example of *some* progress in the declining use of hate speech, ask almost any group of persons under the age of 21 to fill in the blank in the sentence, "Eeny, meeny, meinie mo, catch a _____ by the toe," and they'll likely use either the word *tiger* or perhaps *spider*. My generation and culture learned a different word.

Despite such recent changes, however, there remains in our contemporary society other uses of demeaning language and non-verbal behavior. For example, there have been recent reports of a fraternity hosting a Fiji Islander party, featuring a Harlem Room in which black-faced partygoers ate fried chicken and drank watermelon punch. At another university two caucasians posted a Sambo-like defacement of a picture of Beethoven in the black studies dorm.[4]

Do these reports merely substantiate the claims of those who believe that in any collection of humanity as large and diverse as a university student body there are bound to be some feather-brained zanies who will do anything? Maybe. But racist activities like these aren't confined either primarily or only to university campuses.

To validate this statement, examine your own experience. For example, you probably know that public schools, business firms of all sizes, and governmental and public service agencies employ specialists with the responsibility of improving ethnic and multicultural tolerance, sensitivity, and understanding among students, faculty, and employees. This indicates that there must be a sufficient amount of intolerant and demeaning language and behavior in the larger society that prompts schools, agencies, and businesses to try to do something about it.

This morning I read in my local newspaper about the director of a state agency who has placed a voluptuous light switch cover in his office that depicts a woman with bare breasts. Each morning as he turns on (get it?) the lights, a woman is reduced to her anatomy. Further, Gottlieb claims that movies not only reflect our collective bigotries and hatreds, but also reinforce them. He says this after reviewing a series of Hollywood films which for the past several years have exploited Jewish stereotypes.[5]

Yes, to answer an earlier question, it is a university problem. Intolerant stereotypes, however, apparently extend beyond the campus to the larger society.

I do not pretend to understand all of the reasons for the overt or covert uses of intolerant, prejudicial, and demeaning language. Nor am I posturing, claiming that English language teachers (we precious few) are the sole bastions of sanity in a world gone linguistically loony. On the other hand, I am fairly well convinced that the relationships between thought and language require that you and I attend to language that diminishes and hurts others.

I am proposing that students examine racist or sexist language and behavior following the approach which is advocated in this book for the study of other aspects of language.

To put this idea in a clearer context, and as a brief review, we can recall that prescriptive "Do say" and "Don't say" exhortations are seldom successful. Simply *telling* or *commanding* students "Do not use that term [*homo, coon*, whatever] in this room!" will be, in the long run, about as successful as our trying to dictate to them that "The past tense of *dive* is *dived*, not *dove*! Do not use the term (*dove*) in this room!"

Simply banning or prohibiting certain words and phrases is nothing less than substituting one form of dogmatism for another. As we discussed in earlier chapters, this prescriptive approach seldom motivates students to modify their linguistic behavior in a meaningful manner. We may temporarily suppress a language usage on the surface, but down in the deeper structures the student's attitudes, values, and thought structures, the components of *self*, will either remain unchanged or become more steadfast. (Both *dived* and *dove*, by the way, are entered in most dictionaries and are considered equally grammatical.)

For example, did a teacher ever tell you, "I'm not criticizing you personally, but your writing would be better if you'd only . . . "? Ways of writing and speaking are very personal, extensions and reflections of *person* and *self*. You probably did (and still may) take criticism of your language use personally, despite well-meaning disclaimers.[6] In order to make the grade, however, you tried to accommodate the teacher's request . . . only to revert to prior language use and practice in other classrooms, courses, and social contexts. You weren't convinced of a real need to change, so you didn't.

Similarly, some students are not aware that sentence-initial adverbs, agentless or passive sentences, or any other isolated aspect of language might be offensive to some. Likewise, there are among some of those same students those who are either unaware or are only dimly aware why *girl, cameraman, crip, fag,* or *fox* may be offensive to others or why these words are insulting. Without a fuller awareness, they see little need to modify their language.

I have some crude data on my desk, collected from twenty high school students by a sixteen-year-old friend of mine, which suggest that demeaning and derogatory terms are frequently used without regard to what the terms might mean, but are used as insults almost generally, ambiguously and indiscriminately. For example, one student defined *fag* as "a term you use for anyone you don't like."

Consequently, this chapter presents an approach to demeaning language that is consistent with the approach advocated for all other aspects of language. If learners are going to gain understanding of and greater control over their language, they need to explore language in its social contexts, uses, and outcomes. More intentional and more informed choices will follow.

This chapter examines racist, sexist, and other examples of language of intolerance and discrimination. It is important to stress once more, however, the inseparability of language and context, which includes participants, their relationships and their communicative intent (see *tenor, field,* and *mode* discussion in Chapter 6). While we may agree that *girl* may be considered sexist language in one context, it may not be in another.

For example, a graduate student complained to me one day about one of her professor's habits of constantly referring to the class as "men and girls." He routinely and customarily used this expression, according to the student, consistently throughout the course as a habitual expression.

On the other hand, I have some sixteen- and seventeen-year-old African-American friends who frequently say, "Say, girl . . . " in their conversations with each other.

The former use of *girl* is an example of unexamined, probably unintentional but, nevertheless, sexist language; the latter, in my view, is not. There are many other examples of language use that may be demeaning in one context, but not in another. ("Hey, you old son-of-a bitch! Man, it's good to see you!")

One reason people continue to use hurtful language is that they acquire this language and the semantic houses, fields, and maps it represents just as they acquire all of the other parts of their language of nature and of nurture. They acquire it indirectly and implicitly from their culture. Like their patterns of pronunciation and syntax, these words are a part of the surrounding linguistic atmosphere.

To validate this statement you can conduct some armchair research.

FOR YOUR INQUIRY AND PRACTICE:

Watch television for several hours or for one hour several times. Make a simple tally sheet. Then count the number of products advertised through stereotyped association with female posteriors or cleavage; or, with an association between male decisiveness and dominance linked to female submission.
What are the results of your research?

Must women always be sexy and alluring, and be shown cleaning toilet bowls, scouring dirty pots and pans in the kitchen sink, or shopping for breakfast cereal? These images are not ones I advocate, but they permeate the media.

Must men always be strong, John-Wayne-hair-on-the-chest types who are the center of attention because they make rational and rapid decisions? Many advertising campaigns seem to suggest as much.

Where do these stereotypes come from? Do the advertisements, especially the more ubiquitous ones on television, merely reflect commonly held cultural stereotypes or do they create them? Postman maintains that this question has receded into the background of intellectual thought in the United States because television and its messages have permeated our society to such an extent that "television has gradually *become* our culture."[7] Schultze and his co-authors generally agree with this view and suggest in their book, *Dancing in the Dark: Youth, Popular Culture and the Electronic Media*, that popular culture must be taken very seriously inasmuch as it is both the vehicle and the creator of social attitudes and values.[8]

A tentative answer, then, to the "reflect" or "create" question posed earlier is "Yes." Advertisements both reflect and create stereotypes. Ads seldom are too far ahead of cultural values and probably never lag behind what society might think true and important. Consequently, we can speculate that the advertising agency's images of men, women, and ethnic groups spin in a circular fashion reflecting, reinforcing, creating, hence reflecting and reinforcing society's collective views. If the images violated the public's expectations, they would most likely disappear. So far, they haven't.

It's tempting at this point to cite any number of television commercials that play on male, female, and ethnic stereotypes, none of them flattering. But such a citation would become obsolete as soon as it's printed; the ads change quickly. The stereotypes don't, however, as the armchair research you completed earlier demonstrates.

Advertisements on television are not, however, the sole perpetrators of stereotypes. Also look at display advertisements in popular magazines, tabloids, and some newspapers. You'll discover recurring ethnic and sexual themes. The messages are clear. They signal that it's an either-or world of the beautiful or the ugly, the sexy or the dowdy, the manly or the wimpy.

THE TWO-VALUED ORIENTATION

Korzybski dealt with this simplistic either-or view of the universe in his descriptions of the multiordinality of language. He believed that words have indefinite numbers of meanings, depending upon the contexts to which they are applied. He was concerned because people tend to think with language that is limited to either-or, or biordinal, choices.[9]

Korzybski suggested that people thinking in bipolar opposites leaves little or no room for gradualized positions or ideas in between. Examples of this idea are fairly common. For instance, some people find it convenient to sum up otherwise very complex philosophical, political, or religious ideas on the bumper stickers they place on their cars. "America: Love it or leave it" was popular for awhile. More recently I've seen, "I've found it!" My wife and daughter saw another example a week ago as they drove along one of the major streets in our town. The bumper sticker had the image of the Statue of

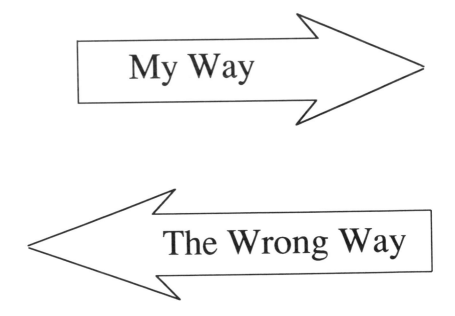

Liberty printed on one side with the two-valued choice, "Speak English or Get the Fuck Out!" printed on the other.

There are more proverbs expressing two-valued views. For example, you've probably heard a few like the following:

1. There are two sides to every question
2. You're either a part of the problem or a part of the solution
3. You're either a Democrat or a Republican
4. You're either right, or you're wrong
5. Either you support the President of the United States, or you're opposed to him
6. Do it my way or the wrong way

Ignoring any middle ground or middle position in circumstances like these illustrates what Korzybski described as a **two-value orientation**, an orientation toward people, events, and circumstances that leads to only two choices.

As you reflect upon two-value orientation, you may conclude that there will be times when it is appropriate and other times when it is inappropriate. For example, you might examine the following and ask yourself whether a two-value orientation is or is not appropriate:

1. Should the ordination of gays and lesbians as clergy be allowed in your church?
2. Should public funds be used to support minority scholarships?
3. Should you force a two-year-old to hold your hand while crossing the street?
4. Is it fair and just to require a sixteen-year-old to observe an 11:00 P.M. curfew?
5. Do you support the establishment of dress codes in schools, especially codes banning gang colors?
6. Should men and women be required by law to register for the Selective Service draft?
7. Should the local, state, or federal government have any authority on membership criteria and quotas at private clubs?
8. Should all employees be required to participate in United Way or Community Chest pledge campaigns?
9. Should the U.S. Constitution be amended to make English the official language of the United States?
10. Should prayer be allowed in public school classrooms?
11. Should women of child-bearing age who are convicted of drug use be forced to have court-ordered contraceptives implanted surgically? Should they be sterilized?
12. Should university athletes with scholarships providing full payment

of tuition, room, board, and books also receive free private tutoring to help them pass their courses?

13. Should fathers of newborn babies be allowed maternity or family leave from their places of employment?

14. Should you adhere to the posted speed limit on the interstate highway at 2:00 A.M.?

15. Should you park in a "Handicapped Only" parking space when you'll be in a supermarket only long enough to pick up a loaf of bread?

Not all the above examples are of equal social, personal, or moral import. Nevertheless, I'm sure you get the idea. Although each of us eventually arrives at a decision in cases such as these illustrations, the decisions are seldom simple yes-no propositions, a fact that will become clearer if you discuss the fifteen statements in a group of three or four people.

We can take the analyses you completed as you considered the fifteen statements above and transpose them into the realm of language marked by racism, sexism, prejudice, and bigotry. If these and other issues are multiordinal, can't we accept the multiordinality of people, too?

THE LANGUAGE OF PREJUDICE

Allport suggests that language plays a major role in the development and maintenance of prejudice, given the interdependent and intimate links among perception, thought, and language. Allport points out that some labels have more powerful emotional connotations than others. He calls the more powerful ones **labels of primary potency**.[10] For example, we may say a person is an expert *speaker*, a thorough *student,* and a faithful *employee.* When we add that the person is also *blind*, then the feature *blind* outweighs all of the other features. Among labels used to describe someone, *blind* is more potent. Many physical and ethnic labels (crippled, disabled, Asian, African American, Native American) are labels of primary potency.

What is at issue here, of course, is the fact that labels of primary potency tend to blind us to other attributes and characteristics an individual might possess. These labels stop thought; they are examples of language "doing" our thinking for us. Labels of primary potency prevent alternative perceptions and descriptions. They refer only to one aspect of a human being, but not any others.

Left-handed people, for example, may also be considered as hard workers and thrifty shoppers. People with black hair may also be good mothers, excellent tennis players, and rapid readers. The various descriptors appear to be relatively equal in emotional connotation, and one feature does not overshadow or diminish another. On the other hand, labels of primary potency conjure up in the minds of some people connotations that are much stronger, almost always negative and hostile, and they do, in fact, overshadow other attributes. Consequently, in such cases, *Jews* are only *Jews* and nothing else. *Hispanics* are only *Hispanics*, and nothing else. *Females* are only *female*. A *crip* is a *crip*. *Wops* arc *wops*. *Gays* arc, wcll . . . you know.

The use of these labels reduces persons to one dimension. A stereotype. End of thinking. End of discussion. These labels prevent our seeing the fuller person, as the writer of the following letter to the editor illustrates:

> Our [gay and lesbian] children have partners celebrating their fifth, tenth, and fifteenth anniversaries. They own homes and mortgages, have car payments, gardens, lawns, neighbors, dogs and cats, and they hold jobs. They pay taxes. They also have brothers and sisters, grandparents, related kinfolks, and friends. . . .[11]

If you are one who cannot or has not been described by one of the labels of primary potency, then you may be less likely to be disturbed by their use in society. Obviously, on the other hand, if you or someone you love have been called *timber-nigger* (a form of double jeopardy aimed at Native Americans) or *porch monkey*, or if you or a friend has been the target of a bumper sticker I saw recently that read, "Save a fish, spear an Indian," then you understand how mean and demeaning they are.

I am not trying to convert either teachers or their students to feminists, or any other kind of -*ists*. I am suggesting, however, that racist, sexist, or demeaning language ought to be understood and avoided, and I am using our earlier definition of good English (see Chapter 6) as the rationale.

> Good English is markcd by succcss in making languagc choiccs so that the fewest number of persons will be distracted by the choices.[12]

Knowing that some will be distracted and offended by the use of *boy, fox, coon*, or any other label of primary and negative potency is reason enough not to use it. We can try to get our own linguistic houses in order in our efforts to help students become more spontaneous, precise, and elaborative with language. Good English is the more traditional educational aim, and we have defined it in such a way that social uses are clearly important.

Look at the matter this way. Regardless of how you may feel personally about the use of *mailman* as opposed to *mail carrier*, or *man* as a generic noun encompassing both male and female, let's review some ideas from Chapter 6. Part of our definition of good English is that the language used will be comfortable to both speaker and listener. If you plan to host a dinner party this weekend and plan to burn incense in an attempt to create the ambience desired, would you insist on burning the incense if you knew one of your guests is allergic to it? Similarly, should we continue to use words and expressions when we know others are distracted by their use?

This determination of good English requires us to re-center the focus of conversation. We refocus from "I" to "we," from "me" to "us."

When conversations, news stories, editorials, television programs, classroom instructional materials, political campaigns, and advertising utilize or exploit labels of primary potency, it makes some people appear to be unidimensional, it is another way of making the targeted group appear less than human. "Anyone who believes that certain people are subhuman will find it easy to treat them as subhuman. The end result can be mountains of baby shoes in storehouses, lamp shades made from human skin, and soap made from human fat."[13]

Given our earlier description of an English teacher as a language cop, not much is likely to be gained by dogmatically banning or prohibiting demeaning language, although its use cannot be condoned. Attempts to control language through prescriptive legislation inevitably fail.

The student explorations at the end of this chapter are examples of classroom activities through which students can become more aware of and sensitive to language and images of intolerance and discrimination. Personal explorations like these are more likely to be effective than teacher- or adult-centered exhortations.

For other aspects of the English language arts curriculum, teachers and school administrators who wish to be more inclusive in their attention to a fuller depiction of nonwhite minorities, will find the statement in Appendix A from the National Council of Teachers of English Task Force on Racism and Bias in the Teaching of English to be helpful.

The sociolinguistic topic of demeaning language must be approached with a fine, sensitive hand in classrooms. It is not to be studied because we want either Caucasian students or young men to feel guilty about racist or sexist language in society. Nor is it to be examined so that beleaguered nonwhite minorities or young women might gain a small measure of smug victory and relief in our classrooms.

It is studied, as Engel reminds us, because we have it in our power either to degrade or to enhance and beautify ourselves and our world by the way we use language.[14] I understand that some may believe this comment hopelessly idealistic, but I leave you with one final challenge and question: If you, a professional language teacher, do not empower your students to use language in ways that will enhance and beautify themselves and their worlds, who will?

Explorations

STUDENT EXPLORATIONS FOR THE LANGUAGE OF INTOLERANCE AND DISCRIMINATION

Exploration: What's Real about Names

DIRECTIONS: We sometimes form opinions, attitudes, and judgments about people because of their names. Here are a number of names for you to think about. Look at each name; then from the two lists at the bottom of the page select the word(s) from list A that you think best "fits" this name; then, from list B select the employment you think this name best represents.

Names

	A	B			A	B
Angie	———	———		Bertha	———	———
Tammi	———	———		George	———	———
Virgil	———	———		Zack	———	———
Mary	———	———		Barbie	———	———
Jason	———	———		William	———	———

List A:		*List B:*	
A. nerd	G. weak	A. model	G. manager
B. attractive	H. alone	B. teacher	H. pastor
C. popular	I. neat	C. delivery person	I. clerk
D. powerful	J. careless	D. athlete	J. reporter
E. plain	K. loyal	E. musician	K. rancher
F. okay	L. friendly	F. scientist	L. driver

1. Compare your answers with those of other members of your group. For those responses you agree on, can you decide *why* you are in agreement?
2. For those responses you *do not* agree on, can you decide why there is disagreement?
3. On what prior information about names, people, jobs, or employment, have you and your classmates based your responses? To put this question another way, on what information, opinions, or values did you base your selections?
4. Where do our notions about the importance of names come from?

183

Exploration: " 'Mawnin!' says Brer Rabbit"

DIRECTIONS: Stereotypes are standardized, uncritical, and unthinking images or prejudgments some people use in viewing of other people and the world. Stereotypes can be found in literature, advertising, television programs, political advertisements, music, and mealtime conversations. Humorous literature frequently uses stereotypes as it pokes fun at people and their behavior. *The Uncle Remus* stories by Joel Chandler Harris, for example, employ heavy use of stereotyped language. Harris's stories depict the way southern white Anglo-Saxons perceived African Americans in the 1800s in the United States. Focusing on the the characters of Brer Fox and Brer Rabbit, the language and action of the stories represent stereotypical black English vernacular. Read the first twenty paragraphs of "The Wonderful Tar-Baby Story," then answer the following questions.

1. List the words in the passage that are used to form the reader's opinion or interpretation of the characters.
2. Explain how these words create stereotypes, and whether they help or harm our interpretations.
3. How do these words and the sentences they're taken from affect the way the reader perceives people living in the South in the 1800s?
4. Based on your understanding of this passage, the words you have been examining, and your general knowledge, do writers continue to use these stereotypes today?

Exploration: Perfect Strangers

DIRECTIONS: "I could fly this plane with both eyes tied behind my back!" This sentence is just one example of many stereotyped uses of language by a nonnative speaker seen on the television program "Perfect Strangers." Balki, the Meiposian visitor, is depicted as having trouble getting English quite right, presumably as many nonnative speakers of English do.

Watch one episode of "Perfect Strangers." Notice in particular the common stereotypes the program's writers use in Balki's speech. Then, be prepared to discuss the following.

1. List some of the language stereotypes used to portray Balki's character.
2. What are some of the words or phrases Balki uses that demonstrate his misunderstanding of English?
3. Do you find Balki's English usage humorous or distracting?
4. Do you believe Balki's English is an accurate representation of nonnative speakers' use of English?
5. Based upon this discussion of one episode of "Perfect Strangers," as well as other television programs you've seen, what can you deter-

mine about television's use of language stereotypes? Are they always funny? Can they be harmful?

Exploration: Are You What You Drive?

DIRECTIONS: "What's a 'rent [parent] doing in a load [great car] like that?" is an example of a sentence you might hear some people say when their stereotyped ideas about the type of automobile a parent *ought* to drive are proved false. Why do so many people associate the type of car a person owns with that person's personality or social status? Or, why do some believe owning a particular type of car automatically bestows upon them either a new personality or a different social position? Using automobile ads clipped from newspapers and magazines, create a collage demonstrating the various ways advertisers use stereotyped language to entice potential buyers.

1. Make a list of the various names of cars appearing in your collage. Can you group them into categories? (For example, under *cats* you could include Cougar, Lynx, Bobcat.)
2. What types of stereotypes do these names and/or categories conjure up? What personality stereotypes do they suggest?
3. How are these examples of stereotyped language used to the advantage of the advertiser? The automobile company? The potential purchaser?
4. Based upon your analyses of stereotyped language in automobile advertising, do you believe society is affected one way or another by this language?

Exploration: All My Ex's Live in Texas

DIRECTIONS: "Don't It Make My Brown Eyes Blue that All My Ex's Live in Texas, Just Three Doors Down from Eighteen Wheels and a Dozen Roses?" You might never read or hear this sentence again! It results from blending the titles of popular country songs, many of which appeal to stereotyped ideas about men and women and their relationships. Listen to a local country radio station and examine the titles of popular songs and the corresponding themes developed through the verses. Are there stereotyped themes, characters, or other patterns you can identify?

1. What are some titles of currently popular country songs? Do the songs use stereotyped language in depicting men, women, or themes?
2. Are these uses of language intentional or unintentional, in your view?
3. Based upon these analyses, what do the titles suggest about people who listen to country music? Is there a stereotyped view of them? Do you agree or disagree with this view?

Exploration: Here Come Angel and Stud-Boy

DIRECTIONS: Terms of endearment are frequently used in spoken exchanges between members of the opposite sex. Some of the terms are positive, but some have negative connotations. Brainstorm with others in your class, listing as many terms of endearment as you can remember hearing people use during the past week.

1. Distinguish between the terms used for men and women. Do the terms group themselves into categories (physical characteristics, special talents, ethnicity, etc.)?
2. What do these categories and terms suggest about possible stereotyped views of men and women? When do we begin to learn these terms?
3. Based upon these discussions, do you think terms of endearment affect people's view of themselves?

Exploration: Cheers

DIRECTIONS: Which character in the cast of the television program "Cheers" is more likely to ask: "Yeah, and how would you like a hook in your mouth?" The characters in the program are defined for the viewer largely through the language they use. Watch an episode or two of "Cheers."

1. Explain how language is used stereotypically by the writers of "Cheers" in order to characterize Frazier and his level of education and training; Carla and her working class social status; or Woody and his midwest origins and values.
2. How would you describe the *tone* of the conversations taking place in the "Cheers" bar? How does this conversational tone provide a setting for the language stereotypes identified in 1?
3. Do you believe that the stereotyped language used by the characters depicted in "Cheers" reflects society in general?

Exploration: Caveat Emptor

DIRECTIONS: Used car advertisements employ language in several unconventional ways. Sometimes "used" cars are called "experienced" or "preowned" cars. In order to lure buyers to the car lot, sales agents describe "easy terms," "instant credit," and the like. Easy for whom? Is it really *instant*? Examine several advertisements for used cars, on television or in newspapers; then prepare a parody of a used car commercial in which you use the stereotypical language you've observed in selling cars. (Select any car you think is a dog.)

1. What are some of the more frequent terms commercials use to describe used cars? In your judgment, are these terms accurate or misleading?
2. How do these terms put the prospective buyer at a disadvantage?
3. What is the general effect of language that distorts? Consider the point of view of both the seller and the buyer.

Exploration: Be A Prudent Thing

DIRECTIONS: George Bush is frequently parodied on television and in political cartoons because of his use of the words "prudent" and "thing." Cartoon creators usually select what they consider a predominant feature or habit of a public personality; then they center their creation around that feature. Find at least three political cartoons of the same public personality.

1. What commonalties do your different cartoons share? How do cartoonists create stereotypes?
2. Do these elements in the cartoons help explain the issue or the personality being featured in the cartoon? Or, do you think they are misleading?
3. Do you believe the stereotypes presented in political cartoons *create* or *reflect* society's views of a public personality?

Exploration: Love Is a Simply Splendored Thing

DIRECTIONS: "Will Zack ever return the searing love Kimberly so desires? Will Kimberly ever find the cache of words in her heart's vocabulary in order to explain to Zack how she yearns for him?" This sentence could have come from one of any number of grocery store romance novels. The language used in these novels is very dramatic, formulaic, and stereotyped as it describes the soft-spoken woman who falls hopelessly in love with an athletic-looking man who inevitably is a member of a different social class. It's the basic Romeo and Juliet story told over and over again, moving around the country from St. Louis to Miami, to Southern California to Anywhere, USA. Only the geography is different. Locate a grocery store romance novel, and select and read a 100-word passage from the beginning, the middle, and the end of the book.

1. What phrases and language cliches are used in the passages to describe the characters? How does this language use affect your view of the characters?
2. Why do these novels rely so heavily on stereotyped language? Is this language use harmful to anyone?

Exploration: The Sexy Toilet Bowl Cleaner

DIRECTIONS: "Don't hate me because I'm beautiful," a woman selling a brand of shampoo on television tells us. Why hate me, she implies, when you can be just as beautiful if you'll wash your hair with this product. The implicit message in this commercial suggests that there is an image of the ideal woman that any female can attain if . . . she uses this shampoo, that toilet bowl cleaner, or washes her family's clothes with a particular detergent. Bring to class several color display advertisements from a variety of popular magazines.

1. What stereotypes of men or women are used in your ads?
2. Are there recurring words or phrases used in the ads, regardless of the product being advertised?
3. What are some results of the stereotyped views of men and women as they are depicted in advertisements?

NOTES

1. Neil Postman, *Amusing Ourselves To Death* (New York: Viking Penguin, 1986), 19.
2. Jere Whiting Bartlett, *Early American Proverbs and Proverbial Phrases* (Cambridge, MA: Harvard University Press, 1977), 496.
3. Peggy Sullivan, *Many Names for Eileen* (Chicago and New York: Follett, 1969).
4. "Hate Speech on the College Campus," *Lex Colligii* 14 (1991): 1 (Nashville, TN: College Legal Information).
5. Walter J. Gottlieb, "Next Comes a Thick Yiddish Accent," *The Washington Post National Weekly*, 9–15 September 1991.
6. Peter Elbow, *What Is English?* (Urbana, IL: National Council of Teachers of English and New York: Modern Language Association of America, 1990), 116.
7. Postman, *Amusing Ourselves*, 79.
8. Quentin J. Schultze, Roy M. Anker, James D. Bratt, William D. Romanowski, John W. Worst, and Lambert Zuidervaart, *Dancing in the Dark: Youth, Popular Culture, and the Electronic Media* (Grand Rapids, MI: Eerdmans, 1991). For related analyses see also: John P. Ferre (ed.), *Channels of Belief: Religion and American Television* (Ames: Iowa State University Press, 1991; and Gregor T. Goethals, *The Electronic Golden Calf: Images, Religion, and the Making of Meaning* (Cambridge, MA: Cowley, 1991).
9. Alfred Korzybski, *Science and Sanity: An Introduction to Non-Aristotelian Systems and General Semantics* 4th ed. (Lakeville, CT: The International Non-Aristotelian Library Publishing Company, 1958), 14.
10. Gordon Allport, "The Language of Prejudice," in Paul Escholz et al. (eds.), *Language Awareness* (New York: St. Martin's Press, 1986), 261–270.
11. Letter to the Editor, *Lincoln* (NE) *Journal-Star*, 7 September 1991.

12. Robert C. Pooley, *The Teaching of English Usage* (Urbana, IL: National Council of Teachers of English, 1974), 5.
13. S. Morris Engel, *The Language Trap* (Englewood Cliffs, N.J.: Prentice-Hall, 1984), 106.
14. Ibid.

Appendix

NON-WHITE MINORITIES IN ENGLISH AND LANGUAGE ARTS MATERIALS

Prepared by the NCTE Task Force on Racism and Bias in the Teaching of English. Printed with permission of the National Council of Teachers of English.

Background

The following statement, "Nonwhite Minorities in English and Language Arts Materials," is a revision of the *Criteria for Teaching Materials in Reading and Literature*. The original version was first accepted by the Executive Committees of the National Council of Teachers of English and the Conference on College Composition and Communication, and then officially adopted by the NCTE Board of Directors at the annual meeting in Atlanta on November 26, 1970. Since 1970, some changes have occurred. In some cases, publishers have included more multiethnic materials in their products. Similarly, teachers, in some cases, have given more attention to multiethnic materials in their classrooms. But problems remain. This revision looks at some of those problems and offers some solutions. Both the original and revised statements were prepared by the Task Force on Racism and Bias in the Teaching of English, Ernece Kelly, Director.

Rationale

Minority groups in the United States, especially the nonwhite minorities— Native Americans, Asian Americans, African Americans, Hispanics, Puerto Ricans, et al.—suffer crippling discrimination in jobs, housing, civil rights, and education. And they continue to face a school curriculum that, for them, is culturally impoverished. Ironically, it is also a curriculum which, in a different fashion, cripples white students and teachers by denying them the opportunity to learn about the history and literature of other Americans who are nonwhites.

During the course of their education, students acquire more than skills and knowledge; they also find and continue to modify images of themselves as they form attitudes toward other persons, races, and cultures. To be sure, the school experience is not the sole force that shapes self-images, nor does it totally influence one's attitude toward others. But to the extent that school does exert influence, it is essential that its materials foster positive student self-images deeply rooted in a sense of personal dignity. School materials should also foster the development of attitudes grounded in respect for and understanding of the diverse cultures of American society.

Classroom teachers are immediately responsible for continuing action to accomplish these ends. However, curriculum planners, textbook selection committees, local, state, and national education authorities, as well as designers of learning systems and publishers, are equally responsible and obligated.

Problems

Print (general anthologies, basal readers, language arts kits, etc.) and nonprint materials (slides, study prints, films, filmstrips, videotapes, illustrations in texts, etc.) used in English and language arts instructions are distorted by

- **A.** misrepresentation of the range of genres within which nonwhites write;
- **B.** misrepresentation caused by inclusion of only popular works by a few "acceptable" nonwhite writers;
- **C.** inclusion of demeaning, insensitive, or inaccurate depictions of nonwhite minorities;
- **D.** biased and out-of-date commentaries resulting from inadequate knowledge of nonwhite minorities; and
- **E.** refusal to acknowledge the influence of nonwhite minority persons on the literary, cultural, and historical developments in America.

Solutions

Book editors and publishers should make certain that

A. anthologies purporting to represent American Literature have more than token representation of works by non-white minorities and that they reflect diversity of subject matter, style, and social and cultural views;

B. texts represent nonwhite minorities in a fashion which respects their dignity as human beings and accurately mirrors their contributions to American culture, history, and letters, meaning that depictions of minority groups be balanced and realistic;

C. illustrations and photographs of nonwhite minorities accurately portray historical and socioeconomic diversity;

D. dialect is realistic, consistent, and appropriate to the setting and characters;

E. editorial and critical commentary includes the roles played by non-white writers in literary developments;

F. texts include criticisms of nonwhite critics on the works of white as well as nonwhite writers; and that

G. historical commentary and interpretations include the range of minority perspectives on social and political history.

Solutions

Teachers and administrators should ask whether

A. their English and language arts curricula include more than token representation of minority writers and/or critics;

B. efforts are consistently made in the classroom to encourage *active use* of materials that have more than a token representation of writers/ critics;

C. illustrations or photographs of nonwhites in the materials are non-stereotyped and unsentimental;

D. illustrations or photographs of nonwhites show them in a variety of roles, including positions of authority;

E. the dialogue of nonwhites is realistic and not exclusively stereotyped;

F. discussions of American literary, social, and political history mention contributions by nonwhites; and whether

G. discussions of American literary, social and political history are also by nonwhites.

If teachers and administrators had to answer no to one or more of these questions, the material being used probably conveys a distorted picture of America and its literature. The NCTE Task Force on Racism and Bias in the Teaching of English urges that such material be balanced by other materials that present positive images of nonwhite minorities. When adopting *new* instructional materials, teachers are urged to use adoption criteria that will assure that classroom materials accurately reflect the literature of America.

Should teachers and administrators elect to replace their present material, the Task Force strongly urges them to write the publishers informing them of their reasons for doing so.

Bibliography

Aitchison, Jean. *Language Change: Progress or Decay?* 16, 222. New York: Universe Books, 1985.

———. *Words in the Mind.* 18–19. Oxford: Basil Blackwell, 1987.

———. *The Articulate Mammal.* 5, 164. London: Unwin Hyman, 1989.

Akmajian, Adrian, Richard D. Demers, Ann K. Farmer, and Robert M. Harnish. *Linguistics: An Introduction to Language and Communication*, 3rd ed. 14, 24. Cambridge: Massachusetts Institute of Technology Press, 1990.

Allport, Gordon. "The Language of Prejudice." In Paul Escholz et al. (eds.). *Language Awareness.* 261–270. New York: St. Martin's Press, 1986.

Anderson, Richard C., Elfrieda Hiebert, Judith Scott, and Ian A.G. Wilkinson. *Becoming a Nation of Readers: The Report of the Commission on Reading.* 76–77. Pittsburgh, PA: National Academy of Education, 1985.

Applebee, Arthur N. *The Teaching of Literature in Programs with Reputations for Excellence in English.* Albany, NY: State University of New York–Albany Center for the Learning and Teaching of Literature, Report 1.1., 1989.

———. *Tradition and Reform in the Teaching of English: A History.* 5–8. Urbana, IL: National Council of Teachers of English, 1974.

———. *Contexts for Learning to Write: Studies of Secondary School Instruction.* Norwood, N.J.: Ablex Publishing Corporation, 1984.

Associated Press. "Wrong turn on foul word spells loss." *The Lincoln* (NE) *Star.* 11, 1991.

Astor, Gerald. *The Baseball Hall of Fame 50th Anniversary Book.* 7. New York: Prentice-Hall, 1988.

Atwell, Nancie. *In the Middle: Writing, Reading and Learning with Adolescents.* Upper Montclair, N.J.: Boynton/Cook, 1987.

Atwood, Margaret. *The Handmaid's Tale.* 26. New York: Ballantine Books, 1985.

Auel, Jean. *The Valley of Horses*. 466–67. New York: Bantam Books, 1982.

Bartlett, Jere Whiting. *Early American Proverbs and Proverbial Phrases*. 496. Cambridge, MA: Harvard University Press, 1977.

Baugh, Albert C., and Thomas Cable. *A History of the English Language*, 3rd ed. 257. Englewood Cliffs, N.J.: Prentice-Hall, 1978.

Berlitz, Charles. *Native Tongues*. 141, 146. New York: Grosset & Dunlap, 1982.

Bolinger, Dwight, and Donald A. Sears. *Aspects of Language*, 3rd ed. 52–53, 134. New York: Harcourt Brace Jovanovich, 1981.

Bostain, James C. "The Dream World of English Grammar." *NEA Journal* 55 (September 1966): 20–22.

Braddock, Richard C., Richard Lloyd-Jones, and Lowell Schoer. *Research in Written Composition*. Urbana, IL: National Council of Teachers of English, 1963.

Brown, Gillian. "The Spoken Language," in Ronald Carter (ed.), *Linguistics and the Teacher*. 75–86. London: Routledge & Kegan Paul, 1982.

Bruner, Jerome S. *Childs Talk*. New York: W.W. Norton, 1981.

Burchfield, Robert. "The Oxford English Dictionary." In Robert Ilson (ed.), *Lexicography: an Emerging International Profession*. 19. Manchester: Manchester University Press, 1986.

Caccia, Paul. "Getting Grounded: Putting Semantics to Work in the Classroom." *English Journal* 80 (1991): 55–59.

Carlson, Robert G. *The Americanization Syndrome: A Quest for Conformity*. 2. New York: St. Martin's Press, 1987.

Carter, Ronald (ed.). *Linguistics and the Teacher*. 75–87. London: Routledge & Kegan Paul, 1982.

Carver, Craig M. *American Regional Dialects*. Ann Arbor, MI: University of Michigan Press, 1987.

Cassidy, Frederick G. (ed.). *Dictionary of American Regional English*, vol. I. Cambridge, MA: Belknap Press of Harvard University Press, 1985.

Chaika, Elaine. "Discourse Routines." In Virginia P. Clark et al., (eds.), *Language: Introductory Readings*. 429–55. New York: St. Martin's Press, 1985.

Chapman, Raymond. "A Versatile Suffix." *English Today* 7 (1991): 39, 41, 52.

Chomsky, Noam. *Syntactic Structures*. The Hague: Mouton, 1957.

Commission on English. *Freedom and Discipline in English*. 20. New York: College Entrance Examination Board, 1965.

Crabtree, Monica, and Joyce Powers. *Language Files*, 5th ed. 327. Columbus, OH: Ohio State University Press, 1991.

Cruz, Isagani R. "A Nation Searching for a Language Finds a Language Searching for a Name," *English Today* 7 (1991): 17.

Crystal, David. *Who Cares About English Usage?* London: Penguin Books, 1984.

Donaldson, Margaret. *Children's Minds*. London: Fontana Press, 1978.

Doughty, Peter, John Pearce, and Geoffrey Thornton. *Exploring Language*. London: Edward Arnold, 1972.

Elbow, Peter. *What is English?* 116. New York: The Modern Language Association and the National Council of Teachers of English, 1990.

Engel, S. Morris. *The Language Trap*. 106. Englewood Cliffs, N.J.: Prentice-Hall, 1984.

Erman, Brit. *Pragmatic Expressions in English: A Study of "You know", "You see" and*

"I mean" in Face-to-face Conversation. 206–207. University of Stockholm, Stockholm Studies in English, 1987.

Evans, Bergan. *The Word-a-Day Vocabulary Builder.* New York: Random House, 1963.

Ferre, John P. (ed.). *Channels of Belief: Religion and American Television.* Ames, IA: Iowa State University Press, 1991.

Finegan, Edward, and Niko Besnier. *Language: Its Structure and Use.* 2, 344, 382, 383. New York: Harcourt Brace Jovanovich, 1989.

Flanders, Ned A. *Analyzing Teaching Behavior.* 89, 90. Reading, MA: Addison-Wesley, 1970.

Flexner, Stuart B. "Preface to *The Dictionary of American Slang.*" In Paul Escholz et al. (eds.), *Language Awareness*, 4th ed. 180, 182, 183. New York: St. Martin's Press, 1986.

Fowler, H. Ramsey. *The Little, Brown Handbook.* Boston: Little, Brown, 1980.

Freire, Paulo. "The Adult Literacy Process as Cultural Action for Freedom." *Harvard Educational Review* 40 (1970): 205–221.

"From Our Files: Bushery." *English Today* 6 (October 1990): 6.

Gee, James Paul. "Literacy, Discourse, and Linguistics: Introduction." *Boston University Journal of Education* 171 (1989) 5–25.

Gere, Ann Ruggles,and Eugene Smith. *Attitudes, Language and Change.* 8–10. Urbana, IL: National Council of Teachers of English, 1979.

Giles, Howard, and W. Peter Robinson. *Handbook of Language and Social Psychology.* 2. New York: Wiley, 1990.

Goethals, Gregor T. *The Electronic Golden Calf: Images, Religion, and the Making of Meaning.* Cambridge, MA: Cowley, 1991.

Goodlad, John. *A Place Called School.* New York: McGraw-Hill, 1984.

Gottlieb, Walter J. "Next Comes a Thick Yiddish Accent." *The Washington Post National Weekly* 8. (September 9–15, 1991): 25.

Greenbaum, Sidney. *Studies in English Adverbial Usage.* 109. Coral Gables, FL: University of Miami Press, 1969.

Grice, Paul. *Studies in the Way of Words.* 26, 27. Cambridge, MA: Harvard University Press, 1989.

Halliday, M.A.K., Agnes McIntosh, and Peter Strevens. *The Linguistic Sciences and Language Teaching.* 105, 142–43, 155. Bloomington: Indiana University Press, 1964.

Halliday, M.A.K., "Linguistics in Teacher Education." In Ronald Carter (ed.), *Linguistics and the Teacher.* 11. London: Routledge & Kegan Paul, 1982.

———. *Learning How to Mean: Explorations in the Development of Language.* 37, 130–32. London: Edward Arnold, 1975.

Harris, Roy. *The Language Myth.* 10. London: Duckworth & Company, 1981.

Hartwell, Patrick. "Grammar, Grammars and the Teaching of Grammar." *College English* 47 (1985): 105–27.

Hasselriis, Peter. "From Pearl Harbor to Watergate to Kuwait: Language in Thought and Action," *English Journal* 80 (1991): 28–37.

"Hate Speech on the College Campus." *Lex Colligii* 14 (1991): 1. Nashville, TN: College Legal Information.

Hatfield, Wilbur N. *An Experience Curriculum in English.* New York: Appleton-Century, 1935.

Hawkins, Eric. *Awareness of Language: An Introduction.* 69. Cambridge: Cambridge University Press, 1987.

Hayakawa, S. I. *Language in Action.* New York: Harcourt, Brace and Company, 1941.

Hayakawa, S.I., and Alan R. Hayakawa. *Language in Thought and Action*, 5th ed. 36. New York: Harcourt Brace Jovanovich, 1990.

Hendrickson, Robert. *American Talk: The Words and Ways of American Dialects.* Chapter 1, 17, 25–34, 194. New York: Penguin Books, 1986.

Hillocks, George. *Research on Written Composition.* Urbana, IL: National Council of Teachers of English, 1986.

Hockett, Charles F. "Logical Considerations in the Study of Animal Communication." In Charles F. Hockett (ed.), *The View from Language.* 145, 147. Athens, GA: University of Georgia Press, 1977.

Hodges, Richard E. *Improving Spelling and Vocabulary in the Secondary School.* 12–13. Newark, DE: International Reading Association, and Urbana, IL: ERIC Clearinghouse on Reading and Communication Skills, 1982.

Hoey, Michael. *On the Surface of Discourse.* 1. London: George Allen & Unwin, 1983.

Hogan, William. *The Quartzsite Trip.* New York: Avon Books, 1980.

Howarth, David. *1066 the Year of the Conquest.* New York: Dorset Press by arrangement with Viking-Penguin, 1978.

Hynds, Susan, and Donald L. Rubin. *Perspectives on Talk and Learning.* Urbana, IL: National Council of Teachers of English, 1990.

Ivins, Molly. *Molly Ivins Can't Say That, Can She?* New York: Random House, 1991.

Jackson, Philip W. *Life in Classrooms.* 70. New York: Holt, Rinehart and Winston, 1968.

Kaplan, Jeffrey. *English Grammar: Principles and Facts.* 21, 86, 87. Englewood Cliffs, N.J.: Prentice-Hall, 1989.

Korzybski, Alfred. *Science and Sanity: An Introduction to Non-Aristotelian Systems and General Semantics*, 4th ed. Lakeville, CT: International Non-Aristotelian Library Publishing Company, 1958.

Kurath, Hans. *A Word Geography of the Eastern United States.* Ann Arbor: University of Michigan Press, 1949

———. *Studies in Area Linguistics.* Bloomington: Indiana University Press, 1972.

Kurath, Hans, and Raven McDavid. *The Pronunciation of English in the Atlantic States.* Ann Arbor: University of Michigan Press, 1961.

Labov, William. "Stages in the Acquisition of Standard English." In Harold Hungerford, Jay Robinson, and James Sledd (eds.), *English Linguistics.* 81–82, 275–302. Glenview, IL: Scott Foresman, 1970.

———. *Language in the Inner City.* Philadelphia: University of Pennsylvania Press, 1972.

———. *The Social Stratification of English in New York City.* Washington, DC: Center for Applied Linguistics, 1966.

———. "Preface" in Uriel Weinrich, *On Semantics.* vii. Philadelphia: University of Pennsylvania Press, 1980.

Labov, William, and David Fanshel. *Therapeutic Discourse: Psychotherapy as Conversation.* 81–82. New York: Academic Press, 1977.

Lee, Laurie. *The Edge of Day: A Boyhood in the West of England.* 45. New York: Morrow, 1960.

Lipton, James. *An Exaltation of Larks*. 13. New York: Viking Penguin, 1991.

Long, C.C. *New Language Exercises for Primary Schools*. 31. Cincinnati and New York: Van Antwerp, Bragg, and Company, 1889.

Lowth, Robert. *A Short Introduction to English Grammar*. Menston, Yorkshire: Scolar Press, facsimile reprint of 1762 first edition, 1967.

Lutz, William. "Notes Toward a Definition of Doublespeak." In William Lutz (ed.), *Beyond Nineteen Eighty-Four: Doublespeak in a Post-Orwellian Age*. 4, 7. Urbana, IL: National Council of Teachers of English, 1989.

Macnamara, John. *Names for Things: a Study in Human Learning*. viii. Cambridge, MA: Massachusetts Institute of Technology Press, 1982.

McCrum, Robert, William Cran, and Robert MacNeil. *The Story of English*. New York: Elisabeth Sifton Books-Viking, 1986.

Mandelbaum, David (ed.). *The Selected Writings of Edward Sapir*. Berkeley: University of California Press, 1949.

Milroy, James and Lesley Milroy. *Authority in Language*. 71–72. London: Routledge & Kegan Paul, 1985.

Nagy, William, and Patricia Herman. "Breadth and Depth of Vocabulary Knowledge: Implications for Acquisition and Instruction." In Margaret McKeown and Mary Curtis (eds.), *The Nature of Vocabulary Acquisition*. 26. Hillsdale, N.J.: Lawrence Erlbaum Associates, 1967.

Nagy, William. *Teaching Vocabulary to Improve Reading Comprehension*. 3. Newark, DE: International Reading Association, 1988.

Noguchi, Rei R. *Grammar and the Teaching of Writing: Limits and Possibilities*. Urbana, IL: National Council of Teachers of English, 1991.

Paulson, Ross Evans. *Language, Science and Action: Korzybski's General Semantics: A Study in Comparative Intellectual History*. 87–88. Westport, CT: Greenwood Press, 1983.

Peck, Robert Newton. *A Day No Pigs Would Die*. New York: Dell, 1972.

Perera, Katherine. "The Language Demands of Schooling." In Ronald Carter (ed.), *Linguistics and the Teacher*. 115. London: Routledge & Kegan Paul, 1982.

———. *Children's Writing and Reading: Analysing Classroom Language*. 156. Oxford: Basil Blackwell, 1984.

Phelan, Patricia. *Talking to Learn*. Urbana, IL: National Council of Teachers of English, 1989.

Piaget, Jean. *The Language and Thought of the Child*. London: Routledge & Kegan Paul, 1965.

Pinker, Steven. *Learnability and Cognition: The Acquisition of Argument Structure*. 6, 11, 199. Cambridge, MA: Massachusetts Institute of Technology Press, A Bradford Book, 1991.

Pooley, Robert C. *The Teaching of English Usage*. 5. Urbana, IL: National Council of Teachers of English, 1974.

Postman, Neil. *Crazy Talk, Stupid Talk*. 9–11, 19, 79, 208, 212. New York: Delacorte Press, 1976.

———. *Amusing Ourselves To Death*. 19. New York: Viking Penguin, 1986.

Richards, Jack, John Platt, and Heidi Weber. *Longman Dictionary of Applied Linguistics*. 234. London: Longman, 1985.

Romaine, Suzanne. *The Language of Children and Adolescents*. 108. Oxford: Basil Blackwell, 1984.

Sampson, Geoffrey. *Schools of Linguistics: Competition and Evolution*. 43–44. London: Century Hutchinson, 1987.

Schultze, Quentin J., Roy M. Anker, James D. Bratt, William D. Romanowski, John W. Worst, and Lambert Zuidervaart. *Dancing in the Dark: Youth, Popular Culture, and the Electronic Media*. Grand Rapids, MI: Eerdmans, 1991.

Sherwin, Stephen. *Four Problems in Teaching English: A Critique of Research*. Scranton, PA: International Textbook Company for the National Council of Teachers of English, 1966.

Shuy, Roger. *Discovering American Dialects*. Champaign, IL: National Council of Teachers of English, 1967.

Snodgrass, Mary Ellen. *The Great American English Handbook*. 27, 36, 38, 92. Jacksonville, IL: Perma-bound, 1987.

Squire, James R., and Roger K. Applebee. *High School English Instruction Today*. New York: Appleton-Century-Crofts, 1968.

Sullivan, Peggy. *Many Names for Eileen*. Chicago and New York: Follett, 1969.

Stubbs, Michael. *Discourse Analysis*. 20–25, 64, 150. Oxford: Basil Blackwell, 1983.

———. "The Sociolinguistics of the English Writing System: Or, Why Children Aren't Adults." In Michael Stubbs and Hillary Hiller (eds.), *Readings on Language, Schools and Classrooms*. 279. London and New York: Methuen & Company, 1983.

———. *Educational Linguistics*. 20–25. Oxford: Basil Blackwell, 1986.

Thornton, Geoffrey, Peter Doughty, and Anne Doughty. *Language Study: The School and the Community*. 130. New York: Elsevier, 1974.

Trudgill, Peter. *Accent, Dialect and the School*. 17, 35. London: Edward Arnold, 1975.

VanDeWeghe, Richard. "Spelling and Grammar Logs." In Candy Carter (ed.), *Nonnative and Nonstandard Dialect Students*. 101–5. Urbana, IL: National Council of Teachers of English, 1982.

Vygotsky, Lev S. *Thought and Language*. Cambridge, MA: Massachusetts Institute of Technology Press, 1962.

Webster's College Dictionary. New York: Random House, 1991.

Weingartner, Charles. "Semantics: What and Why," *English Journal* 58 (1969): 1214–1219.

Wells, Gordon. *The Meaning Makers: Children Learning Language and Using Language to Learn*. 15, 41. London: Heinemann, 1986.

West, Fred. *The Way of Language*. 4. New York: Harcourt Brace Jovanovich, 1975.

Westall, Robert. *Blitzcat*. New York: Scholastic, 1989.

Whorf, Benjamin. "A Linguistic Consideration of Thinking in Primitive Communities." In John Carroll (ed.), *Language, Thought and Reality*. 65–86. Cambridge, MA: Massachusetts Institute of Technology Press, 1956.

Widdowson, Henry. *Explorations in Applied Linguistics*. 138. Oxford: Oxford University Press, 1979.

Wilson, Kenneth G. *Van Winkle's Return: Change in American English, 1966–1986*. 18, 37. Hanover, N.H.: University Press of New England, 1987.

Yule, George. *The Study of Language*. 1, 21, 51–53. Cambridge: Cambridge University Press, 1985.

Index